E V E R E S T

THE
MOUNTAINEERS
ANTHOLOGY

S · E · R · I · E · S

VOLUME IV

EVEREST

EDITED BY PETER POTTERFIELD
FOREWORD BY TOM HORNBEIN

THE MOUNTAINEERS BOOKS

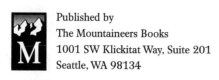

Published by
The Mountaineers Books
1001 SW Klickitat Way, Suite 201
Seattle, WA 98134

First edition, 2003

Published simultaneously in Great Britain by Cordee, 3a DeMontfort Street, Leicester, England, LE1 7HD

Manufactured in the United States of America

Acquiring Editors: Cassandra Conyers, Mary Metz
Project Editor: Kathleen Cubley
Design: The Mountaineers Books
Cover illustration: Ani Rucki
Layout: Mayumi Thompson
Mapmaker: Mayumi Thompson

Library of Congress Cataloging-in-Publication Data
Everest / edited by Peter Potterfield ; foreword by Tom Hornbein.— 1st ed.
    p. cm. — (The Mountaineers anthology series ; v. 4)
Includes bibliographical references.
  ISBN 0-89886-903-X (pbk.)
  1. Mountaineering expeditions—Everest, Mount (China and Nepal)—History. 2. Everest, Mount (China and Nepal)—Description and travel. I. Potterfield, Peter. II. Series.
  GV199.44.E85E82 2003
  796.52'2'095496—dc21
                                                                    2003001334

♻ Printed on recycled paper

CONTENTS

FOREWORD

EVEREST: THE ENDURING CHALLENGE

Mountain shapes are often fantastic seen through a mist: these were the wildest creation of a dream. A preposterous triangular lump rose out of the depths: its edge came leaping up at an angle of about 70 degrees and ended nowhere. To its left a black serrated crest was hanging in the sky incredibly. Gradually, very gradually, we saw the great mountainsides and glaciers and arêtes, now one fragment now another through the floating rifts, until far higher in the sky than imagination had dared to suggest the white summit of Everest appeared. And in this series of partial glimpses we had seen a whole; we were able to piece together the fragments, to interpret the dream. . . .

George Leigh Mallory, 1921

THE MOUNTAIN

One among this earth's protuberances had to be the highest. It is variously called Mount Everest, Sagarmatha, Qomolungma. I have been there once, briefly, forty years ago. Yet with my eyes closed, I can see its form from almost any perspective. The shape is fixed, inert. As my mind's eye zooms in, its surface seems a living thing, in constant motion, scoured and sculpted by wind, bathed by cloud, baked by sun, snow and rock sliding and falling, pulled by gravity toward a place of repose. Inhospitable though it may seem, it is upon this stage that we humans play our game.

EVEREST AS PLAYGROUND

Dick Emerson, a sociologist and my companion on three trips to the Himalaya, posited that motivation is maximized by uncertainty; too great a certainty of failure, or of success, lessens motivation.

Lito Tejada-Flores, in his classic, *Games Climbers Play* (Ascent, 1967), identifies a hierarchy of games, including: the "Bouldering Game," "The Crag Climbing Game," "The Big Wall Game," and "The Expedition Game." At the core of each of these *games* we climbers have created a set of rules that serve to maintain uncertainty, to keep the outcome in doubt.

Thus ladders, a legitimate tool in Everest's Icefall, where their presence scarcely affects the final outcome, would, if placed creatively, subtract from the essence of the Crag and Big Wall Games and completely do away with the *game* in the Bouldering Game. Each rule arises from an ethic concerning personal challenge, a function of our ability and willingness to risk—to savor uncertainty. Such things as familiarity, technological advances, and experience affect the game. As uncertainty diminishes, we create new rules to keep the outcome in doubt.

Using these concepts, we can examine how the game on Everest has evolved over recent decades. As I have watched the human-mountain scene unfold on "The Big E," I have been struck that it has all the characteristics of a maturing, or aging, relationship, albeit with one partner somewhat indifferent. Our human connection with mountains, especially the big, attractive ones (and Everest heads the list) seems to pass through a predictable evolution:

DISCOVERY

For Everest, this took place in 1856 in an office of the Trigonometric Survey of India, when calculations revealed that Peak XV rose 29,002 feet above sea level. That painstaking rod-and-chain number is scarcely different from the recent GPS satellite–determined figure of 29,035 feet (8850 meters).

FIRST ATTEMPTS

It took years of negotiation before Tibet finally granted the permission that launched the 1921 British reconnaissance expedition. The team traveled more than 400 miles overland to Everest's base, then found the way that subsequent expeditions would follow up the East Rongbuk Glacier to reach the North Col.

The Brits attempted to climb Everest in 1922, 1924, 1933, 1935, and 1938, the more successful efforts coming within a thousand feet of the summit before being turned back by a seemingly impenetrable barrier of altitude and circumstances. As a teenager, I was entranced by James Ramsey Ullman's history of Everest, *Kingdom of Adventure*. One of the biggest unknowns seemed to be whether humans could survive on the summit of Everest, much less climb there. Perhaps this question was the seed that grew to be my lifelong interest in how humans adapt to high altitude.

The most notorious of the British pre–World War II attempts occurred in 1924. From below, Noel Odell watched George Mallory and Andrew Irvine heading toward the summit, as clouds rolled in, obscuring the two from view. The rest remained a mystery until Mallory's body was found high on the North Face in 1999. Still, even that discovery did not bring closure to the question of whether one or both climbers might have reached the summit before they died.

In 1949, Nepal opened its borders to outsiders. The following year, H. W. Tilman and Dr. Charles Houston became the first Westerners to view the Icefall guarding access to the Western Cwm. They were not sanguine about prospects for a sane passage. In 1951, Eric Shipton, who had been on all four attempts in the 1930s, led a group, including New Zealander Edmund Hillary, to pursue this option further. They succeeded in climbing the Icefall to its entrance to the Cwm, only to be stopped by a massive crevasse. But the way was defined and boldly exploited by the Swiss in the spring and fall of 1952. The first of these attempts took Raymond Lambert and Tenzing Norgay high above the South Col before a dysfunctional oxygen system put a halt to their dream.

THE FIRST ASCENT

This year, 2003, and this volume (among others), mark the fiftieth anniversary of that day in 1953, May 29, when Edmund Hillary and Tenzing Norgay became the first to stand atop the highest point on earth. The news of their accomplishment came as a gift to British spirits at the very moment that Elizabeth was being crowned queen. In the ensuing decades, Hillary has parlayed the notoriety thrust upon him into giving back to the Sherpas, who enabled the expedition's success; this by building schools and clinics to foster education and health of the inhabitants of the Solu-Khumbu.

SUSTAINING UNCERTAINTY

Once a mountain is climbed, the search for new, more challenging routes follows. Our expedition in 1963 was among the first of this genre on Everest, with the ascent of the West Ridge and the first traverse of a major Himalayan peak. Other handsome examples are the ascent of Everest's Southwest Face by Doug Scott and Dougal Haston in 1975, the 1983 climb of the Kangshung Face in grand expedition style, and that face's 1988 alpine-style ascent by a new route to the South Col, pulled off by an unsupported team of four. Presently, Peter Gillman, in *Everest,* counts fifteen more-or-less separate routes to Everest's top.

A challenge essentially unique to Everest was to climb to the top without the use of supplemental oxygen. This goal was achieved by Reinhold Messner and Peter Habeler in 1978, climbing alongside a conventional expedition using oxygen to enable placing camps and preparing the route. Two years later, Messner transformed this physiologic feat into a truly seminal event, a solo ascent of the North Face, completely unsupported, over the course of three days. I regard this climb as one of the great moments in our human relationship with Everest, noting as I do so the near impossibility these days of enjoying such seclusion on the highest mountain on earth.

Compare, for example, the late Goran Kropp's determined solo ascent of the South Col route in 1996. Kropp peddled a bicycle from Sweden, then carried all his equipment and food without Sherpa support, and even created his own route through the Icefall to avoid using the track made by others. These somewhat artificial restrictions represent the ultimate in creating rules to maximize this one remarkable individual's uncertainty, his attempt to pursue a pure ethic in the midst of a crowd.

Other impressive examples of this stage include the winter ascents, speed ascents, camping out on the summit overnight (by intention), and quick (but controlled) descents by parapent, ski, and snowboard.

A MAGNET FOR MANY

Guided climbing comes to all attractive mountains. What has happened on Everest in the eighteen years since the first for-hire climb by Dick Bass is no exception, no matter how much we aging climbers may view it as diminishing the stature of a magnificent mountain (or perhaps our image of our own stature?). One may debate the propriety, question the added risks of lesser experience, crowding, and queuing and marvel at the numbers putting up their $65,000 to summit the highest point on earth, but the reality is that guided climbing has come of age on Everest. The community for this stage in our relationship with the mountain includes not only those signing on to commercially guided trips but also expeditions mounted by various nationalities or other groups; for example, the small but growing number of individuals with disabilities who seek to demonstrate to themselves and others that their handicap need not disqualify them from pursuing difficult dreams.

I see the panoply of motivations of these individuals as no different from those at prior stages, nor of those who would seek to climb all of Washington's volcanoes, Colorado's Fourteeners, or the seven continental high points. The climbers may be there for the trophy of the summit, the challenge of the journey, testing of the self, the intimidating beauty of the high world around them, or the richness of companionship—the same reasons that compel all climbers of mountains.

This stage differs in one significant way from its predecessors, though. The challenge, the quest, has become exclusively a personal one, absent that additional uncertainty of going where no other human being has gone before.

EVEREST AS LITERATURE

The literature of Everest grows apace with this Everest boom, perhaps only slightly less rapidly than the number of successful ascents (including descents), now nearly 1500 in the half century since the mountain was first climbed. Having made my own contribution to this growing mountain of words, I prefer to be more the observer than the critic. I find it noteworthy that one publisher, The Mountaineers Books, can pull together enough good literature on Everest solely from its own publications to create the rich anthology that you will explore here. These writings are all by or about those who belong to the first stages of the Everest maturation, with an especially rich seasoning from those who first confronted its massive uncertainty. I hope you will enjoy Peter Potterfield's sampler and that your armchair journey will leave you with just the right dose of . . . uncertainty, of course.

Tom Hornbein

Seattle, Washington

INTRODUCTION

For this, the fourth collection in The Mountaineers Books' ongoing series of anthologies featuring the best of mountaineering writing, the theme is the ultimate mountain: Everest. To the Tibetans, it is Chomolungma, to the Sherpa of Nepal, Sagarmatha, but in either culture the highest mountain on earth is "mother goddess." Since its discovery, Everest has motivated climbers (and a few mystics) to take on its irresistible but daunting challenge. The result is a hundred years of colorful history and unparalleled drama, replete with tragedy and triumph. For cultures and peoples all over the world, the mountain remains a place of fascination, even mystery.

Everest was first climbed fifty years ago. The half-century mark seemed an appropriate time to collect in one volume the most compelling literature that has chronicled the suffering, the struggle, and the joy of Everest, and to celebrate the noble human endeavor inspired by the mountain.

The earliest efforts to first find a way to the mountain, and then to climb it, generated enduring narratives of desperate efforts and puzzling mysteries. During the 1924 expedition Edward Norton climbed to an altitude in the Great Couloir less than a thousand feet below the summit, a record that would stand until 1952. Only a few days after his remarkable ascent, the mountain's first great mystery was forged when two other members of the expedition, George Mallory and Sandy Irvine, disappeared in the mists high on the Northeast Ridge. Less than a decade later, the articulate and fearless Frank Smythe would match Norton's altitude record during his own summit bid of 1933, and write eloquently about it. He would also become the first to experience and describe the mysterious "presence" of another, an eerie phenomenon that has since been reported by other climbers high on the mountain. Complex characters such as Smythe make the early climbs on Everest resonate with human interest.

Other talented players made their mark on the mountain. Soon after World War II, the British began to explore the southern approaches to Everest out of necessity; the conventional route, through Tibet, was closed to outsiders when the country was occupied by China. H. W. Tilman in 1950, and Eric Shipton in 1951, led exploratory expeditions that eventually opened up the route by which Everest would first be climbed. The successful summit by Sir Edmund Hillary and Tenzing Norgay, which proved that human ascent of Everest was possible, followed in 1953. Their accomplishment ushered in a half century of unremitting focus in which Everest became a laboratory for the evolution of high-altitude climbing.

While Everest has been a focal point of fascination for people since its discovery, the pre-monsoon season of 1996 brought the mountain to the attention of a much wider modern audience. On May 10 of that year, a fairly ordinary afternoon storm rolled in on the upper slopes of Everest. The timing could not have been worse for dozens of climbers, mostly from guided parties, who remained high on the mountain and would face the fury of the storm. The tragic events of that afternoon and evening changed forever the way Everest was perceived, no doubt because an experienced mountaineering journalist was there to tell the world what happened.

For me, the episode began earlier, in February 1996, with an urgent call from Scott Fischer. Friends and fellow climbers, Fischer and I had climbed Mount Rainier and other Cascade peaks together. A photo of the two of us adorned the back cover of the Cascade climbing guide I wrote with Jim Nelson. My beat as a journalist focused on mountaineering subjects, and Fischer had been featured in a recent cover story I wrote for a major national magazine. The two of us had spent weeks that winter working on my book, *In the Zone,* which included a narrative of Fischer's ascent of K2 with Ed Viesturs.

But Fischer's phone call to me was not a happy one. Scott called to say the *Outside* magazine correspondent—Jon Krakauer—had made a last-minute change of plan. Instead of going to Everest as a client for Fischer's guide service, Mountain Madness, he would instead sign on with New Zealander Rob Hall's company, Adventure Consultants. Fischer, crestfallen at the potential loss of publicity for his fledgling company, asked me to obtain a magazine assignment and come along to Everest with him. His precise closing words to me still resonate: "C'mon, Peter, do it—I'll build you a yellow brick road to the top."

I might well have traveled to Everest with Scott were it not for a long-standing commitment to go that spring to the mountains of Patagonia with photographer Art Wolfe. Instead, it was only when I returned from South America that I listened helplessly, along with everybody else, as the sad news begin to trickle in of the tragic turn of events high on Mount Everest. A few weeks later, over a beer with Krakauer in a pub in the funky Seattle neighborhood of Fremont, I heard from him the grim details. Krakauer, still shaken by the recent traumatic events, knew I was a friend of Fischer's. He generously spent several hours with me to offer a private, first-hand report of the tragedy, the elements of which would later become one of the most famous narratives of Everest history.

The events of May 10, 1996, are now part of the mountain's lore. Eight climbers died on the mountain that day and night when they were trapped by the storm and ran out of oxygen, or descended but could not find their tents at the South Col. The dead included Rob Hall and Scott Fischer, two strong and experienced high-altitude guides. Their almost unbelievable demise stunned the climbing world. In the controversies that would follow in the wake of the disaster—including Anatoli Boukreev's challenge to Krakauer's reporting—the practice of guided climbing on Everest was pilloried by many who knew little about it.

In fact, the previous few years had been a sort of golden age of guided climbing on Everest, with almost no public awareness. It was an era when guides such as Todd Burleson, Rob Hall, Pete Athans, Wally Berg, Guy Cotter, Russell Brice, Eric Simonson, and Ed Viesturs helped dozens of fit and experienced climbers safely to the summit and back down, people who without guides might not have tried for such a lofty goal. Viesturs himself described a guided climb with Hall in 1994 that challenges many assumptions about the practice: "We had six phenomenal clients, all strong, motivated, and experienced. Rob and I just pointed them in the right direction, and we all climbed together to the summit. That fabulous climb proved how successful a guided ascent of the mountain can be."

Despite the deaths of that infamous 1996 incident, some positive things did come out of that spring season: the successful Everest Imax film, directed by David Breashears, and Göran Kropp's remarkable bike ride from Sweden followed by his oxygenless ascent. A few years later, the pall of disaster that seemed to linger over the mountain since the accident would be well and truly dissipated by a new and even more powerful media frenzy over something altogether different: the finding of George Mallory's body.

I remember well the morning of May 23, 1999, as it dawned over the frontier town of Kodari, high above a deep gorge on the Nepal-Tibet border. Ragged streamers of low clouds drifted through the mountains as I stood on the Nepal side of the yellow line demarcating the "no man's land" between the two countries. At the far end of the long, graceful bridge spanning the gorge, two figures with heavy packs appeared and began to walk toward Nepal, and me. I knew them even at a distance by the way they moved: Dave Hahn and Eric Simonson. They looked tired but happy as they trudged slowly across the border, relishing the conclusion of a remarkable effort that had found the long-lost climber, and in doing so had made Everest history anew. I had last seen the pair months earlier in a Seattle restaurant the day Simonson and Hahn dropped off several tons of expedition cargo for their Thai Airways flight to Kathmandu. Before they left for Nepal, the three of us went to lunch to talk over the upcoming expedition, and the dispatches they would send for MountainZone.com

On the eve of their departure, Hahn was visibly uncomfortable at the high-profile nature of their endeavor. "When you say to the world, 'Look at us,'" he said ruefully, "you better not screw up." The expedition, apparently, had taken his words to heart. Far from doing something they would come to regret, Simonson, Hahn, Conrad Anker, and the other members of that expedition would beat some long odds, and with outrageous luck and hard work they would prove once again that Everest holds a deep fascination for people all over the world. I had experienced first-hand the intense interest that followed their stunning find of Mallory's corpse when our servers at MountainZone.com almost melted down as more than a million people logged on that May 1 to get details of the discovery. I had seen up-close the media frenzy that was going on not just in the United States, but in Europe as well.

As I waited for Hahn and Simonson to cross the bridge that chilly morning in Tibet, all I could think of was, "these guys have no idea what they are in for. . . . " So with a few thousand MountainZone.com rupees, I bought every cold beer in Kodari. The entire expedition then clambered not into the waiting chartered bus, but on top of it. Spread out on the roof, ten of us guzzled beer and dodged tree branches as we rocked and rolled along the rough road to Kathmandu. I figured I had about five hours to prepare these guys for what awaited them at the end of the road.

The story of Mallory and Irvine, as well as the discovery of Mallory's body, are some of the pieces featured in this collection of Everest tales. While further ruminations on the events of 1996 are not included—there is little that could be added here—the seminal events of Everest history are represented. Most are told in the first person by those who took part, though some writings are the work of journalists or historians. The pieces include the earliest attempts as well as modern-day summit attempts. The early explorations and first ascent mentioned above are only the beginning of compelling narratives that derive from the action on Everest.

The first traverse of Everest by Tom Hornbein and Willi Unsoeld remains one of the most amazing accomplishments related to the mountain. Doug Scott and Dougal Haston proved that even a technical route and high-altitude bivouac without oxygen was possible. Within a decade of that, the incredible achievements of Reinhold Messner—who climbed the peak without oxygen for the first time, and then made an unsupported solo ascent—would change the very nature of high-altitude climbing. The modern-day realities of climbing on Everest are related by Dave Hahn, who lead a rescue of multiple climbers on the Northeast Ridge in 2001.

The voices represented in these pieces are as diverse as they are irresistible. Smythe writes like the pro he is, smooth and polished, with no hint of self aggrandizement. Hornbein's account of his amazing traverse is told in spare, precise language. Messner, widely regarded as a great climber rather than an inspired writer, produces a gripping narrative of his solo ascent.

Man's evolving approach to Everest during the past century says much about our innate need for risk and adventure. The mountain has become a kind of crucible, where the nature of struggle against long odds has been cooked down into an essence that speaks eloquently about human striving. The pieces included in this collection are the classic tales from Mount Everest, stories that I believe will be read for decades to come, in part because they illustrate the lengths to which we will go to find new ways to challenge our-selves. Together, they offer food for thought, and more—an understanding of what it means to undertake something ineffably difficult.

Peter Potterfield
Seattle, Washington

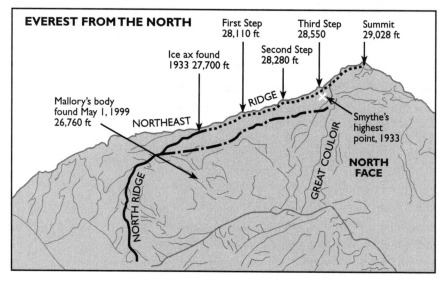

This illustration shows Mount Everest from the north side, or Tibet side, and depicts the Northeast Ridge and North Face routes first attempted by the British expeditions of the 1930s and later by Reinhold Messner on his first solo ascent of the mountain.

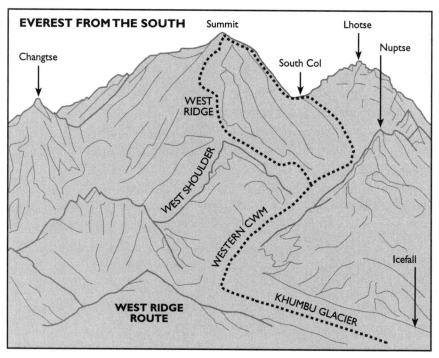

This illustration shows Mount Everest from the south side, or Nepal side, and depicts the South Col route, used by Edmund Hillary on the first ascent, and Jim Whittaker on the first American ascent, and the West Ridge route first climbed by Tom Hornbein and Willi Unsoeld on their first traverse of the mountain (the pair descended via the South Col route).

"VANISHING HOPES"

FROM
The Wildest Dream
BY PETER AND LENI GILLMAN

THE EVENTS OF THE 1924 BRITISH EXPEDITION TO MOUNT EVEREST remain the essence of legend—and enduring mystery. Edward Norton, a member of the landmark expedition, climbed (most of the way with Howard Somervell) to a point in Everest's Great Couloir less than a thousand feet below the summit. The altitude record he set on the peak would stand for almost three decades. A few days later, the most celebrated rope team in climbing history vanished high on the mountain, creating a mystery that has yet to be resolved, and one that forever begs the question: could they have been the first to reach the summit of Everest?

The facts of that fateful climb are these: George Mallory, on his third expedition to attempt Everest, and his protégé, Andrew "Sandy" Irvine, set off for the summit from their highest camp on the morning of June 8, 1924. The pair represented the vanguard of contemporary high-altitude climbing: Mallory and Irvine were part of a well-funded and tightly organized expedition composed almost exclusively of Everest veterans. After five weeks on the mountain the men were in top shape and well acclimated. The pair climbed with the most modern oxygen apparatus of the day, even if it was rudimentary by current standards and cumbersome by any. It is safe to say that, on the heels of Norton's amazing effort a few days before without supplemental oxygen, Mallory and Irvine expected, if not outright success, to make a strong attempt to reach the highest point on earth.

The precise time that Mallory and Irvine departed Camp VI (approximately 26,800 feet on Everest's northern flank) on June 8 is not known with certainty. But expedition member Noel Odell, who was below the high camp at approximately 26,000 feet that day, steadfastly maintains he saw the pair climbing slowly somewhere high on the Northeast Ridge just before 1:00 P.M. The clouds soon closed in, however, and Odell never saw the men again. Odell's sighting is perhaps the single most crucial piece of information regarding the mystery of Mallory and Irvine. But the ambiguity of the climbers' location when they were seen by Odell has frustrated historians. Was it the base of the summit pyramid, as Odell first recorded, or was it at the difficult Second Step—or perhaps even the First Step—as Odell later conceded it might be? Mallory and Irvine were never again seen alive, and the mystery of what transpired that day remains largely unsolved.

The excerpt below comes from *The Wildest Dream,* by British mountaineering journalist Peter Gillman and his wife Leni. *The Wildest Dream* is an in-
sightful and penetrating biography of George Mallory, whose "wild" dream
was to climb Everest. The narrative picks up as Mallory and expedition member Geoffrey Bruce return to the North Col camp on June 2, having
decided to abort their first summit attempt of the 1924 expedition. Ostensibly, the reason for their sudden retreat was the refusal of porters to carry
equipment higher on the mountain, but some historians have speculated that
Mallory wanted to save his strength for a stronger summit bid later, when
camps on the mountain would be better established and when he could climb
with oxygen. Norton and Somervell soon depart on their attempt for the
top, while Mallory and Irvine prepare to move higher for their own fateful
summit bid.

The Gillmans call on a variety of historical resources to report what is
known of the Mallory and Irvine attempt. In this excerpt, George Mallory is
referred to as "George," his wife is "Ruth," and his young daughter is "Clare";
everyone else is identified by their last names. The selection is from *The Wildest Dream,* pages 250–260.

I t is not clear precisely when George decided that his attempt with Bruce
was bound to fail, or when he resolved to revert to his original plan for
making an oxygen attempt with Irvine. But it was the defining moment
of his life. Throughout his mountaineering career he had pushed as hard
and as far as he could, refusing to give up until he was convinced beyond all
possible doubt that he had no other choice. Now that the weather remained
fair, and he was still on his feet, and he had a willing partner, and there was
oxygen equipment at Camp 3, he could not renounce his hope of going to
the summit. It offered him the supreme opportunity of being the climbing
leader who climbed the highest mountain. As he had declared in New York,
a climber was what he was, and this was what climbers did; and this was
how they fulfilled their wildest dreams.

There was more. If he went back to Ruth with Everest unclimbed, he could
face the anguish of wondering whether he should leave her and his children

and their home for yet another try. He could not see how he could inflict that on her again. It was only by making another attempt now that he could be true to Ruth and all they had gone through together, and to the ideals of honesty and integrity they had expressed that were embodied in their love. It was also the only way he knew of redeeming the suffering he had caused Ruth: if he climbed Everest, the conflict at the core of their marriage, the conflict between his dreams and their love, would be reconciled.

That afternoon George descended to Camp 3 with Irvine. While Irvine busied himself with the oxygen equipment, George asked Bruce to see if he could muster enough porters to support their attempt. On the mountain, meanwhile, Norton and Somervell were pushing on. They stayed at Camp 5 that night and the following morning left at 9 A.M., having had a hard struggle to persuade their porters to keep going. At 1:30 P.M. they reached a height of 26,800 feet, pitching the tent that comprised Camp 6 on a precarious platform that they scraped out among the loose stones. Their three remaining porters returned to the North Col, leaving Norton and Somervell to contemplate an awesome panorama of peaks silhouetted against the red evening sky. Somervell felt he was witnessing "a sunset all over the world" and also had the illusion that they were camped in a field close to a wall that marked the limit of their capacities and endurance.

Still Norton was anxious about the monsoon, but on the morning of June 4, the weather held. He had been keen to make an early start but one of the thermos flasks he had filled with tea the previous night had lost its cork, emptying its contents into his sleeping bag. Norton, who knew by then the importance of not becoming dehydrated, insisted on brewing some more tea and it was not until 6:40 A.M. that they left. They now faced a choice of route. George had always favored the line he had identified in 1921, striking up to the crest of the northeast ridge and following it to the summit pyramid. Norton was worried about the two crags that appeared to block the ridge, the First and Second Step, and decided to aim for the great couloir bisecting the face like a great gash beyond the Second Step, hoping it would give easier access to the foot of the summit pyramid.

After an hour, Norton and Somervell reached the Yellow Band, the vast stratum of sandstone that crosses the north face. They found that it consisted of a series of sloping slabs and ledges where they could never be quite sure of their footholds, while the face yawned away beneath them to the Rongbuk Glacier more than 7000 feet below. The altitude was telling on them: Norton set himself the target of taking twenty steps without a pause, but could never manage more than twelve or thirteen, and they had to stop frequently to rest. By noon they were just below the top of the Yellow Band, and not far from the entrance to the couloir. The summit was looming ever closer, a triangle of white rising above the dark slopes below the crest of the northeast ridge and no more than a quarter-mile in distance and 1000 vertical feet away. On a good day in North Wales they would reckon to reach it within an hour but Somervell was at the limit of his strength. He had been in distress all morning from a painfully parched throat, aggravated by a hacking cough, and knew that he was holding Norton up. Finally he sat down on a boulder and told Norton he should go on alone.

Norton continued for another hour. The terrain was more and more treacherous, the ledges steeper and narrower and covered with powdery snow. His best hope was that the couloir would provide easier going, but he found it full of loose, waist-deep snow while the rock beyond was steeper still. He was finding it increasingly difficult to see the way, as he had removed his goggles in the mistaken belief that they were impairing his sight. In fact this was almost certainly a symptom of oxygen deficiency and he had now left himself vulnerable to snow-blindness. At 1 P.M., exhausted, already half-blind, he came to a halt. He was still some 800 to 900 feet below the summit and knew that he had run out of time to reach it and return before nightfall. As he turned back he was nevertheless convinced that there was nothing to prevent a "fresh and fit party" from reaching the summit without oxygen equipment.

Somervell had been photographing Norton as he climbed, taking a series of pictures that showed Norton, bent almost double by exhaustion, framed in the enormity of the sloping face with the snow-covered triangle of the summit tantalizingly close above. When Norton rejoined him, Somervell agreed with the decision to turn back: "We realized that it would be madness to continue, and we were somehow quite content to leave it at that, and to turn down with almost a feeling of relief that our worst trials were over."

Not quite. As dusk fell they had reached 25,000 feet when Somervell succumbed to a renewed bout of coughing. He felt something lodge in his throat and, unable to breathe or to call to Norton, began to choke to death. "I sat in

the snow to die whilst [Norton] walked on, little knowing that his companion was awaiting the end a few yards behind him." In desperation, Somervell
pummeled his chest and coughed up the obstruction into his mouth. It was
part of the mucous membrane of his larynx, which had been damaged by
frostbite. Somervell spat it out, along with some blood, and found that he
could breathe again. "Though the pain was intense," he wrote, "I was a new
man." They continued their descent in the dark, signalling with a torch as
they approached the North Col.

That morning George and Irvine had been watching and waiting at Camp
3. Irvine had patched together two oxygen sets and Geoffrey Bruce had re-
cruited enough porters to support a new attempt. A porter who descended
from the North Col reported that Norton and Somervell had established Camp
6 at around 27,000 feet (later established at 26,800 feet) and spent the night
there. "Great was the excitement in the camp," Irvine wrote. "Noel had his
telephoto camera out and everyone watched unceasingly all day but not a
sign." That afternoon George and Irvine decided to return to the North Col,
"ready," as Irvine put it, "to fetch sick men down or make an oxygen attempt
ourselves a day later." Using oxygen, they reached the col in two and a half
hours. Irvine felt "surprisingly fresh" when they arrived, while Odell, who had
remained skeptical about the benefits of the apparatus, observed that they
seemed "well pleased" with themselves. George thought he could see tracks
leading downwards some 700 feet below the summit. "I hope they've got to
the top," Irvine wrote, "but by God I'd like to have a whack at it myself."

When George saw the torch signals from Norton and Somervell, he and
Odell climbed to meet them some 100 feet above the North Col. They offered them some oxygen but what Norton and Somervell wanted more than
anything was a drink. When they reached the col Irvine plied them with tea
and soup. Their companions, Norton wrote, were "kindness itself," congratulating them on establishing a new height record on Everest—"though we ourselves felt nothing but disappointment at our failure."

Norton, who could barely see, was sharing a tent with George. That night,
after they had crawled into their sleeping bags, George told him that he wanted
to make one more summit attempt, using oxygen equipment. "I entirely agreed
with this decision," Norton wrote, "and was full of admiration for the indomi-
table spirit of the man, determined, in spite of his already excessive exertions,

not to admit defeat while any chance remained, and I must admit—such was his willpower and nervous energy—he still seemed entirely adequate to the task." What did surprise Norton was that George intended to make the attempt with Irvine, and he argued that Odell was not only the more experienced climber, but was also fitter and better acclimatized. Irvine was in fact suffering from both a parched throat and a painfully sunburned face, and had just written in his diary that the previous night "everything on earth seemed to rub against my face and each time it was touched bits of burnt and dry skin came off which made me nearly scream with pain." George would not be deflected, telling Norton that he was taking Irvine because of the skill and initiative he had shown over the oxygen equipment, and because he had greater trust in using oxygen than Odell. Norton realized that George had made up his mind: "It was obviously no time for me to interfere."

To the climbers' delight and surprise, the weather on June 5 remained clear. Although they did not know it, they were in fact experiencing the settled period of ten days or so that often precedes the monsoon on Everest. Ironically, the blazing sun brought still more discomfort. Norton was completely blind and lay in his tent, which was shaded with sleeping bags. Despite intense pain, he crawled to the door to speak to the porters who were to support the attempt, rallying their spirits and telling them it was vital to keep going to Camp 6. Irvine, in equal distress from his sunburn, spent most of the day with Odell's assistance putting the finishing touches on two oxygen sets. That night Irvine wrote his last diary entry. "My face is perfect agony," he concluded. "Have prepared 2 oxygen apparatus for our start tomorrow morning."

George and Irvine were up early on June 6. George was wearing cotton and silk underwear, a flannel shirt from Paine's outfitters in Godalming High Street, a brown long-sleeved pullover, and a patterned woolen waistcoat that Ruth had made. Since he would be wearing the oxygen equipment on his back, he stuffed his personal items into the pockets of his windproof cotton Shackleton jacket and a pair of pouches slung around his neck. They included a pocket knife with a horn handle, a pair of nail scissors in a leather pouch, a box of Swan Vesta matches, and some spare laces and straps. He took a tube of petroleum jelly that he wrapped in a white handkerchief, and two more handkerchiefs, one colored burgundy, green, and blue, the other red, blue, and yellow, both of them monogrammed with his initials, "G. L. M."

He carried several checklists of supplies, together with three recently arrived letters that he carefully wrapped in one of the handkerchiefs.

One of the letters was from his brother, Trafford, written in London on April 2, bringing news of his move with his wife and their two sons to a new house in west London. Another was from his sister Mary, and had been mailed from Colombo on April 12: George had asked her to send regular weather reports in the hope of anticipating the monsoon but, although she had news of a violent tropical storm, her letter had arrived far too late. A third, signed "Stella" and posted in London on April 2, was from Stella Cobden-Sanderson, an Englishwoman George had met in New York during his 1923 lecture tour and whom he had mentioned in his letters to Ruth. She sent gossipy news about going to the theater, a friend of the Mallorys she had dined with the previous day, and her plans to visit the south of France. George had used the envelope of her letter to note down the code numbers and pressures of five oxygen cylinders.

Odell and Hazard were up early too, preparing a breakfast of fried sardines, biscuits, chocolate, and tea. George and Irvine did not finish theirs, Odell observed, "owing to excitement or restlessness." Norton, still blind, came to the door of his tent to shake hands and offer them "a word of blessing." At 8:40 A.M. Odell took a last photograph of them. Irvine is facing away from the camera, with two silvery oxygen cylinders on his back. Both men are wearing their Shackleton jackets, breeches, and puttees. Irvine, hands in pockets, a hat pulled tightly down to protect his face, is looking toward George, who is wearing gloves, goggles, a fur-lined helmet, mitts, and a scarf, and is about to pick up his ice ax. Shortly before 9 A.M. they left with eight porters who were carrying food, bedding, and oxygen cylinders. "The party moved off in silence as we bid them adieu," Odell wrote, "and they were soon lost to view."

Climbing steadily along the line George had followed with Bruce just four days before, they reached Camp 5 in good time. George sent four of the porters back to the North Col, together with an optimistic note: "There is no wind here and things look hopeful." The next day, June 7, using oxygen for part of the way, they and the four remaining porters continued to Camp 6. After reaching the camp, George wrote two brief notes, one for John Noel, the other for Noel Odell.

Knowing that Noel would be at his camera position, a ledge he named
the Eagle's Nest, George told him:

> We'll probably start early tomorrow (8th) in order to have clear
> weather. It won't be too early to start looking for us either cross-
> ing the rock band under the pyramid or going up skyline at
> 8.0 P.M.
>
> Yours ever, G Mallory

The time, "8.0 P.M.," was clearly an error for 8 A.M.

To Odell, George wrote:

> We're awfully sorry to have left things in such a mess—our Unna
> Cooker rolled down the slope at the last moment. Be sure of get-
> ting back to IV to-morrow in time to evacuate by dark, as I hope
> to. In the tent I must have left a compass—for the Lord's sake res-
> cue it: we are here without. To here on 90 atmospheres for the 2
> days—we'll probably go on 2 cylinders—but it's a bloody load for
> climbing. Perfect weather for the job!
>
> Yours ever, G. Mallory

George gave the two notes to the porters to take on their descent. When the
porter Lakpa handed John Noel his note, he told Noel that the two climbers
were well, and that the weather was good. To sustain them on their attempt,
George had selected food that was high on sugar content: cookies, chocolate,
butterscotch, Kendal mint cake, and ginger nuts, plus macaroni and sliced ham
and tongue. They had an Unna cooker to heat the food and melt snow—not
the Unna cooker referred to in George's note to Odell, which he had left at
Camp 5—and were as well provided for as could be. The morning of June 8
was clear, and in the words of Odell, now ensconced in Camp 5 1500 feet
below them, "not unduly cold." From Camp 6, George and Irvine continued
on a diagonal ascent, which brought them to just below the crest of the northeast ridge at 27,760 feet, where they dumped a spent oxygen cylinder. A little
farther on, they faced the choice George had described to John Noel: Should

they veer across the face and traverse the rock band, as Norton had done? Or should they follow the crest of the northeast ridge?

By Odell's account, they chose the ridge. Odell had left Camp 5 at eight o'clock, intending to climb to Camp 6 in support of George and Irvine, using the opportunity to collect geological samples on the way. Soon after he set out banks of mist rolled across the face from the west. Odell was not unduly worried on the two climbers' behalf: although there was an occasional brief squall of sleet or light snow, the mist had a luminous quality that suggested it was not thick and might even remain below the level of the summit pyramid.

At 12:50 P.M., just as Odell had climbed a crag at around 26,000 feet, the mist cleared. Before him was the vision that has become part of the Mallory legend, as he and Irvine continued their seemingly unstoppable progress to the top. "The entire summit ridge and final peak of Everest were unveiled," Odell wrote in a dispatch he compiled for *The Times* a week later. "My eyes became fixed on one tiny black spot silhouetted on a small snow-crest beneath a rock-step in the ridge; the black dot moved. Another black dot became apparent and moved up the snow to join the other on the crest. The first then approached the great rock-step and shortly emerged at the top; the second did likewise. Then the whole fascinating vision vanished, enveloped in cloud once more."

Odell was in no doubt that he had seen George and Irvine, "moving expeditiously" in their bid to reach the summit. He reached Camp 6 around two o'clock, just as the snow began to fall more heavily. Inside the tent he found their sleeping bags and an assortment of spare clothes and scraps of food, together with several oxygen cylinders and spare parts. Ignoring the snowfall, Odell scrambled 200 feet up the face in the hope of seeing George and Irvine, or perhaps meeting them on their way down, but the cloud still obscured his view. By the time he returned to Camp 6 the weather had cleared, and he could see the whole of the north face, and much of the upper section of the ridge, bathed in sunshine. Of George and Irvine, there was no sign. Around 4:30 P.M., in accordance with George's note, he decided to return to the North Col. Before leaving he placed the compass he had retrieved from Camp 5 in a conspicuous place near the door of the tent, so that George would be sure to find it.

Over the next forty-eight hours the members of the 1924 Everest expedition watched and waited for news of their two colleagues. From his camera position, John Noel could only report that he had obtained no sighting of them on their supposed summit day, June 8. Norton was at Camp 3 that day where, still blind, he composed a report of his summit attempt for *The Times*, which he dictated to Geoffrey Bruce. Somervell also contributed an account that ended: "We now await news of Mallory and Irvine, who today are making another attempt, hoping that they may reinforce the feeble summit air by artificially provided oxygen, and by its means be enabled to conquer the chief difficulty of reaching the summit. May the Genie of the Steel Bottle aid them! All of us are hoping that he may, for nobody deserves the summit more than Mallory, the only one of our number who has been at it for three years."

On June 9 Hazard and Odell continued to keep watch on the upper camps from the North Col. At midday Odell could restrain himself no longer and set off with two porters to start a search. He reached Camp 5 that afternoon to find it undisturbed. The next morning, despite a savage wind, he continued alone to the tent at Camp 6. One of the poles had collapsed but otherwise it was exactly as Odell had left it two days before. He set out along the probable route George and Irvine had taken. But, "after struggling on for nearly a couple of hours looking in vain for some indication or clue," Odell accepted that he had no hope of finding them.

Before Odell left the North Col, he and Hazard had agreed on a set of signals that would enable him to convey the outcome of his search. During a lull in the wind, Odell dragged the two sleeping bags from the tent and set them out in the shape of a T. The signal meant: "No trace can be found— given up hope." At the North Col, Hazard used six blankets to set out a similar signal, this time in the form of a cross, for the anxious watchers at Camp 3. John Noel saw it first, through a telescope. Geoffrey Bruce asked what he had seen, but Noel could not bring himself to tell him and handed him the telescope. "We all looked," Noel said. "We all tried to make it different. But it was plainly a cross on the white snow."

⸕   ⸕   ⸕

On June 8, the day George was last seen alive, Ruth and the children were on holiday at Bacton, a seaside resort in Norfolk. On June 19 they were back at Herschel House. That afternoon in London Hinks [Arthur Hinks of the Himalayan Committee] received a coded telegram from Norton that read: "Mallory Irvine Nove Remainder Alcedo." "Nove" meant that George and Irvine had died,

"Alcedo" that the others were unhurt. It thus fell to Hinks to convey the news to Ruth. He composed a telegram that was handed in at the post office at Kensington and dispatched from there to Cambridge, where it arrived at 7:30 P.M.

A short while later a delivery boy carrying the telegram called at Herschel House. Ruth cannot have been too surprised to see him, for in his letter of April 21 George had told her to expect a telegram announcing their success, although this was later than he had led her to expect. When she opened the envelope, this is what she read:

B or C	Charges to pay	POST OFFICE	TELEGRAPHS.	No. of Telegram
Recd from	s. d.			Sent....................M Office Stamp.
By				To....................
				By....................
Prefix	Handed in at	Office of Origin and Service Instructions	Words	Received here at

A 442 7.5 KENSINGTON O 40   7-30 P.M.

MRS MALLORY HERSCHEL HOUSE CAMBRIDGE

COMMITTEE DEEPLY REGRET RECEIVE BAD NEWS EVEREST

EXPEDITION TODAY NORTON CABLES YOUR HUSBAND AND

IRVINE KILLED LAST CLIMB REMAINDER RETURNED SAFE

PRESIDENT AND COMMITTEE OFFER YOU AND FAMILY HEARTFELT

SYMPATHY HAVE TELEGRAPHED GEORGES FATHER HINKS +

Confusion must have compounded Ruth's sense of shock, for almost simultaneously, a reporter from *The Times* arrived at Herschel House. *The Times*, which was entitled to read all Norton's dispatches as part of its contract with the expedition, had been told about the deaths too. When challenged later to explain why it had sent a reporter to Herschel House, *The Times* claimed it was anxious to ensure that Ruth heard the news before reading it in the next day's newspaper.

The most immediate decision Ruth faced was when, and how, to tell the children. By then they were in bed, and she decided to postpone the moment until the morning. She left them in the care of Vi [Violet Meakin, nursemaid], and went for a walk with some friends. In the morning, so Clare recalled seventy-five years later, Ruth took her, Berry, and John into the bed she had shared with George. "She lay between us and told us this bad news," Clare said. "We all cried together."

"CAMP 6"

FROM
The Six Alpine/Himalayan Climbing Books
BY FRANK SMYTHE

THE ENIGMATIC FRANK SMYTHE WAS AT THE CENTER OF world-class climbing for much of his short life, so it is fitting that he made his greatest achievements on Mount Everest. The period between the world wars was a busy one for mountain exploration and climbing, and Smythe—in the prime of his career—was leading the way on both fronts. He pioneered important new approaches and routes in both the Alps and in the Himalaya, including his three separate attempts on Everest during the 1930s.

In addition to his expeditions to Everest, Smythe left his mark on the Himalaya in other important ways: He discovered what would become the eventual route to the summit of Kangchenjunga, made the first ascent of Jonsong Peak, and climbed 25,447-foot Kamet, the highest peak ever climbed at the time. He made notable advances in style, as well, going fast and light in his successful attempts on Nilgiri Parbat and Mana Peak. Smythe clearly loved mountains and climbing, and despite a rather frail constitution, he managed some of the most demanding ascents of his day.

His remarkable success as a climber was mirrored in a pioneering spirit when he became the archetype of the professional climber-writer. Smythe climbed so much, and so widely, that he actually made a living writing about his adventures. The approach was a novel one, and Smythe was successful only because he was as adept with a pen as he was with an ice ax. He spins his tales with relish, and his obvious humility struck a chord in his readers.

Perhaps Smythe's most engaging piece was written about his most remarkable climb: "Camp 6" tells the story of the 1933 British expedition to Everest, and his solo climb to within a thousand feet of the summit. Without oxygen—and without a companion, for his partner Eric Shipton was forced to retreat to high camp—Smythe climbed as high as anyone had ever had climbed on Everest before. His traverse along the friable flanks of the Northeast Ridge toward the Great Couloir took Smythe into an extreme netherworld of hypoxia and hallucination, where his survival underscores his resilient psychological strength.

The following "Camp 6" excerpt joins Smythe's narrative as Lawrence Wager and Percy Wyn-Harris return to Camp Six from their May 30 summit bid. The climbers had been unsuccessful, but they returned to Camp 6 carrying a dramatic find: an ice ax that clearly had belonged to George Mallory or Sandy

Irvine, found a few hundred yards from the First Step on Everest's Northeast Ridge. Wager and Wyn-Harris are met at the high camp by Frank Smythe and his partner, Eric Shipton, awaiting their own turn to go for the summit.

The pair—a strong one by any standards—spent two nights pinned down by high winds in their cramped tent. Finally, at 7:00 A.M. on June 1, the winds abated and the men set out for the summit. Since Wager and Wyn-Harris had reported the crest of the Northeast ridge was blocked by the insurmountable Second Step, the men decided to traverse along the northern flank of the mountain into the Great Couloir—which was known then as Norton's Couloir, after Edward Norton, who had climbed it (most of the way with Howard Somervell) to a point above 28,000 feet in 1924. Smythe and Shipton set out without supplemental oxygen, as the 1933 expedition deemed the apparatus too cumbersome to be helpful. This piece is found in *The Six Alpine/Himalayan Climbing Books*, on pages 619–640.

S uddenly we heard the scrape of boot-nails and a few moments later were welcoming Wyn and Waggers. We did not need to ask them whether they had reached the summit; their bearing was not that of successful men. The first thing Wyn did was to fling down an ice ax at the entrance of the tent. "Found this," he said.

"Must have belonged to Mallory or Irvine."

They squashed themselves into the tent and seated themselves with the thankful sighs of tired men. We asked no questions but set about preparing a hot drink.

When they had rested a little we had their story. Wyn told it; and though for a tired man he was amazingly coherent and intelligible, we had frequently to interrupt him: 27,400 feet does not conduce to clear thinking or description. Yet in the end his story was clear in all its essential details. Following a miserable night, they had risen at 4:30 and, after a very poor meal and the usual exhausting ritual of thawing frozen boots and pulling on windproof clothing, left the tent shortly after 5:30. At this hour the sun had not yet risen above the Northeast Ridge and the cold was so great that they feared frostbite. They traversed the slabs of the yellow band diagonally, gradually gaining height. An hour later, when the sun appeared, they halted and Waggers removed his boots and massaged his numbed feet. Fortunately, there was little or no wind; otherwise both must have been dangerously frostbitten.

Not far beyond this halting-place Wyn discovered the ice ax that can only have belonged to Mallory or Irvine. It was lying on the slabs, which are hereabouts inclined at an angle of 35 degrees–40 degrees unsupported by crack or ledge and dependent on friction alone for its lodgment.

For the time being the ax was left where it was found, and they continued traversing to the foot of the First Step. As we had suspected, it appeared possible to avoid climbing the two towers, which compose the Step, by a traverse to the north of them. The ridge could then be gained above the step. But the objection to this was that the 200-yard-long section of ridge crest between the First Step and Second Step, a jagged saw blade of rock with abrupt gaps fifteen to twenty feet deep, looked difficult. The labor of traversing such an edge at 28,000 feet would be immense, and a gap 15 feet deep, if the sides of it are vertical and unclimbable, is sufficient to stop a party at a much lower elevation. Norton and Somervell had much the same view in 1924, and were so impressed by the difficulty of the ridge and the second step, that they continued traversing the Yellow Band in the hope of circumventing the difficulties. So with Wyn and Waggers.

Their idea was to climb directly upwards, to the foot of the second step, thus short-circuiting the difficult section of the ridge, and with this in view they continued to traverse along the top of the Yellow Band. But the farther they went the steeper and more difficult were the rocks above them. The telescope had revealed a chimney, which Wyn had noted as a possible line, but this they were unable to find. The sole possibility was an oblique gully, which appeared to cut through the steep belt of rock to a point above the Second Step. They reached the foot of this at 10 A.M. and tied on the rope for the first time. Wyn then tried to lead up it, but he found himself in one of the shallow scoops peculiar to the limestone, of which the rocks hereabouts are composed; there were no clean-cut edges, only round knobs affording the poorest of holds, especially as they were covered in snow. The climbing was very steep and at 28,000 feet, where gymnastics are impossible, and the climber cannot accomplish anything in the nature of a strenuous arm pull, it proved hopeless.

Four hours had flown and the net result was that careful examination and a determined attempt had disclosed the apparent impracticability of the ridge route. We could only speculate as to what the result would have been had they gained the ridge immediately above the First Step. The ridge *may* be practicable; the point is, can a party be spared in the future to prove this? They will have no time or strength left for an alternative route should it prove impossible.

Having failed to reach the foot of the Second Step, Wyn and Waggers were now committed to the sole alternative. Norton and Somervell's route; so they continued along the top of the Yellow Band with the steep rock band of the Second Step above them, and presently came to the head of the great couloir. This they crossed, finding, like Norton before them, treacherously loose snow in the bed of the couloir. On the rocks beyond, where the Yellow Band surges outwards in a buttress separating the main couloir from a subsidiary couloir, they encountered steeper and more difficult climbing. And the conditions were bad; the snow of yesterday's blizzard had accumulated on the sloping ledges and in every crack and chimney. Furthermore, Waggers was tired: he thought he might be able to continue for another hour, not longer. Lastly, the time was 12:30 P.M. Even had conditions and the strength of the party rendered the summit accessible, it would have been impossible to return to camp by nightfall and for exhausted men benighted on Everest there is only one ending.

On the way back they again examined the possibilities of reaching the foot of the Second Step, but they were too tired to carry out their intention of gaining the ridge above the First Step. Finally, Waggers managed to reach the ridge below the First Step immediately above the ice ax (Wyn Harris left his own in place of it), whence he gazed down the stupendous ice slopes of the South-East Face. In this connection it is interesting to note that ice is plastered to the south side of the Second Step, and it is just possible that the step can be avoided by an upward traverse on this side, though whether a climber can cut steps in an ice slope of 60° or more, as the angle would appear to be, at 28,000 feet is another unsolved problem of Everest. There are many problems, and each may use up a party, perhaps a whole expedition.

The full story, as I have given it here, Eric and I did not hear until afterwards, but we heard enough to convince us that we must go "all out" for Norton's route and not dissipate our energy between it and the ridge route, as Wyn and Waggers had so unfortunately had to do in their capacity as a reconnaissance party.

We listened to their story with that apathy peculiar to high altitudes. Even the finding of the ice ax, one of the most dramatic discoveries in the history of mountaineering, failed to evoke more than a passing interest.

By dint of a long and miserable effort the methylated cooker mustered sufficient energy to melt some snow. There was no time to heat up a good drink, for time was getting on, and it was essential that Wyn and Waggers should be off down to Camp 5. So contenting themselves with some lukewarm liquid they gathered themselves together and prepared to descend. It must have cost them more than an ordinary effort to face the weary descent, but what would the position have been if they had been too tired to descend, with one small tent at Camp 6, capable of accommodating only two men, and that uncomfortably? And what if there had been a sudden blizzard to make the descent impossible?

A minute or so later, I took a photograph of them; they were following Jack's downward route; their heads were bowed, and they moved in that heavy dragging way peculiar to tired men.

After their departure Eric and I did our best to make ourselves comfortable. Comfort was the only thing in our minds; all else, all plans and thoughts for the morrow could take care of themselves. And there was little enough comfort to be had in that small tent. No platform had been available for it, and one had been constructed of stones, but the party had been too tired to do this efficiently, or to level the floor of the platform, and the result was that the tent canted outwards, whilst sundry large and sharp stones beneath the thin sewn-in ground sheet reminded us forcibly of the hardness of things in general and of Everest in particular. In addition to this, the outer side of the tent was improperly supported and projected beyond the edge of the platform. This reduced the effective width and added greatly to the discomfort.

I do not remember that there was any discussion as to who should have the upper and who the lower position, I only know I found myself in the upper. The net result was that I spent the night rolling at frequent intervals onto Eric, whilst Eric spent the night being rolled on at frequent intervals by me.

Before trying to sleep, we cooked some supper. There was a little store of provisions, enough for three days, perhaps four at a pinch, and ten or a dozen tins of solid methylated fuel. We placed the cooker between us as we lay in our sleeping bags and investigated the provisions. There was condensed milk, sugar, drinking chocolate, tabloid tea, Ovaltine, café au lait, Brand's meat extracts, sardines, cod roes, biscuits, and sweets.

Hot drinks came before everything else and these the wretched little cooker resolutely refused to produce. At 27,000 feet water boils at a temperature many degrees below the boiling point at sea level, but not once during our stay at Camp 6 did we manage to get a boiling drink, and we had to content ourselves with lukewarm concoctions. Our language regarding the solid methylated cooker is unprintable, but it is far too much of an effort to be angry at 27,400 feet.

Our supper consisted principally of Brand's beef extract, which was frozen solid and had to be thawed out before it could be eaten. We had no desire for solids—indeed, no desire for food of any kind; eating was a duty. Drinking was a different matter. Our bodies were desiccated by the intensely dry atmosphere and craved for moisture, which also served as a palliative for sore and congested throats.

Our meal ended with café au lait and condensed milk, which was voted superb. Then, before settling down for the night, we unlaced the tent flaps and glanced outside; everything now depended on the weather.

The evening was calm, the calmest we had known above the North Col. The smooth, outward dipping slabs glowed in the fast setting sun and, at an immense distance beneath, clouds concealed the valleys and lesser peaks. There was nothing to obstruct the tremendous prospect. Seen from Everest, great peaks that dominate the climber as he toils along the East Rongbuk Glacier, and up the slopes of the North Col, show like insignificant ripples at the base of a great ocean roller. Even the North Peak was but a stepping-stone to quick-footed vision.

It was cold. Space, the air we breathed, the yellow rocks, were deadly cold. There was something ultimate, passionless, and eternal in this cold. It came to us as a single constant note from the depths of space. We stood on the very boundary of life and death.

The night spread out of the east in a great flood, quenching the red sunlight in a single minute.

We wriggled by breathless degrees deep into our sleeping bags. Our sole thought was of comfort; we were not alive to the beauty or the grandeur of our position; we did not reflect on the splendor of our elevation. A regret I shall always have is that I did not muster up the energy to spend a minute or two stargazing. One peep I did make between the tent flaps into the night, and I remember dimly an appalling wealth of stars, not pale and remote as they appear when viewed through the moisture-laden air of lower levels, but brilliant points of electric blue fire standing out almost stereoscopically. It was a sight an astronomer would have given much to see, and here were we lying dully in our sleeping bags concerned only with the importance of keeping warm and comfortable.

There is one blessing, if of a negative nature, in high altitude. The physical and mental processes are so slowed down by lack of oxygen that a sleepless night does not drag as interminably as it does at sea level. The climber, though awake, lies semi-comatose, scarcely heeding time's passage. The one thing that stirs his sluggish mental processes into activity is acute discomfort. At times we *were* acutely uncomfortable, and this was due, as already mentioned, to the uneven sloping platform beneath us and the ineffective width of the tent. Between spasms of rapid breathing, sometimes so acute as to amount to a feeling of suffocation, I would drop off into a light slumber only to roll on top of Eric and awake with a resentful elbow in the small of my back. Then we would curse bitterly, not each other but a common fate.

We slept with heads buttressed high by wads of rucksacks, boots, rope, and windproof clothing, as this aids breathing at high altitudes. Balaclava helmets protected our heads, and only eyes, mouths, and noses were exposed. We were reasonably warm and I felt myself to be resting in spite of my sleeplessness.

The night was calm until shortly before dawn. Then, for the first time, a gust of wind tugged at the tent. It was succeeded by another and stronger gust. By dawn a gale was blowing.

We had planned to start at about 5:30 A.M., but it was impossible; to have left the tent even for a few minutes would have meant certain and severe frostbite. It was terribly depressing to lie thus, our hopes destroyed in a single hour, but at the same time I could not suppress a feeling of relief that I did not have to endure the exertion of turning out of my sleeping bag and of struggling into my windproof suit and boots. Ours was not the disappointment of men eager and willing to set off for an unclimbed summit; we only felt that an unpleasant duty had been frustrated. I was tired too, and needed additional rest to recuperate from the exertions of yesterday. Eric felt differently about this. He told me afterwards that so far from recuperating, his strength deteriorated steadily during the day and that his chance of doing himself justice vanished when we were prevented from starting. This physical difference between us crystallized one of Everest's greatest problems—that of two men setting out for the summit, both at the top of their form.

, As daylight increased snow began to fall; we could hear the familiar yet ever hateful patter, swish, and lash of it on the tent.

We breakfasted. The wretched business of having to replenish the saucepan with snow was scarcely compensated for by the lukewarm cup of tea apiece eventually produced by the cooker, yet it served to stimulate a discussion of the position as we lay side by side in our sleeping bags.

If the weather improved would the summit be possible on the morrow? The new snow, even though much of it blew off the mountain as it fell, would inevitably accumulate in every sheltered place, particularly in the vicinity of the Great Couloir. Neither of us voiced the thought to the other, but we knew that unless a miracle happened we were as good as beaten. However, we could at least go as far as possible when the weather mended. But would the weather mend? At the back of our minds was always the thought of the monsoon. At any moment now it might burst on Everest in full force and snow fall for days on end. What then? We had food for another three days, four at a pinch, maybe even five with the strictest rationing, but there was only fuel for another two days, reckoning the use of one tin of solid methylated fuel per meal and three meals a day. Food is useless at 27,400 feet without fuel. Something to warm the stomach is the first essential; without warmth a man cannot live for long; he is too near the point where the oxygen he breathes is insufficient to counteract the cooling of the body by the cold air. For how many days a man can live at 27,400 feet in a small tent supplied with ample food and fuel is a matter for conjecture. I should say not longer than a week. In the event of a continuous snowstorm we should naturally try to descend, but I do not believe a descent from Camp 6 is possible through deep snow even in fair weather; the slabs of the Yellow Band would be impassable.

A heavy snowfall is a risk the climber will always have to face high on Everest, and it militates against a camp on the final pyramid to the west of the great couloir. Here it needs but a sprinkling of snow to render descent impossible, or at least desperately dangerous, and conditions which do not prohibit a descent from a point as high as the ledge beneath the First Step at nearly 28,000 feet, on which we had planned originally to pitch Camp 6, may well make impossible descent from a more westerly point. Yet, whether or not a camp should be pitched on the pyramid may have to be considered. The main point is that Everest cannot be climbed by any route or method, without risks far in excess of ordinary mountaineering risks, and the problem a mountaineer will always have to face is whether or not he is entitled to take risks overstepping the traditional standards of safety in mountaineering in order to gain success. My own belief is that the man who climbs on the upper part of Everest does overstep these standards, and that owing to the unique nature of the problem his conceptions of what is justifiable and what is unjustifiable cannot be based on Alpine standards of safety and danger. One thing only delimits reasoned adventure from unreasoned recklessness—the duty owed by an expedition to its porters. So long as these men are employed their welfare must always determine the manner of climbing Everest, and this helps the climber to gauge his duty to his comrades, and those who anxiously await his safe return.

By the afternoon a full-dress blizzard was raging. We were far too lethargic to be alarmed at the possibility of being marooned permanently. Indeed, our discussion of the possibilities already mentioned was purely academic and on a curiously detached and impersonal plane, almost as though we were scientists discussing an immature experiment, yet our instincts were animal rather than human, inasmuch as we were concerned only with the present, and our complaints were against trivial things which loomed out of all proportion to the possible events of the future. It is probable that we remember each other's grouses without remembering our own—a happy dispensation. Eric had developed a "complex" relating to fresh food. All through the expedition he had been a protagonist of fresh food. The toughest and most indigestible piece of gristle from a Tibetan sheep of Marathon-like build was to him preferable to the most succulent product of Messrs. Fortnum & Mason that came out of a tin. Now in a hoarse, scarcely audible voice, he enlarged on the lack of fresh food at Camp 6. "Oh, for a few dozen eggs!" was his constant plaint; or "This

_____ tinned muck" he would whisper bitterly. I could sympathize, at all events, with his craving for eggs. Certainly an omelette nicely fried and well buttered with a dash of *fines herbs,* would have gone down well, and one of those huge bilberry omelettes known as "palatschinken" in the Tyrol would have been a welcome change from the frozen corpses of sardines in congealed oil.

As I felt I ought to contribute a grouse of my own, I conceived a more and more bitter hatred for a sharp stone beneath the tent. This had been placed at the exact point most convenient for my hipbone. I made a few futile tugs and jabs at it, but it was evidently a large, well-wedged stone and refused to budge. My remarks concerning it were rich in those hyphens and asterisks whereby the deserving printer tries to conceal, and yet, paradoxically, to reveal the niceties of the English language.

Toward evening there was a sudden gleam of light. We looked outside. The clouds had parted, revealing the rapidly declining sun. Its pale light accentuated rather than mitigated the bleakness of the prospect. The wind was still volleying across Everest, raising spirals of loose snow, which hurried in an endless procession across the slabs. Every crack and cranny held its salt-like snow and only the more exposed slabs had been swept clear. In between the flying rags of mist the sky was green, not the warm green of grass and trees, but a cruel feline green utterly unmerciful. Yet the sight of it rekindled a spark of hope. If we could do nothing else on the morrow we might once and for all dispose of the problem of the ridge route and the Second Step.

The wind was moderating as we prepared our meager supper, and only an occasional squall worried the tent. The night was no more comfortable than the last, and to describe it would be to repeat a catalog of discomforts. Now and again would come a fierce squall succeeded by a period of calm, then another squall. But as the night wore on the calm intervals lengthened and the squalls were less violent. Perhaps, after all, we should be able to attempt the summit. In the conditions we could not hope to succeed; we could only do our best.

THE ASSAULT

The sky was clear at daybreak. We had resolved overnight to leave at 5 A.M., but a rising wind and intense cold made this impossible. Cold we could have faced, but the addition of wind is too much for mere flesh and blood on Everest.

Matters appeared hopeless until an hour later when the wind suddenly fell to a complete calm. And it did not return. We listened expectantly for the hateful rush and tug of it, but the calm persisted.

Breakfast eaten, we extricated ourselves foot by foot from our sleeping bags and with much labor and panting pulled on our windproof suits.

Our boots might have been carved out of stone, and they glistened and sparkled inside with the frozen moisture from our feet. I made a vain attempt to soften mine over a candle, but it was useless, and somehow or other I thrust my feet into them, pausing at intervals to beat my bare hands together, or stuff them into my pockets.

We donned every stitch of clothing we possessed. I wore a Shetland vest, a thick flannel shirt, a heavy camel-hair sweater, six light Shetland pullovers, two pairs of long Shetland pants, a pair of flannel trousers, and over all a silk-lined Grenfell windproof suit. A Shetland balaclava and another helmet of Grenfell cloth protected my head, and my feet were encased in four pairs of Shetland socks and stockings. Gloves are always a problem on Everest, and the ideal glove that is warm yet flexible and will adhere to rocks has still to be designed; in this instance, a pair of woollen fingerless gloves inside a pair of South African lambskin gloves, also fingerless, kept my hands moderately warm.

A slab of Kendal mint cake apiece sufficed for food. It was a mistake not to provide ourselves with more food but our repugnance for it had been still further intensified during our enforced stay at Camp 6. Apart from this we carried a length of light climbing line, whilst my Etui camera accompanied me as usual. (With one film pack this weighed one and a quarter pounds.)

At 7 A.M. we emerged from the tent and laced the flaps behind us. It was sadly obvious that Eric was far below his usual form. He had eaten less than I since we had arrived at the camp, and now he complained of stomach pains, and asked me to go slowly—a request I might have made myself had he been fitter.

A shallow snow-filled gully took us diagonally upwards and across the Yellow Band for the best part of 100 feet. There was no difficulty, but every minute or two we had to halt and lean on our ice axes gasping for breath.

The gully petered out into a great expanse of slabs. Again there was no difficulty; advance was merely a matter of careful balance and choice of the easiest route; yet the angle as a whole on the Yellow Band is such that a slip would probably end in a fatal slide, especially as the climber would have little strength left to stop himself. Fortunately, our broad, lightly nailed boots gripped the sandstone well. The snow of yesterday's blizzard had been blown from many of the slabs, but here and there where it had accumulated on the shelving ledges we had to tread circumspectly.

Though we left the camp an hour and a half later than Wyn and Waggers had done, the cold was still intense and there was little warmth in the sun, which was just peeping over the Northeast Ridge.

The first and most lasting impression of the climber on Everest will always be the bleak and inhospitable nature of the great mountain. On the Yellow Band no projecting crags, ridges, or buttresses stimulate the interest or the imagination; there is nothing level and the climber must tread a series of outward-shelving ledges where the rope is useless to him. Never have I seen a more utterly desolate mountainside. And above, still a weary way above, was the summit pyramid set squarely at the end of this vast rocky roof; a last tremendous challenge to our failing strength.

Traversing, and ascending slightly, we made for the foot of the First Step which, from the moment we emerged from the initial gully, appeared close at hand. Its shape reminded me in some curious way of the summit of a Lake District hill, which I had climbed one dewy spring morning before breakfast to "work up an appetite." It had taken me an hour to scale 2,300 feet of turfy bracken-clad fellside, and now with eleven hours of daylight in hand I was doubtful whether we had the time or strength to climb and descend 1,600 feet. Yet, I was going better than I had expected. Exercise was loosening my cramped and stiffened limbs and for the first time since arriving at Camp 6 I was conscious of warm blood flowing vigorously in my veins. But, unhappily, this was not the case with Eric. He was going steadily, but very slowly, and it was more than ever plain that there was something wrong with him.

Not far from the First Step we crossed an almost level platform covered in small screes, a possible site for a future camp, then traversed almost horizontally. We were immediately below the Step when I heard an exclamation behind me. Turning, I saw that Eric had stopped and was leaning heavily on his ice ax. Next moment he sank down into a sitting position.

Many times during the march across Tibet we had discussed what to do in the event of one man of a party of two being unable to continue, and we had agreed that unless he was exhausted and unable to return alone safely his companion should carry on alone, in which decision he would be supported by the expedition and its leader. It was an expedition maxim that no man must go on 'til he reached a point of complete exhaustion, and Eric was far too good a mountaineer to do this. The saving grace in high-altitude climbing is that there is a point at which a man cannot continue to ascend but can still descend relatively easily and quite safely. This is Nature's automatic safety check.

I asked Eric whether he felt fit enough to return to camp safely. He replied unhesitatingly, "Yes," and added that he would follow slowly. This last, though I did not know it at the time, was inspired by generosity. He had no intention of proceeding farther and merely said that he would to encourage me and relieve me from all anxiety as to his safety. It was another example of that good comradeship which will one day take men to the summit of Everest.

Leaving him seated on a rock, I continued. I looked back after a minute or so, but he had as yet made no move.

There was never any doubt as to the best route. The crest of the Northeast Ridge, leading to the foot of the Second Step, was sharp, jagged, and obviously difficult. As for the Second Step, now almost directly above me, it *looked* utterly impregnable, and I can only compare it to the sharp bow of a battle cruiser. Norton's route alone seemed to offer any chance of success, and it follows the Yellow Band beneath a sheer wall to the head of the Great Couloir.

At first there was no difficulty, and a series of sloping ledges at the top of the Yellow Band took me round a corner and out of sight of Eric. Then came a patch of snow perhaps thirty yards wide. There was no avoiding it except by a descent of nearly a hundred feet, but fortunately the snow was not the evil floury stuff I had expected, but had been well compacted by the wind; indeed, such hard snow that step-cutting was necessary.

Step-cutting at nearly 28,000 feet is a fatiguing operation, and the ax seemed unconscionably heavy and unready to do its work. In the Alps one powerful stroke with the adze would have fashioned a step, but sudden spurts of exertion are to be avoided at 28,000 feet, and I preferred the alternative of several light, short strokes. I must have looked like an old hen grubbing for worms, but even so I had to cease work and puff hard after making each step.

High altitudes promote indecision. Projecting through the snow was a rock and at first sight it seemed a good foothold. Then I thought it was too sloping and that I had better cut to one side of it. But I had no sooner changed my mind when I decided that perhaps after all it could be used as a foothold and would save me a step or two. I must have spent a minute or two turning this ridiculous little point over in my mind before doing what was the obvious thing—avoiding it. It is curious how small problems encountered during a great undertaking can assume an importance out of all proportion to their true worth.

When I had crossed the snow I again glanced back, but there was no sign of Eric following me, and I continued on my solitary way.

Contrary to accepted mountaineering practice, I found that the easiest as well as the safest method of traversing the slabs was to keep the ice ax in the outside hand as there were always little cracks and crannies to put it in. It was a third leg to me and an invaluable companion throughout the whole of the day.

Beyond the snow patch the slabs were covered here and there with loose, powdery snow. This had to be kicked or scraped away before I dared stand on the outward-sloping ledges. Progress was slow, though steady, and as I advanced and saw the final pyramid appear above the band of rocks beneath which I was traversing, there came to me for the first time that day a thrill of excitement and hope. I was going well now, better than when I had parted from Eric and for a moment there seemed a chance of success.

The bed of the Great Couloir was hidden, but a subsidiary couloir and a buttress separating it from the Great Couloir were full in view. Both were sheltered from the wind and as a result were still heavily plastered with the snow of yesterday's blizzard. My hopes were dashed as I gazed at the buttress. It was considerably steeper than the rocks I was traversing, and snow filled every crack and was piled deeply on every sloping ledge. Was it climbable in such a condition? In the Alps perhaps, but not at 28,000 feet by a man nearing the limit of his strength. And the subsidiary couloir? Even supposing the traverse of the buttress proved practicable, what kind of snow should I find in this narrow cleft? Most likely unstable powder affording no certain footing and impeding every movement. True, it might be possible to avoid it by climbing the rocks at one side, but these, in their turn, were mostly snow-covered.

Instinctively I looked for an alternative. Could I climb directly upwards to a point above the Second Step and attack the final pyramid without having to continue this long, wearisome, and unprofitable traverse? The wall rose above me like a sea cliff, in places it overhung, and every hold, every wrinkle and crack held its quota of snow. There was no visible break in it until the buttress where there was a gap, possibly the point reached by Norton in 1924, which might prove a feasible alternative to the subsidiary couloir. At all events direct ascent was impossible. One thing alone gave me hope: once the subsidiary couloir had been climbed and the rock band passed there seemed every reason to suppose that the principal difficulties were behind. I could see the face of the final pyramid, and it did not look difficult. There was a scree slope at the base of it and higher a slope of light-colored boulders. Energy alone would be required to surmount it. Of course, it may hold its surprises, for Everest will remain a stubborn opponent to the last; but I feel confident that once the rock band is below, the change from difficult and dangerous climbing to safe and easy climbing will inspire the climber to outlast fatigue and altitude over the remaining 600 feet to the summit.

The angle of the Yellow Band steepened gradually as I approached the Great Couloir. In general direction the ledges were parallel with the Band, but they were not always continuous, and once or twice I had to retrace my steps for a yard or two and seek an alternative route. But the climbing was never difficult—it required only unfailing attention to the planting of each foot on the sloping ledges, especially when these were masked by loose snow.

Presently the bed of the Great Couloir became visible. It was shallow enough not to necessitate any steep descent into it, and was filled with snow, perhaps thirty to forty feet wide, which ended beneath the rock band. Several hundred feet lower was a pitch of unknown height, beneath that the couloir widened out into a small hanging glacier, then fell steeply toward the Rongbuk Glacier, a total height from my position of about 8,000 feet.

It was a savage place. Beyond was the steep and snowy buttress separating me from the subsidiary couloir, and hemming me in above was the unrelenting band of rock, and higher still the final pyramid, a weary distance away, cutting aloofly into the blue.

I approached the couloir along a ledge, which bent round a steep little corner. This ledge was comfortably wide until it came to the corner, then it narrowed until it was only a few inches broad. As far as the corner it was easy going, but to turn the corner I had to edge along, my face to the mountain, in a crab-like fashion. The rocks above projected awkwardly, but it was not a place that would have caused a second's hesitation on an Alpine climb. One step only was needed to take me round the corner. This step I funked. The balance was too critical. With arms spread-eagled above me I sought for steadying handholds. They were not essential; balance alone should have sufficed, but I felt I could not manage without them. I could find none; every wrinkle in the rocks sloped outwards. For a few moments I stood thus like a man crucified, while my heart bumped quickly and my lungs labored for oxygen, and there flashed through my mind the possibility of a backward topple into the couloir and an interminable slide into belated oblivion.

I retired a few yards and apostrophized myself as a fool. I knew that the traverse was possible, and if Eric had been there I should not have hesitated. Being alone made all the difference.

I tried again, and once more found myself in the spread-eagled position but without the courage to take the one step that would have placed me in safety round the corner.

The only alternative was a ledge about twenty feet below. I was loath to lose even twenty feet of height, but there was nothing for it but to descend.

The slabs separating me from the ledge were reasonably rough, and though there were no very definite holds there were wrinkles and folds. For the rest friction should serve. Facing outwards and sitting down I lowered myself gingerly off the ledge on the palms of my hands. The friction was even better than I had hoped for, and the seat of my trousers almost sufficed by itself to maintain me in position without the additional support of the palms of my hands. There was no awkward corner in the lower ledge; it was wide and honest, and though it sloped outwards and supported a bank of snow three or four feet deep, it brought me without difficulty to the snowy bed of the couloir.

Wyn and Waggers had found the same loose, disagreeable snow in the couloir as had Norton in 1924, but I suspect that they traversed the upper ledge and so crossed higher than I. The snow at my level, as a tentative forward dig with the ice ax revealed, had been hardened by the wind and step-cutting was again necessary.

One step, then a pause to gasp, while the snow at my feet and the rocks beyond swam uncertainly before me. Then another step and another bout of gasping.

The snow was very hard and the angle of the Great Couloir at this point fully 50°. About a dozen steps—I was across at last.

Next, how to traverse the buttress? I must climb almost straight up it for about fifty feet before continuing more or less horizontally toward the subsidiary couloir.

The rocks were steep and snow had accumulated on them untouched as yet by the wind. How had the wind swept the snow in the couloir hard and left the slabs at this side unaffected?

When these slabs are snow-free they are probably not much more difficult than the slabs to the east of the Great Couloir. There are numerous ledges, and though the general angle is appreciably steeper, there is no necessity for anything but balance climbing, and I confidently believe no insuperable obstacle will prevent the climber from reaching the subsidiary couloir. But now snow had accumulated deeply on the shelving ledges and it was the worst kind of snow, soft like flour, loose like granulated sugar and incapable of holding the feet in position. As I probed it with my ax, I knew at once that the game was up. So far the climbing had been more dangerous than difficult now it was both difficult and dangerous, a fatal combination on Everest. The only thing I could do was to go as far as possible, always keeping one eye on the weather and the other on the strength I should need to retreat safely.

The weather at all events was fair. In the shelter of the buttress and the wall beyond the subsidiary couloir there was not a breath of wind and the sun shone powerfully—too powerfully, for it seemed to sap my strength and my resolution. I was a prisoner, struggling vainly to escape from a vast hollow enclosed by dungeon-like walls. Wherever I looked hostile rocks frowned down on my impotent strugglings, and the wall above seemed almost to overhang me with its dark strata set one upon the other, an embodiment of static, but pitiless, force. The final pyramid was hidden; if only I were on it away from this dismal place with its unrelenting slabs. The climber who wins across the slabs to the final pyramid must conquer a sickness of spirit as well as a weariness of body.

With both arms at breast-high level I began shoveling the snow away before me; it streamed down the couloir behind me with a soft swishing noise. Several minutes elapsed before a sloping ledge was disclosed, then I heaved myself up, until first one knee, and then the other, were on it. In this position, like a supplicant before a priest, I had to remain while my lungs, intolerably accelerated by the effort, heaved for oxygen. Then with another effort I stood cautiously upright.

More snow had to be cleared before I could tread a smaller ledge on the slab above; then, to my relief, came a step unattended by this prodigious effort of clearing away snow. But relief is short-lived on Everest and the ledge that followed was covered several feet deep in snow beveled into a steep bank, yet without the slightest cohesion.

Presently I had to stop, as apart from the need to rest overstressed heart and lungs, immersing my arms in the snow brought such numbness to my hands, gloved though they were, that I feared I might let slip my ice ax.

So slow and exhausting was the work of clearing the snow that I began to rely on feel alone. That is to say, when I could I trusted my foot to find holds beneath the snow rather than clear the snow away from the slabs until I could see the holds. I realized full well the danger of this, and whenever possible used my ice ax pick as an extra support by jamming it into cracks. This last precaution undoubtedly saved me from catastrophe. There was one steeply shelving slab deeply covered with soft snow into which I sank to the knees, but my first exploring foot discovered a knob beneath it. This seemed quite firm and, reaching up with my ax, I wedged the pick of it half an inch or so into a thin crack. Then, cautiously, I raised my other foot on to the knob, at the same time transferring my entire weight to my front foot. My rear foot was joining my front foot when the knob, without any warning, suddenly broke away. For an instant, both feet slid outwards, and my weight came on the ice ax; next moment I had recovered my footing and discovered another hold. It happened so quickly that my sluggish brain had no time to register a thrill of fear; I had acted purely instinctively and the incident was over almost before I knew it had occurred. I did not even feel scared afterwards as I was climbing now in a curiously detached, impersonal frame of mind. It was almost as though one part of me stood aside and watched the other struggle on. Lack of oxygen and fatigue are responsible for this dulling of the mental faculties, but principally lack of oxygen. It is a dangerous state of mind and comparable to the mental reactions of a drunken man in charge of a car. He may believe that his judgment is unimpaired, even that he can drive more skillfully than usual; in point of fact, as statistics and the police court news reveal, he is much more prone to an accident in this condition.

Just before crossing the Great Couloir I had looked at my watch; it was 10 A.M. Now I looked again. An hour had passed, and I had made about fifty feet of height, not more. At least 300 feet of difficult rocks, all deeply snow-covered, remained to be climbed, before easier ground on the final pyramid was reached. Perhaps I could do another hour or two's work, but what was the use of it? I should only exhaust myself completely and not have the strength left to return.

I shoveled away the floury snow until I had made a space on which I could stand; though I did not dare to sit.

I was high up on the buttress separating the Great Couloir from the subsidiary couloir. Above me was the band of rock beneath which I had been, and was still, traversing. It looked impregnable except where it was breached by the subsidiary couloir, and the place already mentioned a few yards to the east of this couloir. For the rest, it is Everest's greatest defense, and stretches unbroken across the north face of the mountain. The striated limestone rocks composing it actually overhang in places, and the section above the Great Couloir reminded me of the well-known pitch in the Central Gully, on Lliwedd, in North Wales.

It is possible, indeed probable, that weariness and altitude distorted my judgment, but there are two things I believe to be true. Firstly, that Norton's route is practicable, and that when the "tiles," as he calls the slabs, are free of snow, they can be traversed without excessive difficulty to the subsidiary couloir, and this can be climbed on to the face of the final pyramid. Secondly, that it is not a practicable route when snow covers the slabs. But there is no doubt that even in the best conditions this part of the climb will tax a climber's powers to the uttermost. The unrelenting exposure of the slabs, dependence on the friction of boot nails for hours on end, added to the physical and mental weariness and lethargy due to altitude, will require something more than strength and skill if they are to be countered successfully. The summit was just in view over the rock band. It was only 1,000 feet above me, but an eon of weariness separated me from it. Bastion on bastion and slab on slab, the rocks were piled in tremendous confusion, their light-yellow edges ghostlike against the deep-blue sky. From the crest a white plume of mist flowed silently away, like unending volcanic steam, but where I stood there was not a breath of wind and the sun blazed into the hollow with an intense fierceness, yet without warming the cold air. Clouds were gathering, but they were thousands of feet below me. Between them I could see the Rongbuk Glacier, a pure white in its uppermost portion then rugged and uneven where it was resolved into a multitude of séracs and, lower still, a gigantic muddle of moraines as though all the navies in the world had been furiously excavating to no logical purpose. Beyond it, the Rongbuk Valley stretched northwards toward the golden hills of Tibet, and I could make out the Rongbuk Monastery, a minute cluster of minute buildings, yet distinct in every detail through the brilliantly clear atmosphere. With this one exception, I remember no details. My position was too high, my, view too vast, my brain too fatigued to register detail. There was nothing visible to challenge my elevation. The earth was so far beneath; it seemed impossible I could ever regain it. The human brain must needs be divinely inspired to comprehend such a vista, and mine was tied to a body fatigued by exertion and slowed down in all its vital processes by lack of oxygen. Somervell's description of the scene is simplest and best: "A god's view."

More by instinct than anything else, I pulled my camera out of my pocket. The photograph I took is pitifully inadequate.

I cannot enlarge on the bitterness of defeat. Those who have failed on Everest are unanimous in one thing: the relief of not having to go on outweighs all other considerations. The last 1000 feet of Everest are not for mere flesh and blood. Whoever reaches the summit, if he does it without artificial aid, will have to rise godlike above his own frailties and his tremendous environment. Only through a Power within him and without him will he overcome a deadly fatigue and win through to success.

Descending even difficult ground at high altitudes is almost as easy as descending at an Alpine level, and within a few minutes I regained the Great Couloir. Recrossing it, I halted on the broad, comfortable ledge to take a photograph. It is curious that I did not remember taking this photograph or the one from my highest point until the film was developed, so I think my action at the time was more automatic than reasoned, as before starting on the expedition I told myself many times that I must take photographs whenever possible. This lends color to a theory I have long held, that in climbing at great altitudes, when mind and body are in the grip of an insidious lethargy, it is on the subconscious, rather than the conscious, that the climber must rely to push him forwards. Therefore, it is essential that the will to reach the summit of Everest be strengthened by a prior determination to get there. Perhaps it is not too much to say that Everest will be climbed in England.

After taking this photograph it occurred to me that I ought to eat something. I was not in the least hungry, indeed the thought of food was utterly repugnant, especially as my mouth was almost dry, and my tongue leather-like, but in duty bound I pulled a slab of mint cake from my pocket.

And now I must relate the curious incident described in "Everest 1933."

After leaving Eric a strange feeling possessed me that I was accompanied by another. I have already mentioned a feeling of detachment in which it seemed as though I stood aside and watched myself. Once before, during a fall in the Dolomites, I had the same feeling, and it is not an uncommon experience with mountaineers who have a long fall. It may be that the feeling that I was accompanied was due to this, which, in its turn, was due to lack of oxygen and the mental and physical stress of climbing alone at a great altitude. I do not offer this as an explanation, but merely as a suggestion.

This "presence" was strong and friendly. In its company I could not feel lonely, neither could I come to any harm. It was always there to sustain me on my solitary climb up the snow-covered slabs. Now, as I halted and extracted some mint cake from my pocket, it was so near and so strong that instinctively I divided the mint into two halves and turned round with one half in my hand to offer it to my "companion."

It was apparent when I recrossed the couloir that I would do better to return across the Yellow Band by a lower route. The angle of the band west of the First Step is very slightly concave, and on such slabs a degree or two in angle makes all the difference. The western end of the band terminates below in a great cutoff, a sheer precipice which carries the eye in a single bound to the Rongbuk Glacier. My return route lay a few yards above and parallel to the edge of this precipice. There was no difficulty whatsoever. Care alone was needed, especially when crossing some patches of snow which, unlike those on the upper part of the band, were treacherously soft and unstable.

Very soon I found myself below the point where I had parted from Eric, but on looking up, could see no sign of him. I now had to make the choice between climbing up at least 100 feet and joining the ascending route or of traversing directly to the camp. To ascend again at this stage was utterly distasteful. I was too tired, and my legs were leaden; they would descend easily enough or traverse horizontally, but I doubt whether I could have dragged them uphill unless hard pressed. A temptation I had to resist firmly was to slant off down the Yellow Band by Norton and Somervell's route. This was a far easier line than the long, wearisome traverse across a series of shelving ledges to Camp 6. In two or three hours I could have reached Camp 5, even continued on down to the comfort of the arctic tent at Camp 4. Unfortunately, Eric was waiting for me at Camp 6, and if I did not turn up he would naturally assume an accident.

The climbing was simple enough at first, but presently became more difficult. Instead of the easy slabs, which had led us upwards from the camp to the foot of the First Step, I found myself on a series of narrow outward-sloping ledges separated by abrupt little walls. These ledges were never continuous for long, and it was necessary when one petered out to descend to another. However, I could still afford to lose height without descending below the level of Camp 6.

This route took me across the band some distance below the place where Wyn and Waggers found the ice ax, but I did not see any further traces of Mallory and Irvine. I remember glancing down at a wide, gently sloping expanse of snow, screes, and broken rocks below the band and thinking that if the ice ax indeed marked the point where they slipped, it was possible that their bodies might have come to rest there.

Some of the ledges were wider than others and I paused to rest at intervals. It was during one of these halts that I was startled to observe an extraordinary phenomenon.

Chancing to look over the North-East Shoulder, now directly in front of me, I saw two dark objects in the sky. In shape they resembled kite balloons, and my first reaction was to wonder what on earth kite balloons could be doing near Everest, a certain proof that lack of oxygen had impaired my mental faculties; but a moment later I recognized this as an absurd thought. At the same time I was very puzzled. The objects were black and silhouetted sharply against the sky, or possibly a background of cloud; my memory is not clear on this point. They were bulbous in shape, and one possessed what looked like squat, underdeveloped wings, whilst the other had a beak-like protuberance like the spout of a teakettle. But what was most weird about them was that they distinctly pulsated with an in-and-out motion as though they possessed some horrible quality of life. One interesting point is that these pulsations were much slower than my own heartbeats; of this I am certain, and I mention it in view of a suggestion put forward afterwards that it was an optical illusion and that the apparent pulsations synchronized with my pulse rate.

After my first reaction of "kite balloons" my brain seemed to function normally, and so interested was I that, believing them to be fantasies of my imagination, I deliberately put myself through a series of mental tests. First of all I looked away. The objects did not follow my vision, but when my gaze returned to the North-East Shoulder they were still hovering there. I looked away again, and by way of a more exacting mental test identified by name a number of peaks, valleys, and glaciers. I found no difficulty in Cho Oyu, Gyachung Kang, Pumori, and the Rongbuk Glacier, but when I again looked back the objects were in precisely the same position.

Nothing was to be gained by further examination and, tired as I was with the apparently endless succession of slabs, I decided to carry on to Camp 6. I was just starting off when a mist, forming suddenly, began to drift across the North-East Shoulder. Gradually the objects disappeared behind it. Soon they were vague shadows, then as the mist thickened, they disappeared altogether. The mist only lasted a few seconds, then melted away. I expected to see the objects again, but they were no longer there; they had disappeared as mysteriously as they came.

Was it an optical illusion or a mirage? It may be of interest to state that my height was about 27,600 feet and that the objects were a few degrees above the Northeast Ridge about halfway between the position of the 1924 Camp 6 and the crest of the North-East Shoulder. This gives their height as about 27,200 feet, and a line connecting me with them would have ended not in a background of sky, but of clouds and mountains. It is possible, therefore, that imagination magnified some strange effect of mist, mountain, and shadow, yet whatever they were, it was a strange and altogether uncanny experience.

The first light mist was a forerunner of other mists, which quickly gathered and drifted across the mountainside, concealing familiar landmarks. It might not be easy to find Camp 6 among the wilderness of slabs in a mist and I began to feel anxious, especially as I could not see the tent. Fortunately, however, two prominent towers on the Northeast Ridge, which I knew were directly above the camp, showed now and then.

In places the sandstone slabs were intersected horizontally by slippery belts of quartzite. The first intimation I had as to how slippery they were, was when I lowered myself down a steep little wall onto an outward-sloping quartzite ledge. It was far more slippery than the sandstone ledges, and I did not dare trust my bootnails upon it. There was no alternative but to climb up to a sandstone ledge, and this ascent, though it cannot have been more than 20 feet, made me realize how tired I was.

Presently the two rock towers were almost immediately above me, and I halted and looked round expectantly for the camp. It was still not visible. Was I above it or below it? Had my routefinding been at fault? All about me was a vast labyrinth of outward-dipping slabs. Now and then a puff of icy mist would float out of space and pass djinn-like up the mountainside to the crest of the Northeast Ridge where it shredded out and rushed away to join in the ceaselessly moving vapor that boiled upwards and outwards from the south-east precipice.

A few more steps. There was something familiar now about the rocks. Suddenly I came to a shallow, gently sloping gully filled with snow. There were footmarks in the snow; it was the gully immediately above the camp. Next instant I saw the little tent snugly bedded in a corner; small wonder I had not seen it before. What a relief! I let out a hoarse croak of joy and quickly scrambled down to it.

Eric was there. It scarcely needed a word on my part to tell him of my failure; he had seen enough to gauge the conditions. He had descended without difficulty and his stomach was much better. We both talked in whispers, for my mouth and throat had been dried up by the cold air. A hot drink was the first thing; I had not known how thirsty I was, for the intense desiccation of high altitudes takes the body a stage beyond the mere sensation of thirst. And the warmth of it; there was life in that drink.

We discussed plans. Now that we had failed our one desire was for comfort, and there was no comfort at Camp 6. Eric was well rested and strong enough to descend to Camp 5. I, on the other hand, felt very tired; that hour of climbing beyond the Great Couloir had taken it out of me more than many hours of ordinary climbing. We agreed, therefore, that Eric should descend whilst I remained at Camp 6 and descended next morning. It was not a good arrangement; men should not separate on Everest, but another miserable night wedged together in that little tent was not to be borne.

An hour later, at about 1:30 P.M., Eric left. The weather was fast deteriorating, mists had formed above and below and a rising wind was beginning to raise the powdery snow from the face of the mountain. For a few minutes I watched him methodically traversing the sloping shelf, following Jack Longland's descending route; then a corner hid him from sight and I lay back in my sleeping bag for a much needed rest.

For the next hour I lay semi-comatose from fatigue.

I may even have slept. Then I became suddenly conscious of the tent shuddering violently in a high wind. The rest had refreshed me greatly and my brain was beginning to reassert itself over my tired body. I unlaced the tent flaps and looked outside. A blizzard was blowing; nothing was to be seen but a few yards of slabs over which the snow-laden gusts rushed and twisted. Rapidly the wind increased. I could feel the little tent rising and straining against the guy ropes, and, in between the thudding and cracking of its sorely stressed cloth, hear salvos of driven snow spattering viciously against it.

Eric? I was very anxious. He must be having a horrible descent. He would do it all right; he was not one to associate with mountaineering accidents; his calm, detached confidence was a passport to safety in itself. Still, I could not rid myself of anxiety or of a succession of futile yet worrying pictures that flashed through my mind: snow and wind; wind, relentless, battering, snow-filled wind; wind as cold as death; and a lonely, toiling, ice-encrusted figure.

Toward sundown the wind fell appreciably and the clouds blew clear of Everest. Again I looked outside. Every other peak was concealed beneath a roof of clouds stretching in every direction. At that level a tempestuous wind was blowing and now and then a mass seethed upwards as though violently impelled from below and shriveled into nothingness. The sky above was blue-green, never have I seen a colder color, and the declining sun was entirely without warmth. Now and then little twisting devils of wind-driven snow scurried past: small wonder that the Tibetan believes in a cold hell; here were its very flames licking across the slabs of Chamalung.

There was little fuel left and half of it went to cook my supper. It was 6 P.M. when I had finished. I exulted in my comfort. There were now two lots of sleeping bags to keep me warm and I was soon snug with enough below me to defeat the sharpest stone. It did not occur to me that I was spending a night higher than any other human being; I was purely animal in my desire for warmth and comfort. Neither did I feel in the least lonely; in this respect it seemed as natural to spend a night alone in a tent at 27,400 feet as in a hotel at sea level.

I remember nothing more until the following morning. Something heavy was pressing on me when I awoke, and I was astonished to find a snowdrift covering the lower half of my body, reaching almost to the ridge of the tent. How had it got there? Then I remembered a small hole which Eric and I had accidentally burnt in the side of the tent during our cooking operations. It was only an inch or so in diameter, yet large enough for the powdery snow to pour ceaselessly through all night like sand through an hourglass, gathering in a drift which filled nearly a quarter of the tent. There must have been a more than usually severe blizzard.

I looked at my watch: 7 A.M.; I had slept the clock round for the first time since leaving the Base Camp, if not for the first time during the whole expedition. And I was greatly refreshed; as long as I lay without moving I felt almost as though I were at sea level; my heart was beating slowly, steadily and rhythmically, and my brain was more active than it had been since leaving Camp 4. Perhaps I might be able to settle once and for all the vexed question of the Second Step before descending to Camp 4. With this idea in my mind I heaved myself up into a sitting position and began energetically to push away the snow. Instantly the familiar panting supervened, and at the same moment I was aware of the intense cold, the greatest cold I remember during the expedition. Within a few seconds sensation had left my hands and I had to push them into the sleeping bag and put them between my thighs.

The sun had not yet reached the tent, possibly it was behind clouds, and it was useless to think of doing anything until it arrived. It struck the tent a few minutes later, and putting on my gloves I rummaged among the snow for fuel and provisions; it was some time before I found a tin, the last tin, of solid methylated fuel and could prepare a cupful of café au lait. I loathed the sight of food, but I managed to force some down. Then I looked outside. One glance was sufficient: even if I had the strength or inclination (and the latter was now at a low ebb) for a reconnaissance, the appearance of the weather, to say nothing of the lack of fuel, made an immediate descent imperative. High gray clouds were stealing out of the west and overhead a formless murk was gathering in which the sun was struggling with fast diminishing power, whilst the freshly fallen snow had a dull lifeless look. Another blizzard was brewing.

Collecting my few possessions together, I crawled outside and hooked together the flaps of the tent. Then crossing a snow slope I commenced to work along the shelf toward the North-East Shoulder. One backward glance I took at the little tent: it looked strangely pathetic perched amid the desolate rocks and I felt almost as though I were abandoning a friend. It had served us well.

The air was calm and the monsoon clouds thousands of feet beneath almost stationary. This was fortunate, as the shelf proved none too easy. The wind in the night had been too high to allow much snow to collect, but such snow as there was had firmly cemented the screes masking the slabs, and in places, where there were no screes, the slabs were thinly veneered with ice. It was the only time I had seen this disagreeable condition, known to Alpine mountaineers as verglas, above the North Col, and it may have been caused by the sun of the previous day warming the rocks so that the first snow melted and froze, or it may have been due to wind pressure.

Near the North-East Shoulder the shelf petered out into a slope of soft powdery snow resting upon shelving slabs. Except that it was not so steep, it was a replica of the place beyond the Great Couloir. My first impulse was to descend as directly as possible, but I noticed that by descending diagonally across it I would come to some rocks leading down to the screes below the Yellow Band. The snow here had been little affected by the wind and covered the rocks two or three feet deep, and at every step I sank in above the knees. Also, like the snow beyond the Great Couloir, it was so loose that it could not have held me in the event of a slip, and I had an unpleasant feeling that the whole lot might pour off the slabs at any moment, carrying me with it.

After a very slow and careful descent, I reached a shallow chimney by the side of the rocks. The way now was obvious and relatively easy, and I paused for a rest. As I did so I saw a curious fuzziness in the northwest. Quickly it concealed the final pyramid and advanced along the slabs. Scarcely before I had time to realize what it meant, a gust of wind nearly blew me from my holds. Then came another gust and another, and before I had time to move a hurricane was raging.

The situation changed with almost ridiculous suddenness. From climbing slowly, but reasonably comfortably in a still atmosphere, I was reduced to clinging on to the rocks for all I was worth, whilst great waves of wind tried to sweep me from the mountain. Fortunately, easy ground at the foot of the Yellow Band was only about fifty feet below and somehow or other I managed to climb down the rocks to it. But any relief I felt at treading a gentler slope was quickly offset by the hurricane. Muffled up though I was in all my clothing with two helmets on my head, it was impossible to face the driven snow, and with my goggles almost useless I could see little or nothing. So fierce was the wind that there were times when I could only progress on hands and knees, and even so I was several times swept from my balance and only managed to stop myself with my ice ax. All the malignity and intolerance of Everest were concentrated in that withering blast. And the cold was proportional to the wind, the most paralyzing cold I have ever known. It was not content merely to numb my hands and feet; it seized my whole body in a merciless grip.

I have a dim memory of passing the foot of the yellow pinnacle above the 1924 Camp 6 and of bearing instinctively to the right toward the crest of the north ridge. Here with nothing to break its rush, the wind was at its worst, and for minutes at a time progress was impossible. I could feel a kind of deadness creeping up the lower half of my body, something I had never known before, and I remember thinking vaguely that the end would come when it reached my heart. My legs were stiff too, and seemed scarcely to belong to me. The struggle could not be kept up for much longer.

Suddenly I found myself on the crest of the North Ridge and in a familiar place. A few feet below me was the ledge where Eric and I had rested during our ascent to Camp 6; the only place sheltered from the wind.

Slowly and stiffly I half climbed, half slid down to it. There was no wind there and I could actually feel the sun shining dimly through the clouds of wind-driven snow.

For a while I sat too numbed and exhausted to move. Then I began to beat and kick my lifeless hands and feet together. Slowly the dead feeling left my body and circulation painfully returned except to my fingertips and feet, which no amount of kicking could restore to life.

It was astonishingly warm on the ledge, but on the crest of the ridge above me the wind roared ferociously, striking the rocks now and then with a noise like a thunderclap and the clouds of wind-driven snow whirled over my head.

Half an hour later the first fury of the storm had spent itself and I was ready to face the remainder of the descent. I would have remained longer, but the sun had disappeared and with it the warmth.

It was an effort to clamber back over the ridge and endure the wind again. To follow the ridge was impossible, and after passing the remnants of the 1924 Camp 6 I kept below it to the west where the wind was not so strong; even so I had frequently to cling to the rocks to prevent myself from being blown away, and progress was very slow, especially as the rocks are steeper here than those above the camp. Providentially, the wind lessened considerably as I lost height. At about 26,000 feet it was blowing nothing worse than an ordinary gale and visibility had improved to such an extent that there was no risk of missing Camp 5 as I had feared at one time.

Progress should have been more rapid, but if anything it was slower. I was very tired and every wall and slab took a long time to negotiate. By the time the tents of Camp 5 came into view I was descending at a snail-like pace and my legs seemed scarcely to belong to me. I was about 300 feet above the camp when I first saw it, and was just congratulating myself on the prospect of rest, shelter, and a hot drink when two figures emerged from one of the tents. I shouted and waved, but even in my own ears my voice sounded a thin, hoarse wail. They did not hear me; instead, and it was tragic to watch, they busily set about collapsing the only tent left standing.

I shouted again, angrily this time—fate was playing me a scurvy trick— but they neither looked up nor heard me, and a minute or two later set off down to Camp 4 and vanished from sight.

Cursing bitterly, I continued, and it may have been due to this disappointment, but I experienced considerable difficulty in descending some steep slabs interspersed with abrupt little walls. There was one place in particular which I remember vividly where I had to let myself down by the arms onto a snow-covered slab in an angle of which was a bed of hard snow. The lower part of the slab was too steep to descend and I had to cut steps down the snow; it was all I could do to cut them, and they cost me much of my dwindling reserve of strength. Once at the camp and with nothing but the easiest of scrambling before me I decided not to halt and re-erect the collapsed tent, but to continue the descent to Camp 4. I learned later that if I had looked inside the tent I should have found a thermos of hot tea, which Bill [Birnie] had considerately left there.

I was feeling considerably stronger now, owing no doubt to the loss of altitude, and the only thing that bothered me was a curious weakness in my legs, which had developed an annoying habit of giving way under me every few yards. The strange part of it is that I do not remember feeling tired, yet I staggered down the rocks like a Saturday night drunk.

A miserable descent: well-known landmarks were reached and passed with nightmare-like slowness: a small piece of red bunting; two big blocks of rock; Finch's 1922 camp with its tattered green canvas; and scattered oxygen cylinders.

At last the top of the long snow slope; and there I was cheered by seeing some figures issue from the two blister-like arctic tents at Camp 4 and begin slowly to mount the ridge.

It was easy enough descending now, but I could not glissade in my weak condition and had to follow the rock crest all the way, and an incredibly laborious crest it seemed. However, my legs were in better shape; I rested rather than collapsed every few yards, yet, paradoxically, I felt more tired than before, and the explanation of this must lie in the difference between ordinary physical tiredness and exhaustion due primarily to altitude.

Of those who ascended from the camp some stopped with Eric and Bill to assist them down, whilst one came on for me, and after climbing some distance up the ridge halted to wait for me. When I got to him I saw it was Jack. He was half frozen, but he greeted me cheerfully and produced a thermos full of hot tea laced with brandy. The effect was nothing short of miraculous, and within a minute or two my whole body was charged with warmth and renewed strength. Thenceforward there was no need to halt and I was able to keep going continuously.

What a scene when at last we popped our heads in at the arctic tent. Eric, and Bill were there in their sleeping bags, both very tired, whilst Willy was bustling about preparing hot drinks and food, and in general doing all he could for everyone.

In a minute or two my ice-stiffened wind-proofs and boots were off and my dead feet were being energetically rubbed by a porter. I had not escaped unscathed. Some toes were frostbitten and all my fingertips were without feeling. Time would show the extent of the damage.

Not content merely to cook and supply food and hot drinks, Willy [Dr. William McLean] examined us all. He declared me to be perfectly sound except for frostbites, that my pulse rate was only sixty-two, and that my heart showed no signs of strain. Meanwhile Jack telephoned the news of our arrival and our failure to Camp 3. Hugh would be glad to hear we were safely down, far too glad to worry about our failure; still it was terribly hard luck not to be able to send back better news to England. For the moment Everest had won. There was no one else fit enough for another attempt. We had shot our bolt and must go down for a rest. Perhaps, with luck, we should have another crack later.

There were a number of oxygen cylinders in the tent and as an experiment I dosed myself with the gas. As I was now acclimatized to a far greater height, the only beneficial effect was a slight increase of body warmth. Apart from this it made my throat drier and sorer than ever, and I was glad to remove the mask from my face.

Eric had had a terrible descent from Camp 6. The wind was so fierce that at one point he was tempted to return. Fortunately he decided to struggle on; he could never have fought his way back across the Yellow Band in the teeth of the hurricane. Lower, on the awkward slabs above Camp 5, which had given me so much trouble he was nearly killed when a patch of snow gave way beneath him as he was lowering himself onto it from an abrupt little wall. He could find no foothold and had to haul himself back, a supreme effort to an exhausted man at that altitude. He reached Camp 5 absolutely played out.

Although it was a stormy night and snow battered the tent, we slept the sleep of exhaustion; all save Bill, who was in severe pain. How he stuck it out alone at Camp 5 I do not know; the strain had told on him severely and he was frostbitten in both feet and fearfully emaciated. Everest had had the last word and we were a very worn-out party; I doubt whether any of us could have survived more than a day or two longer at or above Camp 5.

"APPROACH TO MT. EVEREST"

FROM
Nepal Himalaya in H. W. Tilman: The Seven
Mountain-Travel Books
BY H. W. TILMAN

WHEN WORLD WAR II ENDED, CLIMBERS TURNED THEIR ATTENTION to Mount Everest for the first time since the 1930s. But the very landscape had changed. In Tibet, through which the traditional approach to Everest had been made, the Dali Lama faced a compelling threat from political turmoil in neighboring China. His greatest fears were realized in 1951, when the Chinese occupation of Tibet became a reality. The outside world was shut off from the country, and with it, the Everest approach route used by the 1920s and 1930s British expeditions.

The only realistic approach option was through the kingdom of Nepal. For the previous fifty years, Nepal had been leery of Westerners, particularly the British, whose colonial activities in neighboring India had not endeared them to the Nepalese. But by midcentury, the ruling powers in Nepal began to see possible benefits in a more open relationship with Western countries. When a party of American scientists was allowed to enter the country in 1948, British Ambassador Sir George Falconer convinced the Nepalese prime minister to allow entry to a British climbing party in 1950.

Predictably, H. W. Tilman, the indefatigable mountaineer-explorer who had already walked through much of central Asia, would find a way to be in that group. Tilman eventually rendezvoused with American Charles Houston, a friend from earlier expeditions, including one to Nanda Devi. Tilman and Houston's travels that year would provide the key to the summit of Everest. By pioneering the Nepal approaches to the mountain via the "unexplored" Khumbu region, they arrived below the Khumbu Icefall and the Western Cwm, showing the way to the beginning of the successful summit route. Strictly speaking, Tilman and Houston weren't the first Western climbers to have seen the Western Cwm. That distinction belongs to George Mallory, who had seen the long, ice-filled valley from the col between Pumori and Lingtren in 1921. But Tilman and Houston blazed the trail for Eric Shipton's 1951 party to make a thorough reconnaissance of the route.

It was November 1950 when Tilman, Houston, and a motley crowd of a half dozen hangers-on set out through the Arun Valley toward Namche Bazar. Called by many the greatest travel writer who ever lived, Tilman's engaging *Nepal Himalaya* recounts a delicious journey through a warm and friendly landscape, replete with Rana royalty and tantalizing views of Himalayan peaks never before seen from that vantage. Houston, whom Tilman describes as "a man who never does anything by halves," and who later would be part of the historic 1953 American attempt on K2, is the perfect partner for the phlegmatic Tilman.

Tilman's account makes a wonderful read. His descriptions of Thyangboche and other landmarks along the now familiar Everest trek resonate with his power of droll observation. Tilman's is a work of wry and subtle wit improved by his cultured world view. He is a man not easily impressed, but who can remain jaded on their first trip through the Khumbu?

The excerpt below begins as Tilman, Houston, and party arrive in Namche Bazar with their Sherpa guides. The story, "Approach to Mount Everest," is part of Tilman's book *Nepal Himalaya,* found in *H. W. Tilman: The Seven Mountain-Travel Books* on pages 876–886

Namche Bazar lies at about 11,000 feet on the ridge between the Dudh Kosi and the Bhote Kosi, facing westwards across the valley to the peak of Kwangde (20,320 feet). Unlike the Manangbhot villages where all are huddled together, the houses are detached as if the owners were men of substance. There are about thirty of these whitewashed, two-storied houses, with low-pitched shingle roofs. The ground floor serves as stables and stores, while above is the one long living room, with an open fire and clay stove against one wall, wooden shelves for fine copperware and cheap china on another, and large trellised window frames set with five or six small panes of glass. To find glass in a Himalayan private house, fourteen days' march from civilization, is a little remarkable.

The extent of cultivation seemed small for the number of people. I imagine that more food is imported and paid for by the trade in salt and rice, which the Sherpas carry on between lower Nepal and Tingri in Tibet over the 19,000-foot Nangpa La. But there are other villages within a few miles of Namche where the acreage of cultivation is much greater in proportion to the number of houses. Kuru (a barley), buckwheat, and potatoes are the crops; wheat is grown in the lower villages like Chaunrikharka and Gumila.

We went at once to our allotted house, and when the crowd had ebbed sufficiently to leave space, the tents were pitched alongside. The women accorded

Gyalgen precedence at the fireplace and the headman took strong measures against the more persistent sightseers. A few privileged intruders were allowed to remain. These were mostly former porters, vouched for by their Himalayan Club service books and numerous carefully cherished "chits" and photographs. They were considered to be sufficiently well disciplined to refrain from laughing at our strange ways and stranger faces. After a meal, fearing rightly that neither beer nor raksi was going to be offered, we went for a walk; partly for privacy—for the Americans were a little dismayed by the attentions of the crowd—and partly in the hope of seeing something of the great mountain which was now less than twenty miles away.

A morning sky freckled with high cirrus clouds had foretold accurately a break in the weather. Low clouds were driving up from the south, and when we had climbed a hill to bring the Lhotse-Nuptse ridge into view, the upper part, over which we should have seen the top of Everest, was obscured. Even in clear weather, however, only the summit is seen. The mountain, in spite of its bulk and height, still eludes the eye of the traveler approaching from the south; who, having outflanked and passed the high white wall of Chamlang, finds himself confronted by a black and higher wall. This is the three-mile-long rock ridge linking Lhotse (27,890 feet), or South Peak, to Nuptse (25,680 feet), the West Peak. The south face of this ridge is too steep to hold snow. Behind it lies the Western Cwm, the deep cleft which separates it from the west ridge of Everest itself.

Although my companions were in ecstasies over Namche Bazar and its friendly people, they were anxious to quit it at once and shrank from staying another night. Charles Houston and I, at any rate, had no time to waste if we were to see anything of the mountain in the six days available. We were due back at Jogbani on December 6 and had therefore to leave Namche by November 21. Thus it was arranged that he and I should start early next morning for Thyangboche and beyond, while the others would follow later and stop at Thyangboche, where there is a monastery of whose beauty and sanctity we had already heard much.

We were astir in pursuit of these plans and were not to be turned from them by a lowering morning with snow falling briskly. Gyalgen was in his element, chaffing the women, haranguing the men, engaging recruits for the glacier party, and cooking for us a very handsome breakfast—hot buckwheat cakes and eggs, tsampa porridge, and fresh milk. With mingled feelings, greed predominating over sorrow, I noticed that their hygienic principles prevented my friends from drinking milk from such dubious sources. Only a timely exclamation of horror vetoed the proposal that it should be boiled, thus rendering it innocuous, and at the same time tasteless. After a few days of intimate life at the monastery where it was obvious that dirt, disease, and death lurked pleasantly in every pot and in every corner of the room, they overcame these scruples and took to milk like cats. All except Mr. Houston, senior, who was made of sterner stuff, who looked upon raw milk as more inimical to health than raw brandy and much less pleasant to take.

The glacier party had with them Da Namgyal, Saki, a musketeer, and Danu, a raw recruit. Although a mere lad, Danu was said to be a brother of the redoubtable Angtharkay, who had begun his climbing career in 1933; be that as it may, he certainly behaved like an Angtharkay. Short, barrel-like, and solemn, he moved about in camp with the portentous tread of a bishop or a muscle-bound all-in wrestler, his hands resting lightly on an incipient stomach. But in action he carried more and went twice as fast as anyone else besides doing the work of three men in camp. He had a passion for building immense campfires, nothing less than a holocaust satisfied him. Long before daybreak one would imagine that the sun had risen untimely, but it was only Danu rekindling the overnight bonfire, so that we could breakfast round it in comfort at first light.

A well-engineered track on which ponies can be ridden leads to Thyangboche. After traversing high it descends gradually to the Dudh Kosi, which it crosses just below its junction with the Imja Khola. This river comes down from Everest, from the northeast, while the Dudh Kosi descends from the north where it rises in the glaciers of the Cho Oyu group. The track then climbs equally gradually to the monastery (c. 12,000 feet), a group of white buildings built on a grassy saddle commanding views up the Dudh Kosi, west to Kwangde, south to the fantastic snow spires of Kangtega, and east to the Lhotse-Nuptse ridge which fills the whole valley. The summit of Everest shows not very prominently over the top of this ridge, but the monks call the whole massif Chomo Lungma. It would be difficult to imagine, much more find, a finer site for worship or for contemplation. Lamas may laugh at our love for climbing mountains, but undoubtedly they themselves take great delight in looking at them. Like Christian monks they seemed to be equally lovers of the picturesque and of good living; on which two counts they have the approval of at any rate one mountaineer.

That morning we saw nothing of this noble prospect. It was snowing steadily, and the monastery yaks scuffled hungrily in the snow. The monks were a little taken aback when we walked boldly into the precincts followed by a crowd of grinning urchins or sucking lamas. However, they placed a couple of braziers in front of us, and when we heard that the rear party had been sighted we decided to lunch with them before going on to Pangboche, the next village up the Imja Khola.

Thyangboche is a very small counterpart of Rongbuk Monastery on the Tibetan side of the mountain, not a quarter of its size and having only a handful of monks. Yet its abbot, a shy smiling youth of reputedly great spiritual power, is held in little less reverence, and its situation is incomparably more beautiful and less austere. It is much less austere inside, too, for they produced a beaker of raksi for our lunch, and when we returned a few days later we found they had the pleasant custom of fortifying their guests with a snorter before breakfast.

Having seen our friends established in an empty house we had no qualms—none, that is, on their behalf—about leaving them in such congenial surroundings. On a fine day it is an entrancing walk from the monastery to the Imja Khola bridge; through open woods of hoary twisted juniper and of glistening silver birch, whose golden leaves were still clinging to branches hung with streamers of pale green lichen. We strolled along, past a little whitewashed hamlet, when suddenly a bend in the path brought into view the white, foaming river and beyond it a massive rock shoulder, like the gray roof of a church, from which sprang the preposterous snow spire of some unnamed, unmeasured peak. The trees ended at the river. As is generally the way, the south-facing side of the valley was bare and bore an abundant crop of stones. Few stretches of the rocky track were without mani walls and chortens, and every convenient boulder had inscribed on it a religious text. Having been warned of sickness at the next village, Pangboche, we camped in a field on the outskirts where there was an empty hut for the men. A dense mist followed the heavy snowfall.

But the storm's malice was spent; after a cold night the morning broke bright and clear. Pangboche, which has few houses and a great many fields, is the last inhabited village. At Dingboche, a few miles up, there are a number of fields but no one lives there in winter. As we walked over flats of coarse brown grass by the river, we had in front of us the long Lhotse-Nuptse rock face with the massive black pyramid of Everest showing above it. One was impressed not so much by its height, for it looked rather squat, but by the suggestion it held of the immensity of its unseen mass. Three miles up, when the valley divided, we took the northern branch; the other continues eastwards, drains the south side of Lhotse, and terminates in a bay a little way south and east of the peak. Makalu, twenty miles away, beyond the head of this valley, bulked big enough, for most of it was in view, yet it was white and shapely and had not the menace of this black fragment of mountain so high above us.

The first two miles of our northern valley consisted of broad, brown pastures dotted with stone huts and grazing yaks. One group of huts is called Pheriche and the uppermost, where we camped, Phalong Karpa. All the living huts were securely locked for the winter but we made ourselves comfortable in one that was used as a hay barn. That afternoon we climbed to about 17,000 feet on the ridge that descends southwest from Nuptse to the fork in the main valley. The glaciers of the eastern branch seemed of no great size and terminated well above the fields of Dingboche, which we now looked down upon. On this bright afternoon with hardly a cloud in sight, we beheld a vast panorama of mountains; from Lhotse, Pethangtse, and Makalu in the east, south to Chamlang and Kangtega, west to Taweche, and north to Cho Oyu and Gyachung Khang. In this galaxy, which included a host of unnamed peaks, neither the lesser nor the greater seemed designed for the use of climbers.

At 14,000 feet at this time of year, mid-November, the nights were bitter. Only a few juniper bushes thrived, yet on returning from this excursion we found Danu Prometheus tending a glorious blaze of sizable logs. Frost soon stilled the murmur of the stream, only the faint note of a bell on some restless yak broke the deep silence. As we sat in the secure circle of the fire, our backs to the stone wall of the hut, the talk turned naturally to the Abominable Snowman. As one might expect they are found in these parts in numbers, especially around Namche Bazar in the depths of winter when the cold drives them lower. Danu affirmed that the previous year, a friend of his named Lakhpa Tensing had had his face so badly mauled by one, on the Nangpa La, that he died. By running downhill, which is, of course, the only way a man can run at these heights, one can usually get away from these creatures whose long hair, falling over their eyes, hampers them; but the unfortunate Lakhpa had apparently tripped and lying half stunned by the fall became an easy prey.

Just above Phalong Karpa is the high terminal moraine of the Khumbu Glacier, which comes down from the northeast, from Pumori, the Lho La, and the Western Cwm. The main valley, also glacier-filled, continues northwards toward the head of the West Rongbuk. They told us of a pass, now disused, at the head of this valley, but I think perhaps they were confusing it with the so-called Nup La which leads from the West Rongbuk into the next valley westwards, the Dudh Kosi. I can find no account of it, but I believe this Nup La was actually crossed by Mr. Hazard (of the 1924 expedition) and a Gurkha surveyor. They camped just on the west side of it and then returned. We turned up the Khumbu valley where we found good going in a warm, grassy ablation valley where gentians were still in flower. As we advanced we brought into view first Pumori, and then the Lho La and the North Peak beyond it. After going for four hours we camped by a little lake beyond the grass almost in the shadow of Nuptse. Our height was about 16,500 feet.

Our afternoon walk toward the foot of the Lho La, whence we hoped to see up the Western Cwm, was very rough. Driven from the friendly ablation valley, now filled with boulders, we took the moraine, and finally sought easier going on the glacier itself. Expecting every moment to round some corner and look up the Cwm, we were baffled by the apparent continuity of the rock and snow wall linking Nuptse with the west ridge of Everest which rises abruptly from the Lho La. Before turning for home and when still a mile from the foot of the Lho La, I struck out across the glacier but still failed to see any break. Some trick of lighting must have concealed it, for we saw it readily enough next morning before we were half way across the glacier. It is, however, the merest slit, not more than three hundred yards across, filled by a broken icefall which falls steeply to the Khumbu Glacier almost at the foot of the Lho La.

As we had only one day left, we thought that, instead of trying to enter the Cwm, our best chance of seeing both its head and the south ridge of the mountain would be from some vantage point on the west side of the glacier. Accordingly we sent the men down to Phalong Karpa, crossed the glacier, and climbed a subsidiary feature of about 18,000 feet to the south of Pumori. The glacier is about a mile wide and only some five miles in length. Its upper part is pinnacled, like the East Rongbuk Glacier, though the ice pinnacles are neither so high nor so continuous. One reason for this comparatively slight glaciation—for it is only half the length of any one of the three Rongbuk Glaciers—is that the southern glaciers start and finish respectively nearly 2000 feet lower than the northern. The south aspect, too, is warmer, and the temperatures must be appreciably raised by the great expanse of bare rock on the south faces of Everest and Lhotse, which are too steep to hold snow.

As we hurried across the glacier under a hard sky that seemed to hold possibilities of evil, we glanced now at the weather and now at the great mountain as bit by bit the terrific sweep of black rock rose above the Western Cwm. So anxious were we to gain our point before any clouds appeared that we forced the pace—if pace it could be called—unwisely; for Houston, who had left New York barely three weeks before, found 18,000 feet quite high enough.

In spite of our height and our distance from it—about seven miles—we could not see the high col between Everest and Lhotse, of which the lowest point is 25,850 feet. A shoulder of Nuptse cut across the south ridge of the mountain, hiding the whole length of the Western Cwm and this col at its head. We could see at most the upper 3000 feet of the south ridge which looked so steep that we dismissed at once any idea of there being a route, even supposing the col could be reached.

From the map, we appeared to be due west of the south ridge and were thus seeing it in profile. On that assumption it seemed to be a waste of time discussing the possibility of reaching it; but I now think we were not looking at its true edge but merely a buttress protruding from the southwest face. For photographs of this high Lhotse-Everest profile, taken during the monsoon from the east by the 1921 reconnaissance party, show a snow-covered slope rising from the col at a much less frightening angle. They also show the east side of the col to be unclimbable. Whether snow lies permanently on the south ridge, and what, at that great height is its consistency, are additional problems. Yet with these pictures in mind, and despite our impressions from the west, one cannot write off the south side as impossible until the approach from the head of the Western Cwm to this remarkably airy col has been seen. (It is a pity that the name Lho La, or South Col, has been appropriated by the col at the foot of the west ridge; but there is perhaps no need to find a name for this true south col, 6000 feet higher than the false, until it has been reached.)

The Western Cwm has been looked at several times from the Lho La. We saw it from there in 1935 and Mr. Shipton secured a photograph of it. All that this shows is a short stretch of level snow above the icefall, the head of the Cwm being well out of sight behind the west ride. It is a trench confined within two more or less precipitous walls, and it somehow seems unlikely that there will be a convenient snow ramp leading from the level floor at, possibly, 21,000 feet to the col at 25,850 feet. Moreover, a trench overhung by these two tremendous walls might easily become a grave for any party that pitched its camp there.

On the whole, whatever one may think of the last 3,000 feet of the south ridge, looked at either from the east or from the west, in my opinion, the chances are against there being any way of reaching it. Of the final 1000 feet, the crux of the whole matter, we have unfortunately no experience. Certainly they cannot be assumed to be easy.

At great heights a route must be easy to be possible, not only because of the extra exertion needed to overcome difficult places but also because of the time so lost. Even in the early days of the 1921 reconnaissance Mallory was aware of this when he dismissed the west ridge as a possible route: "If ever the mountain were to be climbed," he wrote, "the way would not lie along the length of any of its colossal ridges. Progress could only be made along comparatively easy ground. . . . " Mallory, too, had looked into the Western Cwm from the Lho La and even from that restricted view drew some conclusions. He and Bullock had hoped to reach the Western Cwm from the Rongbuk Glacier, but were stopped by the 1500-foot drop to the Khumbu Glacier. He wrote: "It was not a very likely chance that the gap between Everest and the south peak (Lhotse) could be reached from the west. From what we have seen I do not much fancy it would be possible, even if one could get up the glacier" (i.e. up the icefall of the Western Cwm Glacier). Although the weather did not worsen, it remained unkind for photography.

Under a dull, hard sky, with neither sunlight nor shadow playing about its huge faces and ridges, the mountain compelled admiration only by its immensity. Mountains without snow and ice are shorn of the greater part of their splendor, and it is not always realized that in its most familiar aspect Everest is a rock mountain. Above 25,000 feet, from the northeast ridge round to the south, no permanent snow lies except in a few gullies and on odd ledges; and so accustomed are we to associate snow and ice with great height that the fact is not easy to appreciate.

The upper part of the climbing route and what looked like the Second Step were visible, but Camp 6 and the route to it from the North Col were hidden by the northwest shoulder that from here appeared to be a mountain in its own right, with two snow ridges framing a face of rock banded with fluted snow. It was surprising to see the climbing route in perfect condition, free from snow, barely two months after the end of the monsoon. We still have a lot to learn about Everest. It is not yet known how soon after the monsoon the upper rocks are cleared of snow. It has been generally believed that the snow was swept away by gales in late winter, but if this rapid clearing is caused by evaporation toward the end and immediately after the monsoon, then a favorable month for an attempt might be October when the weather is more settled and when there would be no ever-present threat of an untimely "western disturbance" or an early monsoon applying the closure. On the other hand, this rapid clearing may be affected by October gales that would, of course, preclude any attempt at that time. So far as we could tell there was not much wind when we were there in late November, but even if the weather then is generally fine, the intense cold and the shortening days would be deadly disadvantageous for high climbing.

We descended from our little hummock and returned to Phalong Karpa by the true right side of the Khumbu Glacier. From what we had seen we were convinced that the south ridge offered little hope, but of course we had not seen enough. We had not seen the true south ridge, neither had we seen the Lhotse-Everest Col nor the approach to it from the Western Cwm, and until this has been seen one cannot rule out the possibility of there being a route to the summit by the south ridge. From the head of the Western Cwm to the South Col must be nearly 5000 feet; from the head of the East Rongbuk Glacier to the North Col is less than half that and yet it is as steep a place as anyone would like to have to climb with laden porters. One cannot help feeling that the tendency to greater steepness on the south side of the mountain will hold good, and that there will not be any convenient ramp by which the South col will be attainable.

Next morning "Chimpanzee" Saki went down and very nearly out with malaria, so that for the first mile or two he had to be carried. The medicine chest, a very comprehensive one, had been left at Thyangboche, but I happened to have in my pocket a few Paludrin tablets, which worked like a charm. He probably lost the first dose by vomiting, but after the second he began rapidly to perk up and reached Thyangboche on his own feet.

Our friends there had taken to a monastic life with the greatest readiness. Our introduction to it consisted of a large bowl of unexceptionable dai for supper. True we were wakened at 4 A.M. by the din of horns and the clash of cymbals, but we were not expected to rouse out for prayer or meditation, or indeed to do anything beyond reaching for a wooden jorum thoughtfully left in readiness. In this, of course, lurked what we called "lama's milk," which was raksi flavored with cloves.

The jemadar, the escort, and the Dharan men, all of them blue with cold, were waiting to take us down, but first we had to tour the monastery and to receive the blessing of the young abbot. This ceremony resembled a school prize giving, the abbot, in the role of dumb but distinguished visitor, distributing the prizes handed to him by the businesslike secretary. As we sheepishly filed past the dais where the young abbot, attired in full canonicals and a tall cone-shaped hat, sat enthroned, with his cup, copper teapot, silver "dorje," and all the tools of his trade, so to speak, in front of him, we bowed our heads while he draped our necks with the ceremonial scarf and a small silk talisman, at the same time handing us a paper of formidable pills. The talisman consisted of a tightly folded paper of writing and pictures combined, sealed, and neatly bound with red, white, blue, purple, and black threads. In the end curiosity overcame my reluctance to slice open and so destroy this miniature work of art. The monastery possesses a library of 500 wood-bound books, each in its own curtained pigeonhole. Among its rich furnishings are a gilded life-size image of the late abbot of Rongbuk Monastery and some very beautiful religious paintings, temple banners, or "Tang-ka."

Our return journey was remarkable for the size of our retinue. We had thus no transport worries. If we wanted to lengthen our marches all we did was to transfer a few more of our followers to the payroll and so lighten the loads of the rest. Whether they expected to be paid or whether they merely hungered after the privilege of traveling in such distinguished company, a great many Sherpas, men and women, decided to accompany us to Darjeeling if they could raise the money for a ticket. Danu, of course, came, kindling young forest fires all the way. He attached himself to me, and by always having my tent up and bedding out long before any other loads had cast up, gave occasion for some pointed remarks. Another good companion and worker was Sonam Tensing, who is better known in Himalayan circles as the Foreign Sportsman, a familiar figure on a number of expeditions that we had made together in the thirties. Having always returned to his village after each expedition and never resided long in Darjeeling, he seemed quite unspoiled, a visible token of which being the pigtail he still wore. With a voice as deep as of yore, he still crooned what I imagined were prayers, going on sometimes for nearly half an hour without stopping—perhaps the Buddhist prayer known as "Clearing of Obstruction from the Path," which should be a favorite one for wayfarers.

We met with no obstructions at all and only a few slight rubs to mar our felicity. Of these, apart from a few affectionate lice which I shared with Danu until I broke him of the habit of carrying his spare clothes in my rucksack, the most embarrassing was our meeting with a large escort from Okhaldhunga which had been chasing us for nearly a fortnight. It was a case of hail and farewell, for we were on the verge of leaving their district when they caught us up. It was hard to know whom their superior would blame most, us or them, but as we were not going to Okhaldhunga it hardly mattered. We solved the difficulty with a carefully worded note to him and a small cash bonus to them. Our jemadar never got over this. Perhaps he feared this diminution of the prize fund might affect his own prospects, for he never stopped talking of the folly of rewarding men for work they had not done.

To our sorrow we met with further evidence of the long if slightly ineffi-cient arm of Okhaldhunga officialdom, stretching out this time to the detri-ment of our friends of Bung. It seemed that while food grains like rice might be turned into beer, the law drew the line at turning them into spirits. Ac-cordingly a few publicans and sinners, some of Bung's most prominent citizens, had been hauled off to Okhaldhunga to answer for it. Having drunk prematurely a bottle of genuine brandy which had been earmarked for celebrating Thanksgiving Day, we were with difficulty trying to accumulate a stock of the local firewater; a problem not unlike those set in arithmetic papers concerned with the filling of leaking tanks. With confidence well grounded on experience we had looked forward to remedying any deficiency at Bung, and now, of course, the sources of the spring were dry. The lament on this theme, which will not bear repeating, has already been given.

Nevertheless, in the Arun Valley on November 30, the pilgrims had their Thanksgiving dinner—table decorations by Mrs. Cowles, heating and lighting by Danu, solid fare by Gyalgen, fruitcake by Himal Bill, and bottled lightning from the jemadar's private cellar. For my part I gave thanks for past Himalayan seasons, few without their missed opportunities and frustrated hopes, but all of them good, and of which this, I thought, should be the last. The best attainable should be good enough for any man, but the mountaineer who finds his best gradually sinking is not satisfied. In an Early English poem attributed to one Beowulf we are told:

> *Harder should be the spirit, the heart all the bolder,*
> *Courage the greater, as the strength grows less.*

If a man feels he is failing to achieve this stern standard he should perhaps withdraw from a field of such high endeavor as the Himalaya.

"MOUNT EVEREST RECONNAISSANCE EXPEDITION 1951"

FROM
Eric Shipton: The Six Mountain-Travel Books
BY ERIC SHIPTON

AN OBSCURE BUT CRUCIAL EPISODE IN THE DECADES-LONG QUEST to discover a feasible route up Everest was the reconnaissance of 1951, led by Eric Shipton. A hardened climber and explorer with world-wide experience, Shipton was a veteran of all the British attempts on Everest in the 1930s. He was the logical person to make a definitive reconnais-sance of the Khumbu Icefall and the tantalizing potential of the route above. With him were Scottish climbers Bill Murray, Tom Bourdillon (who, with Charles Evans, would become the first to reach Everest's South Summit in 1953), and Mike Ward. Two New Zealanders, Earle Riddiford and Edmund Hillary, would join them later.

In 1950, H. W. Tilman and Charles Houston had pioneered the route through the Solu-Khumbu district of Nepal to the base of the mountain. But their assessment of the route higher up had not been optimistic, as the Khumbu Icefall struck both men as an insurmountable obstacle to the West-ern Cwm above. It was Shipton's 1951 group that first journeyed there to gauge the difficulties of this new "southern" route. Beginning in Dharan, Shipton's team walked for four weeks along the route, much of it in the foot-steps of Tilman and Houston, until they reached the Khumbu Icefall.

Along the way the two New Zealanders joined Shipton, despite the fact that the Himalayan Committee (which had members from both the Royal Geographical Society and the British Alpine Club, and therefore controlled Britain's Everest efforts) had decreed that the reconnaissance be strictly Brit-ish (to prevent the Swiss from coming along and gaining an intelligence advan-tage). Shipton had a soft spot for New Zealand, however. He had been im-pressed by the mettle of Kiwi L.V. Bryant on the 1935 Everest reconnaissance, and had even considered making the island nation his home. From the van-tage point of history, Shipton's capricious decision seems weighted with fate; his invitation to Edmund Hillary was made in an offhand way, but it almost certainly was central to Hillary's inclusion on the 1953 expedition that went on to summit Everest. One may wonder, if it weren't for Shipton's decision in 1951, who would have been first to the top of Everest in 1953?

Once Shipton's expedition reached the site of modern-day Everest base camp, the members climbed high on Pumori for a better view of what lay beyond the deadly chaos of the Khumbu Icefall. What they saw intrigued them:

The Western Cwm seemed to offer a straightforward route to the Lhotse Face and, from there, onto the South Col. But the Icefall was problematic. In a month of climbing through the chaos of ice debris, the team was able to ascend completely through the Icefall itself, only to be blocked from the Western Cwm by a single, large crevasse. Realizing that a strong expedition could force its way into the Western Cwm, the members of the 1951 team had done their work. The way was now clear for a first British attempt on Everest from the south.

The narrative below begins with Shipton's succinct summation of the Icefall problem, and his account of the journey follows. The piece comes from *Eric Shipton: The Six Mountain-Travel Books*, pages 595–617, with some editing for length.

When, in 1924, Norton and Somervell so nearly reached the summit of Mount Everest, it was generally believed that the next expedition, taking advantage of the lessons they had learned, would most probably succeed. For, just as the 1922 parties, by attempting to climb the last 4000 feet to the top in a single day, had completely underestimated the physiological difficulties of climbing at great altitudes, so it seemed that the failure of the 1924 expedition was due to a simple, avoidable cause. That year the climbers had gone high too soon and had become involved in a series of struggles with the early spring blizzards, which had so far drained their strength that, when the time came to launch their attempts upon the summit, the climbers were already exhausted. In 1933 we were confident that, by carefully nursing the climbers and the Sherpas chosen to go high through the preliminary stages and by the use of comfortable, double-skinned tents at Camps 3 and 4, it would be possible to place several successive parties at a camp above 27,000 feet, with their reserves of strength largely unimpaired, and well able to overcome the last 2000 feet.

Once again we found that we had underrated the resources of our opponent. We had been led by the experiences of the previous expedition to assume that at the end of May and beginning of June there would be a period of some two weeks of calm weather before the monsoon wrapped the mountain in a blanket of snow. Moreover, we had not fully realized the extent to which even a small deposit of new snow upon the rocks of the final pyramid would render them unclimbable. Our experiences in the 1930s showed all too clearly that such a spell of favorable conditions immediately before the monsoon could not be relied upon. Indeed, it did not occur in any of the three years when attempts were made during that decade. In 1933 we had perhaps a fleeting chance, but both in 1936 and 1938 the monsoon was upon us before we had even established a camp on the North Col.

Even now we cannot assess the chances in any given year of meeting with a sufficiently late—or, as we used to think "normal"—monsoon to ensure favorable conditions for reaching the top. We cannot say, from the evidence we have, whether 1924 was an exceptional year, recurring perhaps only once or twice in a generation, or whether in the 1930s we perhaps encountered a limited cycle of unfavorable seasons. Whatever the answer, it seemed that the problem of reaching the summit of Mount Everest from the north had been reduced to this one vital question. Three times men had climbed to more than 28,000 feet, unaided by oxygen apparatus; we believed that the climbing on the last thousand feet was no more difficult than that which had already been accomplished, but it was sufficiently difficult to demand good conditions of weather and snow; given these, there seemed to be no reason for failure, without them, success would not be attained. Had it been possible, the obvious solution would have been to send out a small party each successive year until the right conditions occurred. There would have been no lack of personnel, and the modest expense would have been amply justified by physiological and other scientific research. Unfortunately, permission to do this could not be obtained from the Tibetan government.

The attempt to climb Mount Everest, once an inspiring adventure, had become little more than a gambler's throw. To overcome this unhappy situation we had begun, as long ago as 1935, to consider the possibility of finding an alternative approach that would present a different kind of problem, one not so completely dependent for success upon the date of the monsoon.

From the mountains above the Kangshung Glacier, to the southeast, we had seen the ridge running up to the summit from the gap (the South Col) between

Everest and Lhotse. This clearly offered a much easier route up the final pyramid than that across the treacherous slabs of the North Face. It was broad and not so steep, while the dip of the strata would favor the climber. But was there any way of reaching the South Col? We had seen that the eastern side was impossible. The western side of the Col was unknown ground.

The Reconnaissance Expedition of 1921 had discovered in broad outline the geography of the southwestern side of Mount Everest. The three great peaks of the massif, Everest, Lhotse (South Peak), and Nuptse (West Peak), together with their high connecting ridges, enclosed a basin that Mallory named the Western Cwm. (Mallory had climbed a great deal in North Wales and for that reason he used the Welsh spelling of the word "combe.") Any approach to the South Col must lie up this hidden valley, which enclosed the whole of the southern aspect of Mount Everest.

On the 1935 Reconnaissance Expedition, when, with no intention of attempting to climb Everest, we had before us a wide field of mountain travel, our program included an attempt to find a way to the Western Cwm from the north. From the Lho La at the head of the Rongbuk Glacier, and also from a high col on the main watershed farther to the west, where we camped for two nights, we had close views of the entrance to the Cwm, a narrow defile flanked on the south by the great face of Nuptse and on the north by the western shoulder of Everest. Between these lofty portals the glacier of the Cwm poured in a huge icefall, a wild cascade of ice blocks, 2000 feet high. The upper part of the Cwm was screened from view by a northerly bend in the valley, so that we could not see either the South Col or the south face of Everest; nor could we find a practicable route down the precipices on the southern side of the watershed which would have enabled us to reach the foot of the icefall.

Thus the possibility of finding an alternative route up Mount Everest from the southwest could not be put to the test, for the only way of approaching the mountain from that side was through the valley of Sola Khumbu in Nepal. That country had long been forbidden to Western travelers and there was, in those days, no chance of obtaining permission from the government of Nepal to send an expedition to that area. Since the war, however, the Nepalese government began to relax its policy of rigid exclusion, and from 1947 onwards several mountaineering and scientific expeditions—American, French, and British—were permitted to visit various parts of the Nepal Himalaya. In the autumn of 1950, Dr. Charles Houston and his father, together with H. W. Tilman, paid a brief visit to the upper valleys of the Khumbu district. Houston and Tilman spent a day exploring the glacier flowing southward from the Lho La, but did not have time to reach the icefall.

In May 1951, Michael Ward proposed to the Himalayan Committee (a joint committee of the Royal Geographical Society and the Alpine Club, which had handled all previous Everest Expeditions) that permission should be sought for a British expedition to go to Everest that autumn. His suggestion was energetically supported by Campbell Secord and W. H. Murray; formal permission was applied for and, on the assumption that it would be forthcoming, Murray began the preliminary work of organizing the expedition. I was in China at the time, and when I arrived home in the middle of June I had no idea of what was afoot; indeed, nothing was farther from my thoughts than taking part in a Himalayan expedition. After I had been in England for about ten days, I went to London and happened to call on Secord. He said, "Oh, you're back, are you? What are you going to do now?" I told him that I had no plans, to which he replied, "Well, you'd better lead this expedition." I said, "What expedition?" and he explained the position.

At first, I did not take the suggestion very seriously, for it seemed that, owing to the recent political disturbances in Nepal, it was unlikely that permission for an expedition would be forthcoming. But within a few days the Committee heard that, through the courtesy of the Nepalese government and the good offices of Mr. Christopher Summerhayes, the British ambassador at Katmandu, permission for the expedition had been granted. I found the decision to join the expedition a very difficult one to make. Having so lately emerged from Communist China, the freedom of England and the absence of suspicion, hatred, and fear were sheer delight, and the English summer a rare and treasured experience. I found it hard to leave all this and my family again almost immediately. Moreover, I had been away so long from the world of mountaineering that I doubted my value to the expedition.

On the other hand, for twenty years, ever since I had first known the

Sherpas, I had longed, above all else, to visit their land of Sola Khumbu, through which the expedition would travel. I had heard so much about it from the Sherpas; indeed during our journeys together in other parts of the Himalaya and Central Asia, whenever we came upon a particularly attractive spot, they invariably said, "This is just like Sola Khumbu," and the comparison always led to a long, nostalgic discourse about their homeland. It required only an intelligent glance at the map and a little imagination to realize that their praise was not exaggerated; moreover, we had looked down into the upper valleys of Khumbu from the peaks west of Everest. Almost unknown to Western travelers, it had become, to me at least, a kind of Mecca, an ultimate goal in Himalayan exploration. So it was that I finally decided to accept the invitation to lead the expedition.

The possibility of finding a new approach to the summit of Mount Everest from the southwest had assumed a new significance to mountaineers all over the world from the time when the impending "liberation" of Tibet by the Chinese Communist armies had made the old line of approach inaccessible to citizens of Western countries. It was, however, highly improbable that such an alternative existed. No experienced mountaineer can be optimistic about the chances of finding a way up any great Himalayan peak. The vast scale of which these giants are built greatly increases the likelihood of the climber being faced by sheer impossibility—an unclimbable wall, slopes dominated by hanging glaciers, or avalanche-swept couloirs. In addition, his standard of performance is greatly reduced; the fact that heavy loads have to be carried a long way up the mountain to establish camps, the physical disabilities resulting from altitude, the disastrous consequences which threaten from bad weather—these are some of the factors which usually make it impossible for him to accept the challenge of a difficult ridge or face, or to commit himself to a spell of many hours of really hard climbing. When, as in this case, the search for a route is confined to one particular segment of the mountain, the chances of finding a practicable route are obviously still further reduced.

All that we knew of the South Face of Mount Everest and of the western side of the South Col was that they must be approached up a formidable icefall and through a narrow defile which was probably menaced by ice avalanches from the hanging glaciers on the immense precipices above. Beyond the defile was the unknown Cwm, whose southern containing wall, the 25,000-foot ridge connecting Lhotse with Nuptse, obscured all but the very summit of Everest from the south. We estimated that the floor of the Cwm was about 21,000 feet high, nearly 5000 feet below the crest of the South Col. From the fact that, along the whole range, the mountains were far steeper on the southern side of the watershed than on the northern side, we inferred that the slopes below the col would not be easy. That was all we could guess. It did not present a picture upon which we could build great hopes. But the Western Cwm was a freak of mountain architecture and there was no knowing what we might find there. I put the chances against our finding a practicable route at about thirty to one.

Clearly the expedition could only be a reconnaissance; moreover, the time and money at our disposal were not sufficient to organize an attempt to climb the mountain. If, despite the long odds, we found a possible route, we naturally hoped to send a further expedition the following spring to attempt it; for we still believed that, despite its many disadvantages, the spring was the only time of year to tackle the mountain. A case had been argued for making the attempt in the late autumn; that is, after the monsoon instead of before it. So far as I know, this idea had not gained the support of anyone who had been high on the mountain, but it had never been put to a practical test. There were many conflicting theories about the weather and snow conditions likely to be encountered in the autumn; there was little evidence on which to base these theories, and what evidence there was seemed equally conflicting. By visiting the mountain after the monsoon we hoped to furnish answers to some of these questions.

Preparations for the expedition had to be made in a great hurry. It was already July before I had made up my mind to go, and stores and equipment had to be ready for shipment to India by the end of that month. Before the war I used to boast that I could organize a Himalayan expedition in a fortnight. Things had changed since then. Essential materials for equipment, such as eiderdown for sleeping bags, windproof cloth, and rope, were in short supply, and manufacturing firms were busy with priority orders. Whereas before the war it was possible at a moment's notice to obtain passages and cargo space on any of several ships sailing for India each week, especially in the off-season when we usually traveled, now sailings were infrequent and the ships always full. It seemed as though everyone we tried to contact was away on holiday. The problem of raising money to finance the expedition had to be solved quickly. It was a busy and confusing month, and there was little time to enjoy the summer woods at home. Fortunately, Bill Murray had done a great deal of the ground work already, and Campbell Secord allowed his house in Carlton Mews to be used as a dumping ground for stores and equipment as they accumulated. This was very hard on his wife, for the place became a sort of general office and Mrs. Secord had to bear the brunt of endless telephone calls from the press, equipment firms, applicants for a place in the party, inventors of helicopters and portable radio sets, food cranks, money lenders, and members of the expedition. I remember especially the day before our stuff was due to go to the docks; nothing had been packed and we were still hopelessly involved in outside business such as arranging for equipment ordered from abroad to pass from the airport to the docks. I sent an SOS to the W.V.S. (the World War II-era Women's Volunteer Service) to ask if they could send someone to come and pack for us. They responded promptly and worked with such efficiency that everything was packed and listed before evening.

The party had originally consisted of Bill Murray, Michael Ward, Tom Bourdillon, and Alfred Tissiéres, one of the best-known Swiss climbers, who happened to be doing research work in Cambridge at the time. It was also hoped that Campbell Secord would be able to join the party. In its conception it was a purely private party, and, as I have said, the initiative lay with Ward, Murray, and Secord. Unfortunately, in the end, neither Tissiéres nor Secord were able to accompany the expedition. When I was invited to take over the leadership, I stipulated that the Himalayan Committee should assume complete responsibility for financing the expedition and for all matters connected with press coverage. My reason for this was that, although private expeditions have a very great deal to recommend them, Everest expeditions attract a quite disproportionate amount of public interest, so that publicity requires a firm controlling hand. The Himalayan Committee entered into a contract with *The Times* for the publication and the syndication abroad of the official articles and dispatches dealing with the expedition. By this generous contract, *The Times* provided the bulk of the expedition's funds.

Murray and Ward sailed from Tilbury on August 2, 1951, taking with them all the stores and equipment. They reached Bombay on the 18th. Bourdillon and I flew to Delhi, arriving there on August 19. Two days before I left London a cable was received from the president of the New Zealand Alpine Club asking whether two members of the New Zealand Expedition, which was climbing in the Garhwal Himalaya that summer, might accompany our party. I also received a request from the Geological Survey of India to attach one of their officers, Dr. Dutt, to the expedition. I welcomed these suggestions.

⸙   ⸙   ⸙

From India there are four ways of reaching Namche Bazar, the principal village in the district of Khumbu, where we proposed to make our base. The route from Darjeeling, generally used by the Sherpas, is long and very difficult during the monsoon. The route from Katmandu, though easier, is also rather long, while the cost in time and money of transporting a large quantity of baggage from India to the Nepalese capital would be considerable. By far the quickest way would be from Jainagar, the railhead north of Darbhanga in Bihar. But we were advised that it would be impossible to get from there to the foothills by lorry during the rains, while to march through the hot, swampy country would be most unpleasant. So we decided to travel from Jogbani, another railhead in North Bihar farther to the east. Houston's party had gone by this route the previous year after the monsoon was over, and they had succeeded in reaching Namche in a fortnight from Jogbani.

Bourdillon and I reached Jogbani shortly before midnight on August 24. We arrived in Namche Bazar, 12,200 feet above sea level, on the afternoon of September 22.

The journey from Jogbani, which we had expected to cover in a fortnight, had taken us nearly four weeks.

Namche Bazar, which consists of about sixty houses, is the most important village in the district of Khumbu, for it is the last place of any size on the principle route from Eastern Nepal to Tibet, and is therefore a center of trade between the two countries. It is the small metropolis of the Sherpas, who have close connections, both commercial and religious, with Tibet. They are themselves of Tibetan origin and are indistinguishable from the people of the great plateau to the north of the main range. They wear the same kind of clothes and have the same religious beliefs and customs, and, though they have a language of their own, they can all speak Tibetan. They lead a semi-nomadic life; each family owns a house and land in several villages at different altitudes and they move en masse from one village to another according to the seasons, to sow or harvest their fields of potatoes and barley. For this reason, it is common to find a village temporarily deserted while the inhabitants are working at another at a different level. They graze their sheep and goats and yaks in the high valleys, often several days' march from their villages.

We were given a great welcome in Namche, where we spent two days sorting out our stores and equipment and arranging for supplies of local food. I met many old friends from former expeditions, most of whom brought flagons of *chang* and stood by urging us to drink. We were provided with a house. Nearly all Sherpa houses are built on the same pattern. They are oblong, two-storied stone buildings with carved wooden window frames and lattice windows. The front door leads into a dark stable, through which one has to grope, pushing past the oxen or yaks, to a steep wooden ladder leading to a short, narrow passageway on the upper floor. A right-hand turn at the top of the ladder leads to a latrine, a small dark room with a hold in the middle of the floor, which is otherwise deeply covered with grass or pine needles. The other end of the passage leads to the living room, which occupies three-quarters of the upper floor. The alcove between the walled-in ladderway and the front wall is used as a kitchen. The fireplace is set on the floor, and an iron frame is used for holding the cooking pots above the fire. Beyond this is a couch reserved for the women. In the front wall to the right of the fireplace there is a line of windows. Beneath this a platform raised about a foot above the floor is covered with carpets and rugs. Here the men sit, crosslegged, behind a low wooden table. The sear of honor is at the end of the platform nearest the file. The opposite wall, devoid of windows, is lined with shelves full of great copper basins, wooden bowls, china cups, bamboo churns, and other cooking and eating utensils. The far end of the room is cluttered with bags of grain, ropes, wooden ploughs, mattocks, and other farm implements. Beds are made up on the floor as they are required. Some houses belonging to well-to-do people have additional rooms furnished as small Buddhist shrines.

>   >   >

We left Namche on September 25, taking with us supplies for seventeen days. In that time we hoped to make a thorough reconnaissance of the great icefall; if possible, to climb it into the Western Cwm, and to see whether or not there was a practicable route from there to the South Col. If we found a route we would then send down for more supplies, carry a camp into the Cwm and climb as far as possible toward the Col. If, as we expected, there proved to be no practicable route, we would then undertake an extensive exploration of the main range, the southern side of which was almost entirely unknown. We had engaged another five Sherpas, whom we equipped for work on the mountain, bringing the number up to ten. One of them was Angtharkay's young brother, Angphuter, whom I had last met in 1938, when as a lad of fourteen he had come across to Rongbuk from Namche and had carried a load to Camp 3 (21,000 feet) on Everest. Another fifteen men had been engaged to carry our baggage and supplies to our Base Camp at the head of the Khumbu Glacier.

We followed a path across the steep mountainside, 2000 feet above the gorge of the Dudh Kosi, from which we had climbed three days before. On the way we met a very old friend of mine, Sen Tensing, whom I first met in 1935 when he had come across to Tibet to join the reconnaissance expedition. His peculiar appearance in the clothes we gave him had earned him the name of the "Foreign Sportsman." In the years that followed he had been my constant companion in various parts of the Himalaya and Karakoram. In 1936 I had taken him to Bombay, an adventure that he evidently still regarded as one of the highlights of his career. He had heard news of our approach while herding his yaks in a valley, three days' march away, and had hurried down to meet us, bringing gifts of *chang,* butter and curds. He came along with us, and for the rest of the day he regaled me with memories of the past.

After some miles the path descended into the gorge. We crossed the river by a wooden bridge and climbed steeply through the forest for 2000 feet to the monastery of Thyangboche, built on the crest of an isolated ridge dominating the junction of the Dudh Kosi and the large tributary valley, the Imja Khola. The ridge was shrouded in mist that evening, and as it was growing dark when we reached the monastery we saw nothing of our surroundings. The monks welcomed us, and we found that a large Tibetan tent had been pitched for us on a meadow nearby.

During the past few days we had become familiar with the extraordinary beauty of the country, but this did not lessen the dramatic effect of the scene that confronted us when we awoke next morning. The sky was clear; the grass of the meadow, starred with gentians, had been touched with frost that sparkled in the early sunlight; the meadow was surrounded by quiet woods of fir, tree-juniper, birch, and rhododendron silvered with moss. Though the deciduous trees were still green, there were already brilliant splashes of autumn color in the undergrowth. To the south the forested slopes fell steeply to the Dudh Kosi, the boom of the river now silenced by the profound depth of the gorge. To the northeast, 12 miles away across the valley of the Imja Khola, stood the Nuptse-Lhotse ridge, with the peak of Everest appearing behind. But even this stupendous wall, nowhere less than 25,000 feet throughout its 5-mile length, seemed dwarfed by the slender spires of fluted ice that towered all about us, near and utterly inaccessible.

We stayed in this enchanting spot till noon and visited the monastery during the morning. With its cloistered courtyard, its dark rooms smelling of joss sticks and the rancid butter used for prayer lights, its terrifying effigies, its tapestries, and its holy books bound between boards, it resembled most Tibetan monasteries in all save its setting. In the center of the main room or shrine there were two thrones, one for the abbot of Thyangboche, the other for the abbot of Rongbuk. At that time the former was away on a visit to his colleague on the northern side of the great mountain, Chomolungma (Everest). Hanging in one of the windows of the courtyard, we were amused to find an oxygen cylinder. This had evidently been retrieved from the East Rongbuk

Glacier by the Sherpas of one of the early Everest expeditions. It is now used as a gong, which is sounded each evening at five o'clock as a signal for all the women who happen to be there to leave the monastery.

From Thyangboche the way led gently downwards through the woods and across the Imja Khola at a point where the river plunges as a waterfall into a deep abyss, overhung by gnarled and twisted trees with long beards of moss waving in the spray. Beyond the village of Pangboche we left the forest behind and entered highland country of heath and coarse grass. We spent the night of the 26th at Pheriche, a grazing village then deserted, and on the morning of the 27th we turned into the Lobujya Khola, the valley that contains the Khumbu Glacier. As we climbed into the valley we saw at its head the line of the main watershed. I recognized immediately the peaks and saddles so familiar to us from the Rongbuk side: Pumori, Lingtren, the Lho La, the North Peak, and the west shoulder of Everest. It is curious that Angtharkay, who knew these features as well as I did from the other side and had spent many years of his boyhood grazing yaks in this valley, had never recognized them as the same; nor did he do so now until I pointed them out to him. This is a striking example of how little interest Asiatic mountain peasants take in the peaks and ranges around them.

Two days were spent moving slowly up the glacier and getting to know the upper part of the valley. The weather was fine each morning, but each afternoon we had a short, sharp snowstorm. We had some difficulty in finding water along the lateral moraine, but eventually we found a spring in a little sheltered hollow on the west bank of the glacier at the foot of Pumori, and we established our base camp there at an altitude of about 18,000 feet. Later we found that the spring was fed from a small lake a few hundred feet above. There was a small heather-like plant growing on the moraine, which served as fuel and supplemented the supplies of juniper that we had brought from below.

On September 30, Riddiford, Ward, and Bourdillon, with two Sherpas, Pasang and Nima, crossed the glacier to reconnoiter the lower part of the icefall. Hillary and I climbed one of the buttresses of Pumori so as to study the icefall as a whole and, in particular, to examine the position of the hanging glaciers on either side of the gorge leading into the Cwm, and to plot the areas of potential danger from ice avalanches falling from these. We reached a height of just over 20,000 feet. It was a wonderful viewpoint. We could see right across the Lho La to the North Peak and the North Col. The whole of the northwest face of Everest was visible, and with our powerful binoculars we could follow every step of the route by which all attempts to climb the mountain had been made. How strange it seemed to be looking at all those well-remembered features from this new angle, and after so long an interval of time and varied experience: the little platform at 25,700 feet where we had spent so many uncomfortable nights, Norton's Camp 6 at the head of the northeast spur, the Yellow Band and the grim overhanging cliffs of the Black Band, the Second Step and the Great Couloir. They were all deep in powder snow as when I had last seen them in 1938. Straight across from where we stood, Nuptse looked superb, a gigantic pyramid of terraced ice.

But the most remarkable and unexpected aspect of the view was that we could see right up to the head of the Western Cwm, the whole of the west face of Lhotse, the South Col and the slopes leading up to it. Indeed, a view from the interior of the Cwm itself could hardly have shown us more. We estimated that the floor of the Cwm at its head was nearly 23,000 feet, about 2000 feet higher than we had expected. From there we could see that there was a perfectly straightforward route up the face of Lhotse to about 25,000 feet, whence, it seemed, a traverse could be made to the South Col. This long traverse would only be feasible in good snow conditions, and at present conditions were obviously anything but good.

The sudden discovery of a practicable route from the West Cwm to the South Col was most exciting. But we had come here to study the icefall, and this occupation soon sobered our spirits. The total height of this frozen cataract was about 2000 feet. A rough transverse corridor divided it into two equal sections. The glacier descended from the Cwm in a left-hand spiral, so that the lower section of the icefall was facing our viewpoint while the upper half was largely in profile. With the field glasses we picked up two figures on the lower part. From their movements we recognized them, even at that distance, as Riddiford and Pasang. Of the others there was no sign. We heard later that they had taken a different route across the lower glacier and had been forced to turn back by a mass of ice pinnacles before reaching the foot of the icefall. Riddiford and Pasang had made splendid progress, though they were obviously having to work very hard in the soft snow. By two o'clock they had reached a point about four-fifths of the way up the lower section. Here they stayed for an hour and then returned.

Such excellent progress by a party of only two at the very first essay was in itself most encouraging. But from where we were standing, it looked as though the corridor above them was in danger of being swept throughout its length by ice avalanches falling from a great line of hanging glaciers on the left-hand wall of the gorge; it looked, indeed, as though the surface of the corridor was composed entirely of avalanche debris. The right-hand side of the lower icefall and of the corridor were clearly menaced from a mass of hanging glaciers in that direction, while our profile view of the upper icefall made it look very ugly. There was an easy way round the upper icefall to the left, but this was obviously a death trap.

One of the many reasons why an attempt upon a great Himalayan peak offers so very much less chance of success than climbing a mountain of Alpine size is that a great part of the route has to be traversed again and again by parties of laden men carrying supplies to the higher camps. All objective dangers must be judged from this standpoint. The risk, say, of walking for ten minutes under an unstable ice tower, which might be accepted by a party of two or three unladen mountaineers, is obviously increased a hundred-fold in the case of large parties of heavily laden men passing over the same ground dozens of times. The rules of mountaineering must be rigidly observed.

It now seemed that we would be faced with a most difficult decision: to abandon this wonderful new route to the summit of Everest that had appeared like a vision, this chance that we had scarcely dared to hope for, not because the way to it was beyond our powers, but because on a small section of the approach the party, and particularly the Sherpas, must repeatedly be exposed to the risk, however slight at each individual exposure, of extermination.

When we met Riddiford in camp that evening he was much more optimistic about the difficulties on the upper part of the icefall, but he had not been in a position to judge the avalanche danger. On the following day (October 1), while Bourdillon and Angtharkay repeated our visit to the Pumori ridge and climbed to a point some 300 feet higher, Hillary and I made a reconnaissance from another angle. This time we went up to the head of the glacier and climbed again to about 20,000 feet on a ridge of the peak bounding the Lho La on the west. From here, although we could not see into the Cwm, we had a much better view of the upper part of the icefall and of the corridor. We saw that, at this time of year at any rate, the avalanches from the left swept rather less than half the length of the corridor and that a crossing made at about its center would be reasonably safe. We could also trace a good route through the upper part of the icefall.

On October 2, Riddiford, Hillary, Bourdillon, and I, with three Sherpas (Pasang, Dannu, and Utsering), took a light camp up to the foot of the icefall with the intention of making a concentrated attempt to climb from there into the Western Cwm. At this time Murray and Ward were both still suffering from the effects of altitude and remained at the base camp for further acclimatization. The next day the weather was bad. It snowed gently most of the day and we stayed in our tents. The air about us was absolutely calm. At about ten o'clock we heard a dull roar that sounded like an underground railway train. At first we thought it was a distant avalanche somewhere high up in the Cwm. We were quite accustomed to the thunder of these, falling intermittently all around us, from Nuptse, from the great ice cliffs of the Lho La, and from the ridges of Pumori. As a rule, the noise did not last more than a minute or two at a time. When, after a quarter of an hour, this distant roar was still maintained, we began to think that somewhere far away an entire mountainside must be collapsing. However, after an hour, even this theory seemed hardly tenable, and eventually we came to the conclusion that it must be caused by a mighty wind blowing across the Lho La, and over the ridges of Everest and Nuptse. It went on throughout the day. No breeze ruffled the canvas of our tents.

The morning of the 4th was fine and very cold. We started soon after it was light. As we had anticipated, one of the difficulties of working on the icefall, particularly at this time of year, was the fact that the sun reached it so late in the day. At first, we were moving over hard ice, but as soon as we reached the icefall we were up to our knees in soft snow. Our feet became very cold, and once during the morning Hillary and Riddiford had to remove their boots, which were designed for their summer expedition and were only large enough for two pairs of socks, to have their feet massaged back to life. With Riddiford's tracks to follow, we had no difficulty in finding our way through the maze of crevasses and ice walls. After three and a half hours' steady going, we reached his farthest point. Here Bourdillon, who was also still suffering a good deal from the effects of altitude, decided to stop and await our return. The place was just beside a prominent ice-tower, which was thereafter known as "Tom's Sérac." As the sun was now up, he would be able to keep warm enough.

Indeed, our trouble was now exactly the reverse. With the scorching glare of the sun on the fresh snow and the stagnant air among the ice-cliffs, it was rather like working in front of a furnace. This, combined with the altitude, very soon drained our energy and robbed all movement of pleasure. We shed all our upper garments except our shirts, but even so we poured with sweat, and before long our panting produced a tormenting thirst. The going now became far more complicated and laborious. Threading our way through a wild labyrinth of ice walls, chasms, and towers, we could rarely see more than 200 feet ahead. The snow was often hip-deep, so that even with so many to share the labor of making the trail, progress from point to point was very slow. The choice of one false line alone cost us an hour of fruitless toil.

But technically the climbing was not difficult, and even if it had been we had plenty of time for the job. By the middle of the afternoon we seemed to be approaching the top of the icefall. We had decided to turn back not later than four o'clock in order to reach camp by six, when it would be getting too dark to see. Even that was running it rather fine, since it did not allow for accidents, such as the breaking of a snow bridge, and to become involved in such a complication after dark would be to run considerable risk of frostbite.

From the last line of séracs we looked across a deep trough to a level crest of ice marking the point where the glacier of the Cwm took its first plunge into the icefall, like the smooth wave above a waterfall. The trough was really a wide crevasse, partly choked by huge ice blocks, some of which appeared none too stable. Crossing it was the most delicate operation we had encountered.

By 3:50 we reached the final slope beyond the trough, less than 100 feet below the crest, from which we expected to have a clear view along the gently sloping glacier of the Cwm. We had to climb this diagonally to the right, so as to avoid a vertical brow of ice directly above. Pasang, whose turn it was, took over the lead; Riddiford followed, and I came next. When we were on the slope it became obvious that the snow was most unstable and must be treated with great caution. By this time Pasang had advanced about 60 feet. Suddenly the surface began to slide downwards, breaking into blocks as it went. Pasang, who was at the upper edge of the break, managed with great skill to dive over it and ram his ice ax into the snow above. I was only a few yards from Hillary, who had a firm anchorage on an ice block at the beginning of the slope, and I was able without much difficulty to scramble off the moving slope back to him. Riddiford went down with the slope, and was left suspended between Pasang and me, while the avalanche slid silently into the trough. It was a nasty little incident, which might with less luck have had rather unpleasant consequences.

It was now high time to retreat. Going down was, of course, almost effortless compared with the labor of coming up. We had the deep trail to follow and we could jump or glissade down the innumerable little cliffs, each of which had cost a great deal of time and hard work to climb. It was after 5:30 when we reached Bourdillon, who had had a longer wait than he had bargained for, and was by now getting both cold and anxious. Soon after we had started down, the icefall became enveloped in mist. Later, this broke behind us and we saw, high above the darkening Cwm, the north face of Nuptse, a golden tracery of ice lit by the setting sun. We reached camp as it was getting dark, very tired after a strenuous day.

We were well satisfied with this reconnaissance. It was rather disappointing at the last moment to be denied a view into the Cwm from the top of the icefall, though in fact it would not have shown us much more than we had seen already. But we had climbed practically the whole of the icefall in a single day, despite abominable snow conditions and the fact that for the largest and most difficult part we had been working our way over entirely new ground. In time the route could certainly be greatly improved, and the climb would then be done in half the time and with less than half the effort. We thought that the snow conditions would probably improve, but even if they did not, the final slope could certainly be climbed and safeguarded by suspending life-lines from above. Finally, at this time of year at least, the route seemed to be reasonably free from the menace of ice avalanches. We had little doubt that, with a few days' work, we could construct a safe packing route up the icefall into the Western Cwm.

We decided, however, to wait for a fortnight before attempting to do this. There were three reasons for this decision. The first was to allow time for snow conditions on the icefall to improve. Secondly, we had seen that there was still an enormous amount of monsoon snow lying on the upper slopes of Lhotse and Everest, which would make it impossible to climb far toward the South Col, to say nothing of the possible risk of large snow avalanches falling into the Cwm from above. While we knew that at altitudes of 23,000 feet and above this snow would not consolidate, we had reason to believe that by the beginning of November a great deal of it would have been re-moved by the northwesterly winds which were already becoming established. Finally, half the party was badly in need of acclimatization before they could undertake any serious work even in the icefall. We spent the fortnight mak-ing journeys into the unexplored country to the west and south.

On October 19, Hillary and I, who had been working together during this fortnight, returned to Base Camp on the Khumbu Glacier. We had expected the others to get back on the same date, but they did not arrive until nearly a week later. On the 20th and 21st we took a camp to the old site at the foot of the icefall. This time we brought with us a large twelve-man double- skinned dome tent designed for the arctic. It was well worth the labor required to level a sufficiently large area of the ice surface on which to pitch it, for, after the tiny mountain tents we had been using hitherto, it was positively luxuri-ous, and, having more room, we found it a great deal easier to get off to a really early start in the morning. On the 22nd we started work on the icefall. Snow conditions had improved slightly, but a number of new crevasses had opened up across our former route, and these caused us a little trouble to ne-gotiate. However, by the end of the first day's work we had made a solid and completely safe route up as far as "Tom's Sérac." Near this we marked out a site for a light camp from which to work on the upper part of the icefall, but we decided that for the present we would continue to work from our comfortable camp below.

On the 23rd we started early, taking with us Angtharkay and Utsering. It was a glorious morning. With every step of the way prepared, we climbed without effort, breathing no faster than on a country walk at home, and reached "Tom's Sérac" in one hour and twenty minutes. We paused there for a brief rest that we hardly needed, while the sun climbed above the great Nuptse-Lhotse ridge to quicken the frozen world about us. We were in a mood of exultant confidence, for we expected that very day to enter the great Cwm.

But immediately above the sérac we ran into difficulties. A broad crevasse had opened across our former route, and it took us an hour and a half and a lot of very hard work to find a way across it. This check, though a salutary warning against overconfidence, was not serious, and it was not until we were over the crevasse that the real trouble began. Here, about one hundred yards from the sérac, we found that a tremendous change had taken place. Over a wide area the cliffs and towers that had been there before had been shattered as though by an earthquake, and now lay in a tumbled ruin. This had evidently been caused by a sudden movement of the main mass of the glacier, which had occurred some time during the last fortnight. It was impossible to avoid the sober reflection that if we had persisted with the establishment of a line of communication through the icefall and if a party had happened to be in the area at the time, it was doubtful whether any of them would have survived. Moreover, the same thing might happen on other parts of the icefall.

With regard to our immediate problem, however, we hoped that the collapse of the ice had left the new surface with a solid foundation, though it was so broken and alarming in appearance. Very gingerly, prodding with our ice axes at every step, with 100 feet of rope between each man, we ventured across the shattered area. The whole thing felt very unsound, but it was difficult to tell whether the instability was localized around the place one was treading or whether it applied to the area as a whole. Hillary was ahead, chopping his way through the ice blocks, when one of these, a small one, fell into a void below. There was a prolonged roar and the surface on which we stood began to shudder violently. I thought it was about to collapse, and the

Sherpas, somewhat irrationally perhaps, flung themselves to the ground. In spite of this alarming experience, it was not so much the shattered area that worried us as the part beyond, where the cliffs and séracs were riven by innumerable new cracks that seemed to threaten a further collapse. We retreated to the sound ice below and attempted to find a less dangerous route. Any extensive movement to the left would have brought us under fire from the hanging glaciers in that direction. We explored the ground to the right, but here we found that the area of devastation was far more extensive. It was overhung, moreover, by a line of extremely unstable séracs.

We returned to camp in a very different frame of mind from the joyous mood in which we had climbed the lower part of the icefall only a few hours before. It seemed obvious that, though it might be a permissible risk for a party of unladen mountaineers, working on long ropes and taking every available precaution, to attempt the icefall, and even this was doubtful, we would not be justified in trying to climb it with a party of laden porters whose movements are always difficult to control. It looked as though, after all, we were to be faced with the decision which we had dreaded three or four weeks before: to abandon the attempt to reach the Cwm, not because the way was difficult, but because of a danger, which by the very nature of its underlying causes was impossible to assess with any certainty. In this case, however, it did not mean the total abandonment of the route; for the condition of icefalls is subject to considerable seasonal variation, and it was not unreasonable to expect much better conditions in the spring than in the autumn. Nevertheless, it was a bitter disappointment not to be able to proceed with our plan of carrying a camp through into the Cwm and making a close examination of the route to the South Col. We agreed, however, to defer the final decision until we had made another reconnaissance of the icefall with the whole party.

The following day we again climbed the ridge near the Lho La. The view was not very encouraging, for we could see no way of avoiding the shattered area, which was in fact a belt stretching right across the glacier; though the upper part of the icefall above the corridor, so far as we could see, was undisturbed. On the 26th the rest of the party arrived back at Base Camp, and on the 27th we all climbed the ridge of Pumori from which Hillary and I had first looked into the Western Cwm on September 30. We saw that a certain amount of monsoon snow had been removed by the northwest wind from the peak of Everest, though the north face of the mountain was still in an unclimbable condition. There was no apparent change in the snow conditions inside the Cwm, on Lhotse, or on the South Col.

That evening we reoccupied the camp below the icefall, and on October 28 all six of us, together with Angtharkay, Pasang, and Nima, set out for the icefall once more. Our chief object was that the others should examine the situation for themselves so that we could come to a united decision; though Hillary and I, too, were anxious to have another look at it. We arrived at the shattered area by the time the sun reached us. Only minor changes had taken place in the past five days, and this encouraged us, with great care, to cross it and make our way over the delicately poised séracs beyond. Pasang and Angtharkay made no secret of their apprehension and constantly pointed out to me that it was no place to take laden men. Beyond the corridor we found that the upper icefall was in a fairly stable condition, only one sérac having collapsed across our former route. By ten o'clock we reached the final wall dominating the icefall. The steep slopes below this were in the same dangerous condition as they had been at the beginning of the month; but a fin of ice had become detached from the wall, and while other routes were being explored, Bourdillon succeeded in cutting steps up this, thus enabling us to reach the top of the wall. This was a fine effort, for it involved cutting his way through a deep layer of unstable snow into the ice beneath. By keeping to the edge of the fin, he was able to avoid any risk of a snow avalanche, but, as the whole thing overhung a profound chasm into which it might collapse, it was as well to avoid having more than one man on it at a time.

We now stood above the icefall, on the lip of the Western Cwm, and we could look up the gently sloping glacier between the vast walls of Everest and Nuptse to its head. But we soon found that we had by no means overcome all the difficulties of entry into this curious sanctuary. A little way farther on a vast crevasse split the glacier from side to side, and there were indications of others equally formidable beyond. To cross these in their present state would have taken many days of hard work and a good deal of ingenuity, and unless we could carry a camp up to this point we were not in a position to tackle them. I have little doubt that in the spring they would be a great deal easier. We sat for nearly an hour contemplating the white, silent amphitheater and the magnificent view across the Khumbu Glacier to Pumori, Lingtren, and the peaks beyond the Lho La. Then we returned down the icefall.

The fact that we had now climbed the icefall without mishap made the decision to abandon the attempt to carry supplies through into the Cwm all the more difficult. We discussed it at great length. The next day Ward and Bourdillon climbed the ridge near the Lho La to satisfy themselves that there was no alternative route, while Hillary and I paid one more visit to the icefall. Angtharkay and Pasang were still convinced that it would be madness in the present conditions to try to carry loads through it and unfair to ask the Sherpas to do so. There was nothing for it but to submit, hoping that we would get another chance in the spring.

"THE SUMMIT"
BY SIR EDMUND HILLARY

FROM
The Ascent of Everest
BY SIR JOHN HUNT

WITH ERIC SHIPTON'S RECONNAISSANCE OF THE KHUMBU ICEFALL in 1951, all feasible routes to Everest had been explored. As historian Walt Unsworth put it: "There was no possible approach to Everest that had not been traveled at least once. This was Shipton at his best—the brilliant penetration of a blank on the map—and the thing he was happiest in doing."

But confidence in Shipton's ability to make a successful attempt on Everest was waning among the all-powerful Himalayan Committee. The man himself conceded to a "dislike of large expeditions" and an "abhorrence of a competitive element in mountaineering." The urgency for a British success was heightened in 1952, when a Swiss expedition led by Raymond Lambert and including the veteran Sherpa climber from Darjeeling, Tenzing Norgay, climbed to within a few hundred meters of the summit. The die was cast. Shipton, the man who for decades had been at the vanguard of the British quest for Everest, would not be invited to lead the most promising attempt yet on the world's highest mountain.

The leadership of the British 1953 attempt fell to Col. John Hunt, an army officer whose father had actually climbed with Edward Whymper. By 1952, Hunt himself had climbing seasons in the Alps and the Himalaya to his credit. And though not politically well connected with the British Alpine Club, he had a champion on the Himalayan Committee who was essential to his eventual appointment. Hunt, a superb organizer and effective leader of men, was to prove a successful field marshal of the almost paramilitary-style 1953 "assault" on Everest.

The all-out attempt included a successful but hard-won route through the dangerous Khumbu Icefall, then a retracing of the 1952 Swiss route up the Lhotse Face to the South Col. A number of important firsts marked the 1953 climb. Tom Bourdillon and Charles Evans not only pushed beyond the Swiss high point (reached by Lambert and Tenzing) above the South Col, setting a new mark for the highest point yet climbed on earth, the pair actually reached the South Summit of Everest on May 26. Just 300 feet below the main summit, the climbers were tantalizingly close to the ultimate goal, but the exhausted men could climb no farther.

It was the New Zealand beekeeper, Edmund Hillary, who had accompanied Shipton on his 1951 reconnaissance to the Icefall, and the venerable

Everest powerhouse, Tenzing Norgay, who would follow Bourdillon and Evans and push to the top of the world on May 29, 1953. With the news of their success arriving in London (in code) just as Queen Elizabeth's coronation was to begin, the first ascent of Everest had an aura of inevitability, as if the effort put into the attempts of the 1920s, 1930s, and 1950s was fated to be rewarded at a time when Britain entered a new era.

The full story of the expedition is carefully told by John Hunt, who was eventually knighted (along with Hillary), in his book, *The Ascent of Everest*. The excerpt below, recounting the final push to the summit, comes from Hunt's book, but from a chapter written by Hillary himself. The narrative picks up as Hillary, Tenzing, George Lowe, and Alf Gregory awake on the morning of May 27 in a tent on the South Col. The story can be found in Sir John Hunt's *The Ascent of Everest*, on pages 203–213.

E arly on the morning of May 27 I awoke from an uneasy sleep feeling very cold and miserable. We were on the South Col of Everest. My companions in our Pyramid tent, Lowe, Gregory, and Tenzing, were all tossing and turning in unsuccessful efforts to gain relief from the bitter cold. The relentless wind was blowing in all its fury and the constant loud drumming on the tent made deep sleep impossible. Reluctantly removing my hand from my sleeping bag I looked at my watch. It was 4 A.M. In the flickering light of a match, the thermometer lying against the tent wall read –25° C.

We had hoped to establish a camp high on the South-East Ridge that day, but the force of the wind obviously made a start impossible. We must, however, be prepared to go on if the wind should drop. I nudged the uncomplaining Tenzing with my elbow and murmured a few words about food and drink, then callously snuggled my way back into my bag again. Soon the purring of the Primus and the general warming of the atmosphere stirred us into life and while we munched biscuits and drank hot water flavored with lemon crystals and heaps of sugar, Lowe, Gregory, and I discussed rather pessimistically our plans for the day.

At 9 A.M., the wind was still blowing fiercely, and clad in all my warm clothing I crawled out of the tent and crossed to the small Meade tent housing John Hunt, Charles Evans, and Tom Bourdillon. Hunt agreed that any start under these conditions was impossible. Ang Temba had become sick and was obviously incapable of carrying up any farther, so we decided to send him down with Evans and Bourdillon when they left for Camp VII about midday. Hunt decided at the last moment to accompany this party, owing to Bourdillon's condition, and George Lowe and I assisted a very weary four-some to climb the slopes above the camp and then watched them start off on their slow and exhausting trip down to Camp VII.

All day the wind blew furiously and it was in a somewhat desperate spirit that we organized the loads for the establishment of the Ridge Camp on the following day. Any delay in our departure from the South Col could only result in increased deterioration and consequent weakness. The violent wind gave us another unpleasant night, but we were all breathing oxygen at 1 liter per minute and this enabled us to doze uneasily for seven or eight hours.

Early in the morning the wind was still blowing strongly, but about 8 A.M. it eased considerably and we decided to leave. However, another blow had fallen—Pemba had been violently ill all night and was obviously not capable of going on. Only one Sherpa porter, Ang Nyima, was left to carry for us out of our original band of three. Our only alternative was to carry the camp ourselves, as to abandon the attempt was unthinkable. We repacked the loads, eliminating anything not vitally necessary and having no choice because of our reduced manpower but to cut down vital supplies of oxygen.

At 8:45 A.M. Lowe, Gregory, and Ang Nyima departed, all carrying over 40 pounds each and breathing oxygen at 4 liters a minute. Tenzing and I were to leave later so that we could follow quickly up the steps made by the other party and so conserve energy and oxygen. We loaded all our personal clothing, sleeping bags, and air mattresses, together with some food, on to our oxygen sets and left at 10 A.M. carrying 50 pounds apiece.

We followed slowly up the long slopes to the foot of the great couloir and then climbed the veritable staircase hewn by Lowe in the firm steep snow of the couloir. As we moved slowly up the steps we were bombarded by a con-stant stream of ice chips falling from well above us where Lowe and Gregory were cutting steps across to the South-East Ridge. We reached the ridge at midday and joined the other party. Nearby was the tattered ruin of the Swiss tent of the previous spring, and it added an air of loneliness and isolation to this remarkable viewpoint. From here Lambert and Tenzing had made their gallant attempt to reach the summit after a night spent without sleeping bags.

It was a wonderful spot with tremendous views in every direction and we indulged in an orgy of photography. We were all feeling extremely well and confident of placing our camp high up on the South-East Ridge. We heaved on our loads again and moved 150 feet up the ridge to the dump made by Hunt two days previously. The ridge was quite steep but the upward-sloping strata of the rocks gave us quite good footholds and the climbing was not technically difficult, although loose snow over the steep rocks demanded care. The dump was at 27,350 feet, but we considered that this was still far to low for an effective summit camp, so somewhat reluctantly we added all this extra gear to our already large loads. Gregory took some more oxygen, Lowe some food and fuel, and I tied on a tent. Apart from Ang Nyima, who was carrying just over 40 pounds, we all had loads of from 50 to 63 pounds. We continued on up the ridge at a somewhat reduced rate. Despite our great burdens we were moving steadily, though very slowly. The ridge steepened onto a slope of firm snow and Lowe chipped steps up it for 50 feet. By 2 P.M., we were beginning to tire and started looking for a campsite. The ridge appeared to have no relief at all and continued upwards in one unbroken sweep. We plugged slowly on, looking for a ledge without success. Again and again we hopefully labored up to a prospective site only to find that it was still at a 45-degree angle. We were getting a little desperate until Tenzing, remembering the ground from the previous year, suggested a traverse over steep slopes to the left, which finally landed us on to a relatively flat spot beneath a rock bluff.

It was 2:30 and we decided to camp here. All day the magnificent peak of Lhotse had commanded our attention, but now its summit was just below us. We estimated our height at 27,900 feet. Lowe, Gregory, and Ang Nyima dropped their loads on the site with relief. They were tired but well satisfied with the height gained, and to them must go a great deal of the credit for the successful climb on the following day. Wasting no time, they hurried off back to the South Col.

It was with a certain feeling of loneliness that we watched our cheerful companions slowly descending the ridge, but we had much to do. We removed our oxygen sets in order to conserve our supplies and set to work with our ice axes to clear the tiny platform. We scratched off all the snow to reveal a rock slope at an angle of some 30 degrees. The rocks were well frozen in, but by the end of a couple of hours' solid work we had managed to prise loose sufficient stones to level out two strips of ground a yard wide and 6 feet long, but almost a foot different in levels. Even though not breathing oxygen, we could still work quite hard, but rested every ten minutes or so in order to regain our breath and energy. We pitched our tent on this double level and tied it down as best we could. There were no suitable rocks around which to hitch our tent guys, and the snow was far too soft to hold aluminum tent pegs. We sank several of our oxygen bottles in the soft snow and attached the guys to these as a somewhat unreliable anchor. Then, while Tenzing began heating some soup, I made a tally of our limited oxygen supplies. They were much less than we had hoped. For the assault we had only one and two-thirds bottles each. It was obvious that if we were to have sufficient endurance we would be unable to use the 4 liters per minute that we had originally planned, but I estimated that if we reduced our supplies to 3 liters per minute we might still have a chance. I prepared the sets and made the necessary adjustments. One thing in our favor was that Evans and Bourdillon had left two bottles oxygen, still one-third full, some hundreds of feet above our camp. We were relying on this oxygen to get us back to the South Col.

As the sun set we crawled finally into our tent, put on all our warm clothing and wriggled into our sleeping bags. We drank vast quantities of liquid and had a satisfying meal out of our store of delicacies: sardines on biscuits, tinned apricots, dates, and biscuits and jam and honey. The tinned apricots were a great treat, but it was necessary first to thaw them out of their frozen state over our roaring Primus. In spite of the great height, our breathing was almost normal until a sudden exertion would cause us to pant a little. Tenzing had his air mattress on the lower shelf, half-overhanging the steep slope below, and calmly settled down to sleep. I made myself as comfortable as possible half-sitting and half-reclining on the upper shelf with my feet braced on the lower shelf. This position, while not particularly comfortable, had decided advantages. We had been experiencing extremely strong gusts of wind every ten minutes, and whenever I received warning of the approach of such a gust by a shrilling whine high on the ridge above, I could brace my feet and shoulders and assist our meager anchors to hold the tent steady while it temporarily shook and flapped in a most alarming manner. We had sufficient oxygen for only four hours' sleep at 1 liter per minute. I decided to use this in two periods of two hours, from 9 to 11 P.M. and from 1 to 3 A.M. While wearing the oxygen we dozed and were reasonably comfortable, but as soon as the supply ran out we began to feel cold and miserable. During the night the thermometer read –27° C, but fortunately the wind had dropped almost entirely.

At 4 A.M., it was very still. I opened the tent door and looked far out across the dark and sleeping valleys of Nepal. The icy peaks below us were glowing clearing in the early morning light and Tenzing pointed out the monastery of Thyangboche, faintly visible on its dominant spur 16,000 feet below us. It was an encouraging thought to realize that even at this early hour the lamas of Thyangboche would be offering up devotions to their Buddhist gods for our safety and well being.

We started up our cooker and in a determined effort to prevent the weaknesses arising from dehydration we drank large quantities of lemon juice and sugar, and followed this with our last tin of sardines on biscuits. I dragged our oxygen sets into the tent, cleaned the ice off them and then completely rechecked and tested them. I had removed my boots, which had become a little wet the day before, and they were now frozen solid. Drastic measures were called for, so I cooked them over the fierce flame of the Primus and despite the very strong smell of burning leather managed to soften them up. Over our down clothing we donned our windproofs and on to our hands we pulled three pairs of gloves—silk, woolen, and windproof.

At 6:30 A.M., we crawled out of our tent into the snow, hoisted our 30 pounds of oxygen gear onto our backs, connected up our masks and turned on the valves to bring life-giving oxygen into our lungs. A few good deep breaths and we were ready to go. Still a little worried about my cold feet, I asked Tenzing to move off and he kicked a deep line of steps away from the rock bluff that protected our tent out onto the steep powder-snow slope to the left of the main ridge. The ridge was now all bathed in sunlight and we could see our first objective, the South Summit, far above us. Tenzing, moving purposefully, kicked steps in a long traverse back toward the ridge and we reached its crest just where it forms a great distinctive snow bump at about

28,000 feet. From here the ridge narrowed to a knife-edge and as my feet were now warm I took over the lead.

We were moving slowly but steadily and had no need to stop in order to regain our breath, and I felt that we had plenty in reserve. The soft unstable snow made a route on top of the ridge both difficult and dangerous, so I moved a little down on the steep left side where the wind had produced a thin crust which sometimes held my weight but more often than not gave way with a sudden knock that was disastrous to both balance and morale. After several hundred feet of this rather trying ridge, we came to a tiny hollow and found there the two oxygen bottles left on the earlier attempt by Evans and Bourdillon. I scraped the ice off the gauges and was greatly relieved to find that they still contained several hundred litres of oxygen—sufficient to get us down the South Col if used very sparingly. With the comforting thought of these oxygen bottles behind us, I continued making the trail on up on the ridge, which soon steepened and broadened into the very formidable snow face leading up for the last 400 feet to the southern summit. The snow conditions on this face were, we felt, distinctly dangerous, but as no alternative route seemed available, we persisted in our strenuous and uncomfortable efforts to beat a trail up it. We made frequent changes of lead on this very trying section and on one occasion as I was stamping a trail in the deep snow a section around me gave way and I slipped back through three of four of my steps. I discussed with Tenzing the advisability of going on and he, although admitting that he felt very unhappy about the snow conditions, finished with his familiar phrase, "Just as you wish." I decide to go on.

It was with some relief that we finally reached some firmer snow higher up and then chipped steps up the last steep slopes and cramponed on to the South Peak . It was now 9 A.M. We looked with some interest at the virgin ridge ahead. Both Bourdillon and Evans had been depressingly definite about its problems and difficulties and we realized that it could form an almost insuperable barrier. At first glance it was certainly impressive and even rather frightening. On the right, great contorted cornices, overhanging masses of snow and ice, stuck out like twisted fingers over the 10,000-foot drop of the Kangshung Face. Any move onto these cornices could only bring disaster. From the cornices the ridge dropped steeply to the left until the snow merged with the great rock face sweeping up from the Western Cwm. Only one encouraging feature was apparent.

The steep snow slope between the cornices and the rock precipices seemed to be composed of firm, hard snow. If the snow proved soft and unstable, our chances of getting along the ridge were few indeed. If we could cut a trial of steps along this slope, we could make some progress at least.

We cut a seat for ourselves just below the southern summit and removed our oxygen. Once again I worked out the mental arithmetic that was one of my main preoccupations on the way up and down the mountain. As our first partly full bottle of oxygen was now exhausted, we had only one full bottle left. Eight hundred liters of oxygen at 3 liters per minute? How long could we last? I estimated that this should give us four and a half hours of going. Our apparatus was now much lighter, weighing just over 20 pounds, and as I cut steps down off the southern summit I felt a distinct sense of freedom and well-being quite contrary to what I had expected at this great altitude.

As my ice axe bit into the first steep slope of the ridge, my highest hopes were realized. The snow was crystalline and firm. Two or three rhythmical blows of the ice axe produced a step large enough even for our oversized high-altitude boots and, the most encouraging feature of all, a firm thrust of the ice axe would sink it halfway up the shaft, giving a solid and comfortable belay. We moved one at a time. I realized that our margin of safety at this altitude was not great and that we must take every care and precaution. I would cut a 40-foot line of steps, Tenzing belaying me while I worked. Then in turn I would sink my shaft and put a few loops of the rope around it and Tenzing, protected against a breaking step, would move up to me. Then once again as he belayed me I would go on cutting. In a number of places the overhanging ice cornices were very large indeed and in order to escape them I cut a line of steps down to where the snow met the rocks on the west. It was a great thrill to look straight down this enormous rock face to see, 8000 feet below us, the tiny tents of Camp 4 in the Western Cwm. Scrambling on the rocks and cutting handholds in the snow, we were able to shuffle past these difficult portions.

On one of these occasions I noted that Tenzing, who had been going quite well, had suddenly slowed up considerably and seemed to be breathing with difficulty. The Sherpas had little idea of the workings of an oxygen set and from past experience I immediately suspected his oxygen supply. I noticed that hanging from the exhaust tube of his oxygen mask were icicles, and on closer examination found that this tube, some two inches in diameter, was completely blocked with ice. I was able to clear it out and gave him much-needed relief. On checking my own set I found that the same thing was occurring, though it had not reached the stage to have caused me any discomfort. From then on I kept a much closer check on this problem.

The weather for Everest seemed practically perfect. Insulated as we were in all our down clothing and windproofs, we suffered no discomfort from cold or wind. However, on one occasion I removed my sunglasses to examine more closely a difficult section of the ridge but was very soon blinded by the fine snow driven by the bitter wind and hastily replaced them. I went on cutting steps. To my surprise I was enjoying the climb as much as I had ever enjoyed a fine ridge in my own New Zealand Alps.

After an hour's steady going we reached the foot of the most formidable-looking problem on the ridge—a rock step some 40 feet high. We had known of the existence of this step from aerial photographs and had also seen it through our binoculars from Thyangboche. We realized that at this altitude it might well spell the difference between success and failure. The rock itself, smooth and almost holdless, might have been an interesting Sunday afternoon problem to a group of expert rock climbers in the Lake District, but here it was a barrier beyond our feeble strength to overcome. I could see no way of turning it on the steep rock bluff on the west, but fortunately another possibility of tackling it still remained. On its east side was another great cornice, and running up the full 40 feet of the step was a narrow crack between the cornice and the rock. Leaving Tenzing to belay me as best he could, I jammed my way into this crack, then kicking backwards with my crampons I sank their spikes deep into the frozen snow behind me and levered myself off the ground. Taking advantage of every little rock hold and all the force of knee, shoulder, and arms I could muster, I literally cramponed backwards up the crack, with a fervent prayer that the cornice would remain attached to the rock. Despite the considerable effort involved, my progress although slow was steady, and as Tenzing paid out the rope I inched my way upwards until I could finally reach over the top of the rock and drag myself out of the crack onto a wide ledge. For a few moments I lay regaining my breath and for the first time really felt the fierce determination that nothing now could stop us reaching the top. I took a firm stance on the ledge and signaled to Tenzing to come on up. As I heaved hard on the rope Tenzing wriggled his way up the crack and finally collapsed exhausted at the top like a giant fish when it has just been hauled from the sea after a terrible struggle.

I checked both our oxygen sets and roughly calculated our flow rates. Everything seemed to be going well. Probably owing to the strain imposed on him by the trouble with his oxygen set, Tenzing had been moving rather slowly but he was climbing safely, and this was the major consideration. His only comment on my inquiring of his condition was to smile and wave along the ridge. We were going so well at 3 liters per minute that I was determined now if necessary to cut down our flow rate to 2 liters per minute if the extra endurance was required.

The ridge continued as before. Giant cornices on the right, steep rock slopes on the left. I went on cutting steps on the narrow strip of snow. The ridge curved away to the right and we had no idea where the top was. As I cut around the back of one hump, another higher one would swing into view. Time was passing and the ridge seemed never-ending. In one place, where the angle of the ridge had eased off, I tried cramponing without cutting steps, hoping this would save time, but I quickly realized that our margin of safety on these step slopes at this altitude was too small, so I went on step-cutting. I was beginning to tire a little now. I had been cutting steps continuously for two hours, and Tenzing, too, was moving very slowly. As I chipped steps around still another corner, I wondered rather dully just how long we could keep it up. Our original zest had now quite gone and it was turning more into a grim struggle. I then realized that the ridge ahead, instead of still monotonously rising, now dropped sharply away, and far below I could see the North Col and the Rongbuk Glacier. I looked upwards to see a narrow snow ridge running up to a snowy summit. A few more whacks of the ice axe in the firm snow and we stood on top.

My initial feelings were of relief—relief that there were no more steps to cut, no more ridges to traverse, and no more humps to tantalize us with hopes of success. I looked at Tenzing and in spite of the balaclava, goggles, and oxygen mask all encrusted with long icicles that concealed his face, there was no disguising his infectious grin of pure delight as he looked all around him. We shook hands and then Tenzing threw his arm around my shoulders and we thumped each other on the back until we were almost breathless. It was 11:30 A.M. The ridge had taken us two and a half hours, but it seemed like a lifetime. I turned off the oxygen and removed my set. I had carried my camera, loaded with color film, inside my shirt to keep it warm, so I now produced it and got Tenzing to pose on top for me, waving his axe on which was a string of flags—United Nations, British, Nepalese, and Indian. Then I turned my attention to the great stretch of country lying below us in every direction.

To the east was our giant neighbor Makalu, unexplored and unclimbed, and even on top of Everest the mountaineering instinct was sufficiently strong to cause me to spend some moments conjecturing as to whether a route up that mountain might not exist. Far away across the clouds the great bulk of Kangchenjunga loomed on the horizon. To the west, Cho Oyu, our old adversary from 1952, dominated the scene and we could see the great unexplored ranges of Nepal stretching off into the distance. The most important photograph, I felt, was a shot down the north ridge, showing the North Col and the old route that had been made famous by the struggles of those great climbers of the 1920s and 1930s. I had little hope of the results being particularly successful, as I had a lot of difficulty in holding the camera steady in my clumsy gloves, but I felt that they would at least serve as a record. After some ten minutes of this, I realized that I was becoming rather clumsy-fingered and slow-moving, so I quickly replaced my oxygen set and experienced once more the stimulating effect of even a few liters of oxygen. Meanwhile, Tenzing had made a little hole in the snow and in it he placed various small articles of food—a bar of chocolate, a packet of biscuits and a handful of lollies. Small offerings, indeed, but at least a token gift to the gods that all devout Buddhists believe have their home on this lofty summit. While we were together on the South Col two days before, Hunt had given me a small crucifix that he had asked me to take to the top. I, too, made a hole in the snow and placed the crucifix beside Tenzing's gifts.

I checked our oxygen once again and worked out our endurance. We would have to move fast in order to reach our lifesaving reserve below the South Peak. After fifteen minutes we turned to go. We had looked briefly for any signs of Mallory and Irvine, but had seen nothing. We both felt a little tired, for reaction was setting in and we must get off the mountain quickly. I moved down off the summit onto our steps. Wasting no time, we cramponed along our tracks, spurred by the urgency of diminishing oxygen. Bump followed bump in rapid succession. In what seemed almost miraculous time, we reached the top of the rock step. Now, with the almost casual indifference of familiarity, we kicked and jammed our way down it again. We were tired, but not too tired to be careful. We scrambled cautiously over the rock traverse, moved one at a time over shaky snow sections and finally cramponed up our steps and back onto the South Peak.

Only one hour from the top! A swig of sweetened lemonade refreshed us and we turned down again. Throughout the climb we had a constant nagging fear of our return down the great snow slope, and as I led down I packed each step with as much care as if our lives depended on it, as well they might. The terrific impression of exposure as we looked straight down onto the Kangshung Glacier, still over 9000 feet below us, made us move with the greatest caution, and every step down seemed a step nearer safety. When we finally moved off the slope onto the ridge below, we looked at each other and without speaking we both almost visibly shrugged off the sense of fear that had been with us all day.

We were now very tired but moved automatically down to the two reserve cylinders on the ridge. As we were only a short distance from camp and had a few liters of oxygen left in our own bottles, we carried the extra cylinders down our tracks and reached our tent on its crazy platform at 2 P.M. Already the moderate winds of the afternoon had wrenched the tent loose from some of its fastenings and it presented a forlorn sight. We had still to reach the South Col. While Tenzing lit the paraffin stove and began to make a lemonade drink heavily sweetened with sugar, I changed our oxygen sets to the last partly filled bottles and cut down our flow rates to 2 liters per minutes. In contrast to the previous day, when we were working vigorously without oxygen at this camp, we now felt very weak and exhausted. Far below on the South Col we could see minute figures moving and knew that Lowe and Noyce would be waiting for our descent. We had no extra sleeping bags or air mattresses on the South Col, so reluctantly tied our own onto our oxygen frames. Then with a last look at the camp that had served us so well we turned downwards with dragging feet and set ourselves to the task of safely descending the ridge.

Our faculties seemed numbed and the time passed as in a dream, but finally we reached the site of the Swiss Ridge Camp and branched off on our last stage down on to the great couloir. There an unpleasant surprise greeted us. The strong wind that had been blowing in the latter part of our climb had completely wiped out all our steps and only a hard, steep, frozen slope lay before us. There was no alternative but to start cutting again. With a grunt of disgust I chipped steps laboriously downwards for 200 feet. Gusts of driving wind whirling down off the ridge tried to pluck us from our steps. Tenzing took over the lead and cut down another hundred feet, then moved into softer snow and kicked a track down the easier slopes at the bottom of the couloir. We cramponed wearily down the long slopes above the South Col.

A figure came towards us and met us a couple of hundred feet above the camp. It was George Lowe, laden with hot soup and emergency oxygen.

We were too tired to make any response to Lowe's enthusiastic acceptance of our news. We stumped down to the Col and slowly ground our way up the short rise to the camp. Just short of the tents my oxygen ran out. We had had enough to do the job, but by no means too much. We crawled into the tent and with a sign of sheer delight collapsed into our sleeping bags, while the tents flapped and shook under the perpetual South Col gale. That night, our last on the South Col, was a restless one indeed. The bitter cold once again made any deep and restful sleep impossible and the stimulating effects of our success made us so mentally active that we lay there for half the night re-living all the exciting incidents and murmuring to each other between chattering teeth. Early the following morning we were all very weak and made slow but determined preparations for our departure.

The 200-foot slope above the South Col was a great trial, and even when we commenced the long traverse down towards Camp 7 we found it necessary to move very slowly and to have frequent rests. The upper part of the Lhotse Glacier seemed very steep to us and as we came down the ice steps towards Camp 7 our main wish was to rest. We were only 30 yards from the camp when a cheerful shout attracted our attention and there to greet us was Charles Wylie and several of the Sherpas, all looking fresh and strong and with the same question trembling on their lips. The hot drinks they pressed into our hands and their joyful acceptance of our news were a great stimulant in themselves, and we continued on down the Lhotse Glacier mentally if not physically refreshed.

As we approached Camp 4, tiny figures appeared from the tents and slowly drifted up the track. We made no signal to them but wearily moved down the track towards them. When only 50 yards away, Lowe with characteristic enthusiasm gave the "thumbs up" signal and waved his ice axe in the direction of the summit. Immediately the scene was galvanized into activity and our approaching companions, forgetting their weakness, ran up the snow toward us. As we greeted them all, perhaps a little emotionally, I felt more than ever before that very strong feeling of friendship and cooperation that had been the decisive factor throughout the expedition.

What a thrill it was to be able to tell them that all their efforts amongst the tottering chaos of the icefall, the disheartening plunging up the snowy inferno of the Western Cwm, the difficult technical ice work on the Lhotse Face, and the grim and nerve-racking toil above the South Col had been fully rewarded and that we had reached the top.

To see the unashamed joy spread over the tired, strained face of our gallant and determined leader was to me reward enough in itself.

POSTSCRIPT

It is forty years since Tenzing Norgay Sherpa and I stood on the summit of Mount Everest and much has happened in the lives of all the expedition members since then. Certainly for me the Everest story has faded a little into the past. Like all my companions, I have had many exciting moments and challenges: driving tractors to the South Pole; raising a couple of million dollars to build Himalayan schools and medical facilities; taking jet boats up Mother Ganga from the Ocean to the Sky; and four and a half years as New Zealand High Commissioner in Delhi. But when I look back on it all there is no doubt that reaching the summit of Everest on May 29, 1953, was a major turning point in my life.

When we returned to Base Camp after the ascent I had no comprehension of the impact that our climb would have in the outside world. After all, I was just an unsophisticated antipodean. I expected reasonable interest from mountaineers, but what had climbing a mountain to do with the ordinary public?

As we trekked from the mountain back to Kathmandu my innocence was quickly dispelled. Every day, mail runners were meeting us with masses of telegrams and newspaper cuttings indicating the immense impact the climb had universally made. When I was finally handed a letter from John Hunt addressed to "Sir Edmund Hillary" I was horrified but reluctantly forced to realize that my life, and indeed the lives of all the expedition members, had irrevocably changed.

Perhaps it was my independent New Zealand background, but fortunately I refused to take the publicity or myself particularly seriously. I had all too clear an understanding of my modest abilities, although I accepted that I was fitter than most and had a good deal of enthusiasm. In the hectic months after the climb John Hunt understandably made great efforts to emphasize the team nature of our success. I was doing the same myself, although it wasn't always easy, because I was one of the guys "who got to the top," and this seemed important to the media and public. Finally I stopped running down my own contribution and became more balanced and rational in my approach. I accepted that I had made a not inconsiderable effort too.

I haven't the slightest doubt that we who were attempting Everest in 1953 were the lucky ones. We were not driven by ideas of fame and fortune (or certainly I wasn't). All we wanted to do was climb a mountain that had been a constant challenge for more than thirty years. But how things have changed! So many remarkable efforts and so many disasters. Prima donnas have come and gone; huge expeditions have moved side by side with small Alpine-style efforts; the mountain has been cluttered with junk; and many of the expeditions are now outright commercial undertakings at $35,000 (US) a customer. With a dozen or more expeditions together at Base Camp, the sense of freedom and challenge has long disappeared.

Why were we successful when so many other good expeditions had failed? Our climbers were competent, although not exceptional compared with the best modern standards. Our organization was sound and our equipment adequate. Our physiologists impressed on us the importance of taking plenty of liquid and this we did, although I still lost twenty pounds from the time we established Base Camp to when we came off the mountain. The physiologists were also unsure as to whether it was humanly possible to reach the summit of Everest and survive, so we had that barrier to overcome too.

We were undoubtedly fit and strongly motivated; our oxygen equipment was erratic but effective; and we had that little bit of luck with the weather at the right time. So it was a combination of circumstances. I had the feeling that, in a sense, the mountain was waiting to be climbed—and we were the ones who were ready, willing, and able to do it at the right moment.

Ed Hillary
Auckland, 1993

"EVEREST"

FROM
A Life on the Edge
BY JIM WHITTAKER

JIM WHITTAKER'S CLIMB WITH NAWANG GOMBU TO THE SUMMIT of Everest in 1963 made him America's most famous climber for decades to come. His summit, ten years after the mountain's first ascent by Edmund Hillary and Tenzing Norgay, was only the tenth ever, by anyone, and only the seventh via the South Col route. "Big Jim" Whittaker would occupy a place in history as the first American on the summit of Everest.

Perhaps most ironic is that an American would come before any British climber to the top of a peak universally regarded as the province of English mountaineers. Since the 1920s, most of the important attempts on Everest had been by British teams; and while the first successful ascent came on the British expedition of 1953, the summit climbers were from New Zealand and India (Tenzing moved to Darjeeling in the 1930s). Dougal Haston and Doug Scott would become the first British climbers to reach the summit, but not until 1975.

Put in that historical context, the 1963 American Mount Everest Expedition was a defining one. Norman Dyhrenfurth, a Swiss filmmaker who had been to Everest in 1952 on the Swiss attempt that came within a few hundred meters of the goal, became the unlikely leader of the U.S. expedition when his application to climb Everest was approved in 1961. He spent the next two years raising money, putting together impressive sponsorships—including the patronage of the National Geographic Society—and assembling a team of the strongest and most versatile American climbers of the day.

Three-time Himalaya veteran Willi Unsoeld, cutting-edge rock climbers Al Auten, Dick Pownall, Barry Corbet, and Jake Breitenbach, and mountaineers Whittaker, Thomas Hornbein, and Barry Bishop made up the heart of an impressive climbing team. On a sad personal note, Jim Whittaker's twin, Lou Whittaker, decided not to go, a decision that created a rift between the famous brothers of Mount Rainier that, Jim Whittaker told me in 2002, took years to heal. In his forthright autobiography, A Life on the Edge, Whittaker tells the story: "Here he was—my twin brother, my other half, my best friend with whom I had shared virtually every major event of my life—telling me he wasn't going to Everest with me. Actually, it was worse than that because he didn't tell me. He let a stranger do it."

Without his twin, Whittaker was still part of a driven team. Even the

tragic death of Jake Breitenbach in the Khumbu Icefall early in the expedition could not dissuade them from a successful effort. And while climbers
around the world remember the 1963 expedition primarily for its historic
first traverse of Everest by Hornbein and Unsoeld, the expedition is more
popularly known for its first ascent by an American, a fact that made Jim
Whittaker—along with astronaut John Glenn—the most admired Americans of the 1960s.

Whittaker narrates the story of his ascent with Nawang Gombu in his
autobiography. The excerpt below picks up the narrative as Whittaker and
Gombu arrive at Camp II, in the Western Cwm, on their way to the top of
the world. The piece can be found in A Life on the Edge, pages 104–115.

We were now in the Western Cwm. Cwm is a Welsh word
for a high, glacier-scooped valley; this one was surrounded
by the mightiest walls on earth. To our left was Everest,
29,028 feet; ahead, Lhotse, 27,890 feet; and on our right,
Nuptse, 25,790 feet.

The next day, Gil [Roberts], Barry Prather, and I searched out a route to
what would become Camp II, our Advance Base Camp. It was a bit like
threading a needle; we had to find a route that would avoid as many of the
huge transverse crevasses in the center of the glacier as possible (two would
eventually have to be bridged) and, at the same time, steer clear of the avalanches sweeping down to the edge of the glacier from Nuptse and the west
shoulder of Everest. Eventually, halfway up the Cwm at an altitude of 21,350
feet, we found a terrific site. This would be the second-largest camp on the
mountain and our home for the next three weeks as we established camps
on the upper slopes.

The process of scaling a mountain like Everest is not linear. The first job
is scouting a route. After we found one, we would then install fixed rope
on the steeper sections and ascend until we located a good site for the next
camp. There we would dig platforms in the snow and ice, put up tents, and
then descend to the previous camp and begin the laborious process of haul-
ing up food and equipment—not just for that camp but for all the camps

yet to be established. It was exhausting work, even with Sherpa help, and as the altitude increased, we could feel our bodies and brains rebelling. At this stage in the ascent, I hadn't yet experienced the altitude headaches and nausea that others had, but I was struggling with a hacking cough and chronic shortness of breath. I dreamed of lying on a warm beach somewhere.

Above Base Camp, Camp II would prove to be our most comfortable site, but it still had its thrills. Huge avalanches poured off the walls of Everest, Lhotse, and Nuptse toward our campsite. By the time they reached our tents, they were just blasts of wind and powder snow, but that didn't make them trouble-free. More than once, squatting over the pit toilet 50 feet from the nearest tent, we would hear the avalanche coming and, our pants at half mast, start running for the tents. Those who didn't make it would be blasted with snow and ice crystals. For those of us out of harm's way, of course, it was a source of great hilarity.

Back in the States, the team had debated how to make the final ascent and had planned to climb Lhotse and Nuptse as well. Norman was focused on summiting and was fine with following the route up the South Col that the British and Swiss expeditions had used. Instead of climbing Lhotse and Nuptse, Tom Hornbein and Willi Unsoeld were determined to create a new route up the West Ridge. The competition between the "West Ridgers" and the "South Colers" was pitched but remarkably friendly, although serious issues were at stake, including the distribution of oxygen tanks and Sherpa support. It was from Camp II that we planned to split into two smaller expeditions. The South Col team, spearheaded by Lute Jerstad, Dick Pownall, Gombu, and me, would follow the established route to the summit. The West Ridge team, which included Barry C. Bishop, Barry Corbet, Dave Dingman, Tom Hornbein, and Willi Unsoeld, aimed to push the new route. Most of the rest of our expedition group, including our scientists and Jimmy Roberts, our logistics coordinator, did not often go higher than the lower camps.

On April 3, Lute, Gombu, and I did a reconnaissance climb to locate a site for the South Col team's Camp III, and two days later we had put in a tent and cached oxygen bottles at 23,900 feet at the base of Lhotse. By now we were really struggling to breathe, and we finally began to use bottled oxygen.

A week later, thanks to bad weather and exhaustion, we still hadn't established Camp IV. Frustrated with being stuck at Camp III, I wrote in my diary on the twelfth, "I am leaving early tomorrow to put in the route to IV or know the reason why!" The next day, with the weather clear and windless, that's exactly what Gombu and I did, high on the Lhotse Face at 24,900 feet. The next step would be to cut across the face to Everest's South Col, but for the time being, we headed down again to Advance Base to rest.

At this point, the process of ferrying supplies from Advance Base to Camp IV began in earnest. Dozens of loads had to be shifted first to Camp III and then to Camp IV. The days dragged by—two weeks of days spent humping heavy loads from one camp to the next camp higher, descending to sleep, then getting up the next morning and doing the same thing all over again. And again. And again.

Finally, with all the camps to Camp IV stocked, Norman selected me, Gombu, Ang Dawa, and himself for the first assault team. As expedition leader, he hadn't originally planned to be in the first group, but we needed a photographer/filmmaker. Dan Doody was laid up with a blood clot, and at least at that point, Barry C. Bishop was working with the West Ridge team members, who were still struggling to put in their own route. He had no choice. Meanwhile I had my own worries. I had shrunk from 200 pounds at Base Camp to a scrawny 175, and I hoped I had what it would take to reach the summit.

We left for Camp III on April 27 with thirteen Sherpa, carrying the gear for Camps V and VI on our backs. It had snowed in the interim and that meant breaking trail all over again. I kicked steps all the way up to Camp III. Then the next day, I kicked steps again, all the way up the Lhotse Face to Camp IV. And on April 29, with the weather deteriorating, I kicked steps across the Lhotse Face and up to the South Col, following a route Lute and Dick had set in a reconnaissance climb days earlier. There, at 26,200 feet and in rising wind, we set up Camp V. Norman, Ang Dawa, and a group of Sherpa carrying cameras and supplies followed soon after. Others had reached this point before; their trash littered the high plateau. But few had gotten much farther.

Finally, on April 30, eight Sherpa, Norman, Ang Dawa, Gombu, and I climbed to 27,450 feet, carrying on our backs everything needed for Camp

VI—High Camp. Desperately slowly, not using oxygen in order to conserve it for the final summit push, we hacked a platform out of the ice and set up two tents. By radio, I advised Base Camp of our progress and learned that high winds were forecast. I cut our 120-foot climbing rope in half and, using pieces of it, pitoned the tents to a rock outcrop.

As the Sherpa turned to begin their descent, I was shocked to see them pick up oxygen bottles.

"No!" I shouted. "Those stay here. Sahibs and Sherpa both go down mountain *without* oxygen." But they continued as if they hadn't heard me.

"Gombu, explain to them!" I pleaded. It had always been the plan that we would conserve our oxygen for the ascent; we simply did not have enough. But they didn't listen to Gombu either. Only one relented; the other seven left with oxygen bottles.

Norman and Ang Dawa waged the same battle with them farther down the slope, but they had no more success than we had. Meanwhile the wind was gaining strength. Exhausted, brain-numb from the altitude, we crawled into our tents—the highest shelters on earth—melted snow, drank liquids, tried to force down some solid food, and waited for the storm we knew was coming.

The night was fierce. Sleep was impossible. Lightning flashed around us. The wind shrieked and howled and tore at the tents. Inside, Gombu and I lay breathing a thin half-liter flow of oxygen per minute. Moisture, condensed from my breath, trickled out of my mask, ran down my neck, and froze on the sleeping bag. As the storm intensified, I heard a whistling. Half-conscious, I imagined things. An Abominable Snowman? No, just the wind in the ropes. And still the wind intensified, gusting over 80 miles an hour. The temperature dropped to twenty below.

⸙   ⸙   ⸙

May 1, 4:00 A.M. I sat up. The storm outside raged on, the tent poles whistled, and the nylon walls hammered my head and shoulders. I turned to Gombu, pointed my forefinger up, and said, "We go up." He nodded. To the extent that I could think at all, what I was thinking was "Dammit, we've come this far, I'll crawl the rest of the way if I have to." On Mount Rainier, you always have a second chance; here, I knew there wasn't going to be one. With only two bottles of oxygen apiece, enough to last approximately seven hours, we couldn't wait another day for the weather to improve.

I lit the stove and started melting ice to fill our water bottles. Gombu protested; he was trained to do these housekeeping tasks. But as far as I was concerned, we were a team now, equals before the mountain. Many times in the past weeks, Gombu had made me think of the line from Kipling's poem, " . . . by the living God that made you, you're a better man than I am, Gunga Din." On this morning, I felt honored to make his breakfast. Without appetite, but knowing we'd need whatever fuel and liquid we could take in, we forced down freeze-dried crabmeat, tea, and two cups each of hot, sugary Jell-O, mixed double-strength.

At 6:00 A.M. I yelled over to Norman that we were going up. He shouted back from his tent that they would follow soon. Then Gombu and I crawled out of our tent into a raging ground blizzard.

Overhead, the sun was brilliant. But from my chest down, it was a white-out. Snow and ice crystals were screaming past us at 60 miles an hour. Gombu was an eerie-looking goggled head sitting on top of this layer of blowing snow.

We set off anyway. Ahead, I could just make out the Southeast Ridge that was our first goal, but I couldn't see my feet. The howling wind cloaked the terrain in a four- to five-foot-deep cloud of swirling and drifting snow. The going was terribly slow. We kicked steps in the snow, alternating leads. Kick. Pause. Step. Rest. Suck oxygen. In two hours of climbing, we gained only about 700 vertical feet.

My pack, jammed with two oxygen bottles, two cameras, a radio (that never worked), two water bottles, a first-aid kit, food, extra clothing, a flashlight, a picket with the American flag attached, and a minus-thirty-degree sleeping bag (just in case we had to bivouac overnight), weighed 45 pounds but felt like a ton of bricks. High on the ridge, about 700 feet below the South Summit at what I estimated to be the halfway point to the summit, Gombu and I decided we would each cache our partly used bottle for the return and use the remaining bottle for the summit. At 13 pounds apiece, leaving one behind would make a huge difference.

Then we were off again. But now I had a new problem: the relentless wind and ice crystals blowing up under my goggles had frozen my left eyeball and I couldn't see clearly. Without binocular vision, it was hard to judge distances. In addition, I was terribly thirsty, but my water bottles were frozen solid. Stupid from lack of oxygen, I had put them in the outside pockets of my pack earlier and now they were completely useless. (Even stupider, it had not occurred to me to cache them with the spare oxygen bottle to lighten my pack.) The only liquid I'd had since Camp VI was the icicle that kept forming on the oxygen mask from my exhaled breath—periodically, I broke it off and slipped the ice behind the mask into my mouth. I was drinking my own breath.

Even on a 2-liter-per-minute flow of oxygen, climbing just 200 vertical feet an hour, we had to take five or six breaths with every step. In addition, we were continually being knocked over by the wind. The less steep the slope, the more we staggered; we came to prefer climbing to walking—at least we had something to hold on to. We kept plodding ahead, half-crawling, half-climbing, becoming more exhausted with each labored step. I felt like a tarantula in a 90-mile-an-hour gale.

The ridge we were climbing had a heavy cornice of windblown snow and ice stretching out to the right over the void, and it was impossible to determine where the rock ended and the overhanging snow cornice began. If we went out on the cornice too far, we courted disaster; if we moved too far to the left, we faced difficult rock climbing. It was guesswork. Watching for signs in the texture of the snow, I chose the best route I could, hoping we were following the true ridge.

We crested the South Summit at about 11:30 A.M. and, for the first time, could see the true summit above us to the north. There was a sharp drop ahead of us and then a saddle between us and the next obstacle, a steep rock face that we'd have to climb. During the 1953 British expedition, Charles Evans and Tom Bourdillon had stood where we were now, looked at that pitch, then turned around and descended. The valves on their oxygen sets had frozen, and they couldn't go on. The following day, New Zealander Ed Hillary and Sherpa Tenzing Norgay scaled it, and ever since it had been known as "the Hillary Step."

We squatted on the South Summit and climbed the Step with our eyes. Then we descended to the saddle and crossed over to it. At the base of the

Step, buffeted by the wind, we rested again. From here, it was practically straight up—rock on the left, snow cornice on the right. The cornice clung to the rock, but there were wind-cut cracks and hollows. Beneath the cornice, the Kangshung Face of Everest dropped thousands of feet into Tibet.

"If we fall," I thought to myself, "it'll be one hell of a border crossing. And I don't have my passport."

As Gombu belayed and anchored me, I wiggled and pried myself up through a slot between the lee side of the rock and the cornice, gasping for breath and cursing my pack for its weight and awkwardness. At last, I crawled out on top to a good belay spot, took in the slack, and jerked on the rope for Gombu to come up after me. Slowly, I coiled in the rope as he climbed up alongside me. We sprawled flat and took another break.

Finally, Gombu and I stood again and turned. Moving once more and near complete exhaustion, I suddenly realized I was sucking on an empty oxygen bottle. I had thought one bottle each would take us to the summit and back to our cache, but the ascent had taken longer—and taken more out of us— than I had expected. Gombu, smaller than I, used less oxygen and still had some left, but he would be out soon too. If my brain had been functioning normally, I probably would have been frightened. Instead, about the only thing that registered was "Keep moving." And we were close, with only a gentle slope ahead of us.

About 50 feet from the top, I coiled in the rope again, and Gombu came up beside me. I leaned toward him and shouted against the wind, "You first, Gombu!"

"You first, Big Jim!" he shouted back. Even with his oxygen mask I could see him grinning.

We compromised. Side by side, we staggered the last few feet until, at 1:00 P.M., we stood together at the highest point on earth—29,028 feet above the sea. The sky above us was that deep, dark blue you only see when you've climbed above most of the earth's atmosphere. We were on the edge of space.

Though the sky above was clear, the view was limited. Tibet was completely hidden by the plume of snow blowing past our feet to the north, but we could see into Nepal. Close by, Makalu, the world's fifth-highest mountain, and Lhotse, the fourth-highest, looked back at us.

We dropped our packs. I pulled out a 4-foot aluminum picket, placed the point of the stake on the highest part of the summit, and drove it into the snow, pounding it in with my ice ax. At long last, the American flag, and the flag of the National Geographic Society, flew over Mount Everest. Gombu deposited a *kata*, a Buddhist friendship scarf, and held the flag of the Himalayan Mountaineering Institute as I snapped his picture. He snapped mine as well, stepping back and turning the camera sideways to fit me into the frame.

I looked around the summit for any sign of previous climbs. Deep down, I hoped to find some clue that Mallory and Irvine had, in their final effort, made it to the top in 1924. They had disappeared in the clouds at 28,000 feet, never to be seen again. But there was no trace of them or anyone else.

At this moment, I did not feel expansive or sublime; I felt only, as I said later, "like a frail human being." People—mostly nonclimbers—talk about "conquering" mountains. In my mind, nothing could be further from the truth. The mountain is so huge and powerful, and the climber so puny, exhausted, and powerless. The mountain is forever; Gombu and I, meanwhile, were dying every second we lingered.

And that thought brought me back to reality. The wind continued at hurricane force. The temperature was thirty below. We were out of oxygen, cold, exhausted, and in danger. Weeks later, at a press conference, Gombu was asked what he was thinking when he reached the summit. He got a big laugh when he said, slowly, "How . . . to . . . get . . . down." But at the summit of Everest, I was just responding automatically to my body, which was screaming, "Get down! Get off! Go lower now! Climb down to the oxygen!" So after more than two years of planning and more than two months of climbing, Gombu and I spent only twenty minutes on top before we began our descent—every bit as dangerous as the climb itself. What happened next was a bizarre combination of comedy and nightmare.

Gombu took the lead while I belayed and anchored him. Already, the roaring wind had almost filled our uphill tracks with snow. Gombu was 60 feet ahead of me. We had not gone far when, suddenly and without warning, the entire cornice directly before me simply dissolved and slid off into Tibet. There was no noise; the roaring wind drowned out any other sound. I stared dumbfounded at the gigantic hole in front of me. The fracture line began 30 feet to my left, ran up literally to my feet, and turned sharply down the slope, following our tracks for 60 feet or so. Then it cut back to the edge again. I looked up, and to my relief, Gombu stood safe on the other side of the void. Exhausted and oxygen-starved, this was my thoughtful reaction: "Gee, I guess I'd better move over a foot or two." And we continued our stumbling and lurching descent.

I belayed Gombu off the steep Hillary Step, then scrambled down myself. At the foot of the Step, in the saddle formed by the lower South Summit, Gombu led off again. As I watched him disappear over the rise of the South Summit, however, I was suddenly hit with an urgent need to . . . take a crap. There was nothing to do but stop, lay down a few coils of rope, throw off my pack, and drop my pants, answering what had to be the highest call of nature yet dictated to a human being. There I was, squatting bare-assed on the down-slope to Nepal—in the Throne Room of the Mountain Gods—crampons flat on the surface and all points secured, with a ground blizzard freezing my private parts. It was a humbling—not to mention numbing—experience. I felt very mortal.

Dressing quickly, I grabbed my pack and struggled toward the South Summit. Gombu, who had no idea what was going on, had begun pulling on the now-taut rope, thinking it was snagged on a rock. A hard tug threw me off balance and turned me sideways. As I fell, my pack tipped and one of my cameras fell out, rolling about 30 feet down the West Face. "To hell with it," I thought to myself. Then I thought again; it was my old friend John Day's expensive Leica. I stared down at it for a few seconds, then changed my mind. As I started down the slope, Gombu felt the rope go taut again. This time, though, he backed up to give me some slack. I retrieved the camera, stuffed it in my pack, and climbed back up the slope. (Three weeks later, I realized how dangerous this gambit had been; on the second assault, Lute Jerstad followed the faint outline of my footprints heading down the West Face, thinking they must lead to the summit. He had gone a long and perilous way toward the edge before he realized the track went nowhere.)

Without oxygen and severely dehydrated because of my frozen water bottles, I barely managed the uphill stretch from the saddle to the South Summit. We rested briefly, then headed down toward our oxygen cache, hooked up the bottles, turned on a 2-liter flow, took a few wonderful deep breaths, and continued our descent to High Camp. Even on oxygen, though, we moved slowly, placing our crampons carefully, thankful that we could see our feet now that the wind had at last lessened and the ground blizzard was gone. Three hours later, just before dark, we staggered into High Camp, where Norman and Ang Dawa awaited us, having themselves been frustrated from summiting because of oxygen problems. I was so wasted I almost crawled into my sleeping bag with my crampons on. We melted ice to make drinks, and Norman and Ang Dawa passed us hot Jell-O and more hot water—but I was still desperately thirsty when I finally fell asleep.

At midnight I ran out of oxygen again. Lying in my sleeping bag, I could feel the cold work its way up my extremities. My body was telling me it was slowly dying, and it was moving my blood to my vital organs. The cold crept toward my middle, and my feet and hands grew numb. I lay there, inert, waiting for daylight.

Sunrise. Thank God, the sun. The wind had died down, and the sky was clear all the way into Tibet. Norman wanted to stick around and do some filming, but I could think only of getting down to thicker atmosphere. Gombu and I descended to Camp V on the South Col, meeting the second assault team on their way up. Seeing the shape we were in, and recognizing the general shortage of oxygen, they abandoned their summit attempt, took us down, and cared for us at Camp V, doing the same for Norman and Ang Dawa when they caught up. After a couple of hours of rest, Gombu and I, with Dick Pownall roped in with us, headed down again, still without oxygen. Not long afterward, the rest of the team followed. We continued almost nonstop through Camps IV and III. As we descended, I could feel the air getting thicker and heavier, the breathing easier. The numbness in my extremities had started to dissipate by the time we reach Camp II—Advance Base—at 5:30 that evening. Ecstatic, we arrived to a great celebration.

⟩   ⟩   ⟩

It was a feeling that wouldn't last. Amid all the congratulations and backslapping, I was already worrying about the Khumbu Icefall.

I had stayed above the Icefall most of the expedition, working from Advance Base upward. In all I had spent thirty days at 21,350 feet and above, and I had lost more than 25 pounds, my body deteriorating in the thin air. Now it suddenly hit me that perhaps we had committed a great transgression on that remote summit; we had stolen a jewel from the breast of the Goddess Mother of the Earth, and Chomolungma might strike back. What better place to bring us up short than at the very gate of escape, the Khumbu Icefall, before we could get the jewel to Base Camp. As I lay in my sleeping bag, my old night fears returned in earnest.

Gombu and I left early the next morning. It was now spring, and it would be hot by midafternoon. Eager to reach the Icefall before it began melting, we half-walked, half-ran as we entered the top of the labyrinth. We threaded our way down, listening for movement in the ice, running in some places and balancing precariously in others. But this time, the Icefall was quiet. Nothing moved. The descent went smoothly and—with broad smiles and full lungs—we walked into Base Camp, our jewel in hand.

With the Icefall behind me, I finally relaxed. Dear God, it felt so good to take off my clothes and lie naked on a slab of rock in the warmth of the spring sun. The tips of the big toes and second toes on both my feet were black from frostbite, so I sat soaking them in a metal tub. I had frostbite scars on my face, where the mask and goggles had not covered my skin, and frostbite blisters on my left (Nepal side) wrist, where there had been a gap between my glove and parka. But all signs of frostbite would go away in a few weeks. It was the same with Gombu.

By now the entire team was down at Base Camp, and we were fielding congratulatory telegrams left and right. President Kennedy wrote:

> *I am most pleased to learn of the success of the American Expedition on Mount Everest. These American climbers, pushing human endurance and experience to their farthest frontiers, join the distinguished group of Swiss and British mountaineers who have performed this feat. I know that all Americans will join me in saluting our gallant countrymen.*

We had taken a vote and agreed no names would be released to the press until the other groups had had a shot at the summit, which we figured would be in another couple of days.

In the end, it took three weeks. (And in the meantime, the expedition had been pressured into revealing that it had been Gombu and me who had summited.) While the first summit team rested in Base Camp, the rest of our crew launched a two-pronged summit attempt, aiming for the record books a second time. The idea was for Tom Hornbein and Willi Unsoeld's West Ridge group to meet the second South Col group, led by Lute Jerstad and Barry C. Bishop, on the summit, then descend together down the South Col route. If they could pull it off, Tom and Willi would have to their credit not only the ascent of Everest by a new route but also an unprecedented traverse of an 8000-meter peak.

"MILES TO GO"

FROM
Everest: The West Ridge
BY TOM HORNBEIN

IN THE FINAL FEW DAYS OF THE 1963 AMERICAN MOUNT EVEREST Expedition, Tom Hornbein and Willi Unsoeld made an indelible mark in the annals of mountaineering. The two climbers ascended Everest by a new route, in virtual alpine style above their highest camp, and then descended via the South Col to complete the first traverse of the world's highest mountain. Forced by darkness to bivouac just below the summit, the pair's survival is almost as unbelievable as their accomplishment, widely viewed to be decades ahead of its time.

Unsoeld and Hornbein's bold ascent almost never happened. The large American expedition of 1963, led by Norman Dyhrenfurth, had from the beginning stated objectives of putting the first American on the summit of Everest as well as attempting a new route. In fact, it was the appeal of a new route on Everest that had most attracted anesthesiologist Tom Hornbein to the expedition. As the expedition approached the mountain, his fervor for the West Ridge grew. In *Everest: The West Ridge*, Hornbein writes, "Growing excitement lured my thoughts again and again to the West Ridge. My dreams were of the reconnaissance of the West Shoulder and the possibilities that lay above."

Inevitably, however, as the large expedition approached at the mountain, the scale of what they were trying to accomplish brought sobering realities to the forefront. The internal politics of the expedition began to shift: a failure to put an American on top would have been an embarrassment. And the West Ridge, on closer inspection, seemed to harbor even more difficulties than the climbers had suspected. To ensure an American success, the preponderance of resources was directed toward the effort to summit via the South Col route.

That development came as a bitter disappointment to Hornbein, who remained committed to at least making a strong attempt of a new route. The tragic death of Jake Breitenbach in the Khumbu Icefall on March 23 had a demoralizing effect on team members. Some members questioned whether pursuing any route made sense. But the strength and commitment of this American team was not to be underestimated. When Jim Whittaker reached the summit with Nawang Gombu on May 1, any sense of internal conflict ended. Now, the West Ridge effort should get the resources it needed.

Hornbein had ensured a new route would be tried. An exasperated Dyhrenfurth later remarked that he wished he had known before leaving the States that "Tom was going to be so fanatical about the West Ridge."

Unsoeld, Hornbein, Barry Corbert, Al Auten, Dick Emerson, and a few other climbers and Sherpas immediately set about establishing and stocking the final high camps on the West Ridge route. From the traditional Camp 2 in the Western Cwm, three more camps were established on the West Shoulder and West Ridge: 3W, 4W, and, eventually—just in time—5W. The effort was hampered by persistent bad weather and one devastating storm. Finally, three weeks after Whittaker's summit with Gombu, Unsoeld and Hornbein left Camp 5W, which had been placed and supplied by Corbert and Auten and five Sherpas the day before, and headed for the summit. That same day, May 22, Lute Jerstad and Barry Bishop would leave Camp 6 on the Southeast Ridge for a second attempt via the South Col route. The plan was for the two teams to meet up on the summit and descend the South Col route together.

The narrative that follows describes one of the great Himalayan climbing epics. In the end, it is the magnificent story of two friends who believed they could climb more than 2000 feet of an unknown and unclimbed ridge above 8000 meters, reach the highest point on earth, and descend a route that was also unknown to them. Their rendezvous with Jerstad and Bishop below the summit, and the risky, unplanned bivouac at 28,000 feet that ensued, complete one of the most gripping episodes of mountaineering history.

The excerpt below picks up Hornbein's narrative as he and Unsoeld awake at Camp 5W on the morning of their attempt. The piece is in Hornbein's book, *Everest: The West Ridge*, on pages 158–181.

At four the oxygen ran out, a most effective alarm clock. Two well-incubated butane stoves were fished from inside our sleeping bags and soon bouillon was brewing in the kitchen. Climbing into boots was a breathless challenge to balance in our close quarters. Then overboots, and crampons.

"Crampons, in the tent?'"

"Sure," I replied, "It's a hell of a lot colder out there."

"But our air mattresses!"

"Just be careful. We may not be back here again anyway. I hope."

We were clothed in multilayer warmth. The fishnet underwear next to our skin provided tiny air pockets to hold our body heat. It also kept the outer layers at a distance, which, considering our weeks without a bath, was respectful. Next came Duofold underwear, a wool shirt, down underwear tops and bottoms, wool climbing pants, and a lightweight wind parka. In spite of the cold, our down parkas would be too bulky for difficult climbing, so we used them to insulate two quarts of hot lemonade, hoping they might remain unfrozen long enough to drink during the climb. Inside the felt inner liners of our reindeer-hair boots were innersoles and two pairs of heavy wool socks. Down shells covered a pair of wool mittens. Over our oxygen helmets we wore wool balaclavas and our parka hoods. The down parka lemonade-muff was stuffed into our packs as padding between the two oxygen bottles. With camera, radio, flashlight, and sundry mementos (including the pages from Emerson's diary), our loads came close to forty pounds. For all the prior evening's planning it was more than two hours before we emerged.

I snugged a bowline about my waist, feeling satisfaction at the ease with which the knot fell together beneath heavily mittened hands. This was part of the ritual, experienced innumerable times before. With it came a feeling of security, not from the protection provided by the rope joining Willi and me, but from my being able to relegate these cold gray brooding forbidding walls, so high in such an unknown world, to common reality—to all those times I had ever tied into a rope before: with warm hands while I stood at the base of sun-baked granite walls in the Tetons, with cold hands on a winter night while I prepared to tackle my first steep ice on Longs Peak. This knot tied me to the past, to experiences known, to difficulties faced and overcome. To tie it here in this lonely morning on Everest brought my venture into context with the known, with that which man might do. To weave the knot so smoothly with clumsily mittened hands was to assert my confidence, to assert some competence in the face of the waiting rock, to accept the challenge.

Hooking our masks in place we bade a slightly regretful goodbye to our tent, sleeping bags, and the extra supply of food we hadn't been able to eat. Willi was at the edge of the ledge looking up the narrow gully when I joined him.

"My oxygen's hissing, Tom, even with the regulator turned off."

For the next twenty minutes we screwed and unscrewed regulators, checked valves for ice, to no avail. The hiss continued. We guessed it must be in the valve, and thought of going back to the tent for the spare bottle, but the impatient feeling that time was more important kept us from retracing those forty feet.

"It doesn't sound too bad," I said. "Let's just keep an eye on the pressure. Besides if you run out we can hook up the sleeping T and extra tubing and both climb on one bottle." Willi envisioned the two of us climbing Everest in lockstep, wed by six feet of rubber hose.

We turned to the climb. It was ten minutes to seven. Willi led off. Three years before in a tent high on Masherbrum he had expounded on the importance of knee-to-toe distance for step-kicking up steep snow. Now his anatomical advantage determined the order of things as he put his theory to the test. Right away we found it was going to be difficult. The Couloir, as it cut through the Yellow Band, narrowed to ten or fifteen feet and steepened to fifty degrees. The snow was hard, too hard to kick steps in, but not hard enough to hold crampons; they slid disconcertingly down through this wind-sheltered, granular stuff. There was nothing for it but to cut steps, zigzagging back and forth across the gully, occasionally finding a bit of rock along the side up which we could scramble. We were forced to climb one at a time with psychological belays from axes thrust a few inches into the snow. Our regulators were set to deliver two liters of oxygen per minute, half the optimal flow for this altitude. We turned them off when we were belaying to conserve the precious gas, though we knew that the belayer should always be at peak alertness in case of a fall.

We crept along. My God, I thought, we'll never get there at this rate. But that's as far as the thought ever got. Willi's leads were meticulous, painstakingly slow and steady. He plugged tirelessly on, deluging me with showers of ice as his ax carved each step. When he ran out the hundred feet of rope he jammed his ax into the snow to belay me. I turned my oxygen on to "2" and moved up as fast as I could, hoping to save a few moments of critical time. By the time I joined him I was completely winded, gasping for air, and sorely puzzled about why. Only late in the afternoon, when my first oxygen bottle was still going strong, did I realize what a low flow of gas my regulator was actually delivering.

Up the tongue of snow we climbed, squeezing through a passage where the walls of the Yellow Band closed in, narrowing the Couloir to shoulder width.

In four hours we had climbed only four hundred feet. It was 11 A.M. A rotten bit of vertical wall forced us to the right onto the open face. To regain the Couloir it would be necessary to climb this sixty-foot cliff, composed of two pitches split by a broken snow-covered step.

"You like to lead this one?" Willi asked.

With my oxygen off I failed to think before I replied, "Sure, I'll try it."

The rock sloped malevolently outward like shingles on a roof—rotten shingles. The covering of snow was no better than the rock. It would pretend to hold for a moment, then suddenly shatter and peel, cascading down on Willi. He sank a piton into the base of the step to anchor his belay.

I started up around the corner to the left, crampon points grating on rusty limestone. Then it became a snowplowing procedure as I searched for some sort of purchase beneath. The pick of my ax found a crack. Using the shaft for gentle leverage, I moved carefully onto the broken strata of the step. I went left again, loose debris rolling under my crampons, to the base of the final vertical rise, about eight feet high. For all its steepness, this bit was a singularly poor plastering job, nothing but wobbly rubble. I searched about for a crack, undipped a big angle piton from my sling, and whomped it in with the hammer. It sank smoothly, as if penetrating soft butter. A gentle lift easily extracted it.

"Hmmm. Not too good," I mumbled through my mask. On the fourth try the piton gripped a bit more solidly. Deciding not to loosen it by testing, I turned to the final wall. Its steepness threw my weight out from the rock, and my pack became a downright hindrance. There was an unlimited selection of handholds, mostly portable. I shed my mittens. For a few seconds the rock felt comfortably reassuring but cold. Then not cold any more. My eyes tried to direct sensationless fingers. Flakes peeled out beneath my crampons. I leaned out from the rock to move upward, panting like a steam engine. Damn it, it'll go; I know it will, T, I thought. But my grip was gone. I hadn't thought to turn my oxygen up.

"No soap," I called down. "Can't make it now. Too pooped."

"Come on down. There may be a way to the right."

I descended, half rappelling from the piton, which held. I had spent the better part of an hour up there. A hundred feet out we looked back. Clearly we had been on the right route, for above that last little step the gully opened out. A hundred feet higher the Yellow Band met the gray of the summit limestone. It had to get easier.

"You'd better take it, Willi. I've wasted enough time already."

"Hell, if you couldn't make it, I'm not going to be able to do any better."

"Yes you will. It's really not that hard. I was just worn out from putting that piton in. Turn your regulator clear open, though."

Willi headed up around the corner, moving well. In ten minutes his rope was snapped through the high piton. Discarding a few unsavory holds, he gripped the rotten edge with his unmittened hands. He leaned out for the final move. His pack pulled. Crampons scraped, loosing a shower of rock from beneath his feet. He was over. He leaned against the rock, fighting for breath.

"Man, that's work. But it looks better above."

Belayed, I followed, retrieved the first piton, moved up, and went to work on the second. It wouldn't come. "Guess it's better than I thought," I shouted. "I'm going to leave it." I turned my oxygen to four liters, leaned out from the wall, and scrambled up. The extra oxygen helped, but it was surprising how breathless such a brief effort left me.

"Good lead," I panted. "That wasn't easy."

"Thanks. Let's roll."

Another rope-length and we stopped. After six hours of hiss Willi's first bottle was empty. There was still a long way to go, but at least he could travel ten pounds lighter without the extra cylinder. Our altimeter read 27,900. We called Base on the walkie-talkie.

Willi: West Ridge to Base. West Ridge to Base. Over.

Base (Jim Whittaker, excitedly): This is Base here, Willi. How are you? How are things going? What's the word up there? Over.

Willi: Man, this is a real bearcat! We are nearing the top of the Yellow Band and it's mighty tough. It's too damned tough to try to go back. It would be too dangerous.

Base (Jim): I'm sure you're considering all about your exits. Why don't you leave yourself an opening? If it's not going to pan out, you can always start working your way down. I think there is always a way to come back.

Willi: Roger, Jim. We're counting on a further consultation in about two or three hundred feet. It should ease up by then! Goddammit, if we can't start moving together, we'll have to move back down. But it should be easier once the Yellow Band is passed. Over.

Base (Jim): Don't work yourself up into a bottleneck, Willi. How about rappeling? Is that possible, or don't you have any *reepschnur* or anything? Over.

Willi: There are no rappel points, Jim, absolutely no rappel points. There's nothing to secure a rope to. So it's up and over for us today . . .

While the import of his words settled upon those listening 10,000 feet below, Willi went right on:

Willi (continuing): . . . and we'll probably be getting in pretty late, maybe as late as seven or eight o'clock tonight.

As Willi talked, I looked at the mountain above. The slopes looked reasonable, as far as I could see, which wasn't very far. We sat at the base of a big, wide-open amphitheatre. It looked like summits all over the place. I looked down. Descent was totally unappetizing. The rotten rock, the softening snow, the absence of even tolerable piton cracks only added to our desire to go on. Too much labor, too many sleepless nights, and too many dreams had been invested to bring us this far. We couldn't come back for another try next weekend. To go down now, even if we could have, would be descending to a future marked by one huge question: what might have been? It would not be a matter of living with our fellow man, but simply living with ourselves, with the knowledge that we had had more to give.

I listened, only mildly absorbed in Willi's conversation with Base, and looked past him at the convexity of rock cutting off our view of the gully we had ascended. Above—a snowfield, gray walls, then blue-black sky. We were committed. An invisible barrier sliced through the mountain beneath our feet, cutting us off from the world below. Though we could see through, all we saw was infinitely remote. The ethereal link provided by our radio only intensified our separation. My wife and children seemed suddenly close. Yet home, life itself, lay only over the top of Everest and down the other side. Suppose we fail? The thought brought no remorse, no fear. Once entertained, it hardly seemed even interesting. What now mattered most was right here: Willi and I, tied together on a rope, and the mountain, its summit not inaccessibly far above. The reason we had come was within our grasp. We belonged to the mountain and it to us. There was anxiety, to be sure, but it was all but lost in a feeling of calm, of pleasure at the joy of climbing. That we couldn't go down only made easier that which we really wanted to do. That we might not get there was scarcely conceivable.

Willi was still talking.

Willi: Any news of Barry and Lute? Over.

Jim: I haven't heard a word from them. Over.

Willi: How about Dingman?

Jim: No word from Dingman. We've heard nothing, nothing at all.

Willi: Well listen, if you do get hold of Dingman, tell him to put a light in the window because we're headed for the summit, Jim. We can't possibly get back to our camp now. Over.

I stuffed the radio back in Willi's pack. It was 1 P.M. From here we could both climb at the same time, moving across the last of the yellow slabs. Another hundred feet and the Yellow Band was below us. A steep tongue of snow flared wide, penetrating the gray strata that capped the mountain. The snow was hard, almost ice-hard in places. We had only to bend our ankles, firmly plant all twelve crampon points, and walk uphill. At last, we were moving, though it would have appeared painfully slow to a distant bystander.

As we climbed out of the Couloir the pieces of the puzzle fell into place. That snow rib ahead on the left skyline should lead us to the Summit Snowfield, a patch of perpetual white clinging to the North Face at the base of Everest's final pyramid. By three we were on the Snowfield. We had been climbing for eight hours and knew we needed to take time to refuel. At a shaley outcrop of rock we stopped for lunch. There was a decision to be made. We could either cut straight to the northeast ridge and follow it west to the summit, or we could traverse the face and regain the West Ridge.

From where we sat, the Ridge looked easier. Besides, it was the route we'd intended in the first place.

We split a quart of lemonade that was slushy with ice. In spite of its down parka wrapping, the other bottle was already frozen solid, as were the kippered snacks. They were almost tasteless but we downed them more with dutiful thoughts of calories than with pleasure.

To save time we moved together, diagonaling upward across downsloping slabs of rotten shale. There were no possible stances from which to belay each other. Then snow again, and Willi kicked steps, fastidiously picking a route between the outcropping rocks. Though still carting my full load of oxygen bottles, I was beginning to feel quite strong. With this excess energy came impatience, and an unconscious anxiety over the high stakes for which we were playing and the lateness of the day. Why the hell is Willi going so damned slow? I thought. And a little later: He should cut over to the Ridge now; it'll be a lot easier.

I shouted into the wind, "Hold up, Willi!" He pretended not to hear me as he started up the rock. It seemed terribly important to tell him to go to the right. I tugged on the rope. "Damn it, wait up, Willi!" Stopped by a taut rope and an unyielding Hornbein, he turned, and with some irritation anchored his ax while I hastened to join him. He was perched, through no choice of his own, in rather cramped, precarious quarters. I sheepishly apologized.

We were on rock now. One rope-length, crampons scraping, brought us to the crest of the West Ridge for the first time since we'd left camp 4W yesterday morning. The South Face fell eight thousand feet to the tiny tents of Advance Base. Lhotse, straight across the face, was below us now. And near at hand a hundred and fifty feet higher, the South Summit of Everest shone in the afternoon sun. We were within four hundred feet of the top! The wind whipped across the ridge from the north at nearly sixty miles an hour. Far below, peak shadows reached long across the cloud-filled valleys. Above, the Ridge rose, a twisting, rocky spine.

We shed crampons and overboots to tackle this next rocky bit with the comforting grip of cleated rubber soles. Here I unloaded my first oxygen bottle though it was not quite empty. It had lasted ten hours, which obviously meant I was getting a lower flow than indicated by the regulator. Resisting Willi's suggestion to drop the cylinder off the South Face, I left it for some unknown posterity. When I resaddled ten pounds lighter, I felt I could float to the top.

The rock was firm, at least in comparison with our fare thus far. Climbing one at a time, we experienced the joy of delicate moves on tiny holds. The going was a wonderful pleasure, almost like a day in the Rockies. With the sheer drop to the Cwm beneath us, we measured off another four rope-lengths. Solid rock gave way to crud, then snow. A thin, firm, knife-edge of white pointed gently toward the sky. Buffeted by the wind, we laced our crampons on, racing each other with rapidly numbing fingers. It took nearly twenty minutes. Then we were off again, squandering oxygen at three liters per minute, since time seemed the shorter commodity at the moment. We moved together, Willi in front. It seemed almost as if we were cheating, using oxygen; we could nearly run this final bit.

Ahead the North and South Ridges converged to a point. Surely the summit wasn't that near? It must be off behind. Willi stopped. What's he waiting for, I wondered as I moved to join him. With a feeling of disbelief I looked up. Forty feet ahead, tattered and whipped by the wind, was the flag Jim had left three weeks before. It was 6:15. The sun's rays sheered horizontally across the summit. We hugged each other as tears welled up, ran down across our oxygen masks, and turned to ice.

⋎   ⋎   ⋎

Just rock, a dome of snow, the deep blue sky, and a hunk of orange-painted metal from which a shredded American flag cracked in the wind. Nothing more. Except two tiny figures walking together those last few feet to the top of the earth.

For twenty minutes we stayed there. The last brilliance of the day cast the shadow of our summit on the cloud plain a hundred miles to the east. Valleys were filled with the indistinct purple haze of evening, concealing the dwellings of man we knew were there. The chill roar of wind made speaking difficult, heightening our feeling of remoteness. The flag left there seemed a feeble gesture of man that had no purpose but to accentuate the isolation. The two of us who had dreamed months before of sharing this moment were linked by a thin line of rope, joined in the intensity of companionship to those inaccessibly far below, Al and Barry and Dick—and Jake.

From a pitch of intense emotional and physical drive it was only partly possible to become suddenly, completely the philosopher of a balmy afternoon. The head of steam was too great, and the demands on it still remained. We have a long way to go to get down, I thought. But the prospect of descent of an unknown side of the mountain in the dark caused me less anxiety than many other occasions had. I had a blind, fatalistic faith that, having succeeded in coming this far, we could not fail to get down. The moment became an end in itself.

There were many things savored in this brief time. Even with our oxygen turned off we had no problem performing those summit obeisances, photographing the fading day (it's a wonderful place to be for sunset photographs), smiling behind our masks for the inevitable "I was there" picture. Willi wrapped the kata given him by Ang Dorje about the flag pole and planted Andy Bakewell's crucifix alongside it in the snow; Lhotse and Makalu, below us, were a contrast of sun-blazed snow etched against the darkness of evening shadow. We felt the lonely beauty of the evening, the immense roaring silence of the wind, the tenuousness of our tie to all below. There was a hint of fear, not for our lives, but of a vast unknown which pressed in upon us. A fleeting feeling of disappointment—that after all those dreams and questions this was only a mountain top—gave way to the suspicion that maybe there was something more, something beyond the three-dimensional form of the moment. If only it could be perceived.

But it was late. The memories had to be stored, the meanings taken down. The question of why we had come was not now to be answered, yet something up here must yield an answer, something only dimly felt, comprehended by senses reaching farther yet than the point on which we stood; reaching for understanding, which hovered but a few steps higher. The answers lay not on the summit of Everest, nor in the sky above it, but in the world to which we belonged and must now return.

Footprints in the snow told that Lute and Barrel had been here. We'd have a path to follow as long as light remained.

"Want to go first?" Willi asked. He began to coil the rope.

Looking down the corniced edge, I thought of the added protection of a rope from above. "Doesn't matter, Willi. Either way."

"O.K. Why don't I go first then?" he said, handing me the coil. Paying out the rope as he disappeared below me I wondered, "Is Unsoeld tired?" It was hard to believe. Still he'd worked hard; he had a right to be weary. Starting sluggishly, I'd felt stronger as we climbed. So now we would reverse roles. Going up had been pretty much Willi's show; going down would be mine. I dropped the last coil and started after him.

Fifty feet from the top we stopped at a patch of exposed rock. Only the summit of Everest, shining pink, remained above the shadow sea. Willi radioed to Maynard Miller at Advance Base that we were headed for the South Col. It was 6:15 P.M.

We almost ran along the crest, trusting Lute and Barrel's track to keep us a safe distance from the cornice edge. Have to reach the South Summit before dark, I thought, or we'll never find the way. The sun dropped below the jagged horizon. We didn't need goggles any more. There was a loud hiss as I banged my oxygen bottle against the ice wall. Damn! Something's broken. I reached back and turned off the valve. Without oxygen, I tried to keep pace with the rope disappearing over the edge ahead. Vision dimmed, the ground began to move. I stopped 'til things cleared, waved my arms and shouted into the wind for Willi to hold up. The taut rope finally stopped him. I tightened the regulator, then turned the oxygen on. No hiss! To my relief it had only been jarred loose. On oxygen again, I could move rapidly. Up twenty feet, and we were on the South Summit. It was 7:15.

Thank God for the footprints. Without them, we'd have had a tough time deciding which way to go. We hurried on, facing outward, driving our heels into the steep snow. By 7:30 it was dark. We took out the flashlight and resumed the descent. The batteries, dregs of the expedition, had not been helped by our session with Emerson's diary the night before; they quickly faded. There was pitiful humor as Willi probed, holding the light a few inches off the snow to catch some sign of tracks. You could order your eyes to see, but nothing in the blackness complied.

We moved slowly now. Willi was only a voice and an occasional faint flicker of light to point the way. No fear, no worry, no strangeness, just complete absorption. The drive that had carried us to a nebulous goal was replaced by simple desire for survival. There was no time to dwell on the uniqueness of our situation. We climbed carefully, from years of habit. At a rock outcrop we paused. Which way? Willi groped to the right along a corniced edge. In my imagination, I filled in the void.

"No tracks over here," Willi called.

"Maybe we should dig in here for the night."

"I don't know. Dave and Girmi should be at 6."

We shouted into the night, and the wind engulfed our call. A lull. Again we shouted. "Helloooo," the wind answered. Or was it the wind?

"Hellooo," we called once more.

"Helloo," came back faintly. That wasn't the wind!

"To the left, Willi."

"O.K., go ahead."

In the blackness I couldn't see my feet. Each foot groped cautiously, feeling its own way down, trusting to the pattern set by its predecessor. Slowly left, right, left, crampons biting into the snow, right, left, . . .

"Willeeee!" I yelled as I somersaulted into space. The rope came taut, and with a soft thud I landed.

"Seems to be a cornice there," I called from beneath the wall. "I'll belay you from here."

Willi sleepwalked down to the edge. The dim outline of his foot wavered until it met my guiding hand. His arrival lacked the flair of my descent. It was well that the one of lighter weight had gone first.

Gusts buffeted from all directions, threatening to dislodge us from the slope. Above a cliff we paused, untied, cut the rope in half, and tied in again. It didn't help; even five feet behind I couldn't see Willi. Sometimes the snow was good, sometimes it was soft, sometimes it lay shallow over rocks so we could only drive our axes in an inch or two. With these psychological belays, we wandered slowly down, closer to the answering shouts. The wind was dying, and so was the flashlight, now no more than an orange glow illuminating nothing. The stars, brilliant above, cast no light on the snow. Willi's oxygen ran out. He slowed, suddenly feeling much wearier.

The voices were close now. Were they coming from those two black shapes on the snow? Or were those rocks?

"Shine your light down here," a voice called.

"Where? Shine yours up here," I answered.

"Don't have one," came the reply.

Then we were with them—not Dave and Girmi, but Lute and Barrel. They were near exhaustion, shivering lumps curled on the snow. Barrel in particular was far gone. Anxious hungering for air through the previous night, and the near catastrophe when their tent caught fire in the morning, had left him tired before they even started. Determination got him to the top, but now he no longer cared. He only wanted to be left alone. Lute was also tired. Because of Barrel's condition he'd had to bear the brunt of the climbing labor. His eyes were painfully burned, perhaps by the fire, perhaps by the sun and wind. From sheer fatigue they had stopped thinking. Their oxygen was gone, except for a bit Lute had saved for Barrel; but they were too weak to make the change.

At 9:30 we were still a thousand feet above Camp 6. Willi sat down on the snow, and I walked over to get Lute's oxygen for Barrel. As I unscrewed Lute's regulator from the bottle, he explained why they were still there. Because of the stove fire that had sent them diving from the tent, they were an hour late in starting. It was 3:30 P.M. when they reached the summit. Seeing no sign of movement down the west side, they figured no one would be any later than they were. At 4:15 they started down. Fatigue slowed their descent. Just after dark they had stopped to rest and were preparing to move when they heard shouts. Dave and Girmi, they thought. No—the sounds seemed to be coming from above. Willi and Tom! So they waited, shivering.

I removed Barrel's regulator from his empty bottle and screwed it into Lute's. We were together now, sharing the support so vigorously debated a week before. Lute would know the way back to their camp, even in the dark. All we had to do was help them down. Fumbling with unfeeling fingers, I tried to attach Barrel's oxygen hose to the regulator. Damn! Can't make the connection. My fingers scraped uncoordinatedly against cold metal. Try again. There it goes. Then, quickly, numb fingers clumsy, back into mittens. Feeling slowly returned, and pain. Then, the pain went and the fingers were warm again.

Willi remembered the Dexedrine I had dropped into my shirt pocket the evening before. I fished out two pills—one for Barrel and one for Lute. Barrel was better with oxygen, but why I had balked at his communal use of Lute's regulator, I cannot say. Lack of oxygen? Fatigue? It was fifteen hours since we'd started our climb. Or was it that my thoughts were too busy with another problem? We had to keep moving or freeze.

I led off. Lute followed in my footsteps to point out the route. Lost in the darkness sixty feet back on our ropes, Willi and Barrel followed. The track was more sensed than seen, but it was easier now, not so steep. My eyes watered from searching for the black holes punched in the snow by Lute's and Barrel's axes during their ascent. We walked to the left of the crest, three feet down, ramming our axes into the narrow edge. Thirty feet, and the rope came taut as Barrel collapsed in the snow, bringing the entire caravan to a halt. Lute sat down behind me. Got to keep moving. We'll never get there.

We had almost no contact with the back of the line. When the rope came taut, we stopped, when it loosened we moved on. Somewhere my oxygen ran out, but we were going too slow for me to notice the difference. Ought to dump the empty bottle, I thought, but it was too much trouble to take off my pack.

Heat lightning flashed along the plains to the east, too distant to light our way. Rocks that showed in the snow below seemed to get no closer as the hours passed. Follow the ax holes. Where'd they go? Not sure. There's another.

"Now where, Lute?"

"Can't see, Tom." Lute said. "Can't see a damn thing. We've got to turn down a gully between some rocks."

"Which gully. There's two or three."

"Don't know, Tom."

"Think, Lute. Try to remember. We've got to get to 6."

"I don't know. I just can't see."

Again and again I questioned, badgering, trying to extract some hint. But half-blind and weary, Lute had no answer. We plodded on. The rocks came slowly closer.

Once the rope jerked tight, nearly pulling me off balance. Damn! What's going on? I turned and looked at Lute's dim form lying on the snow a few feet farther down the Kangshung Face. His fall had been effectively if uncomfortably arrested when his neck snagged the rope between Willi and me.

We turned off the crest, toward the rocks. Tongues of snow pierced the cliffs below. But which one? It was too dangerous to plunge on. After midnight we reached the rocks. It had taken nearly three hours to descend four hundred feet, maybe fifteen minutes' worth by daylight.

Tired. No hope of finding camp in the darkness. No choice but to wait for day. Packs off. Willi and I slipped into our down parkas. In the dark, numb fingers couldn't start the zippers. We settled to the ground, curled as small as possible atop our pack frames. Lute and Barry were somewhere behind, apart, each alone. Willi and I tried hugging each other to salvage warmth, but my uncontrollable shivering made it impossible.

The oxygen was gone, but the mask helped a little for warmth. Feet, cooling, began to hurt. I withdrew my hands from the warmth of my crotch and loosened crampon bindings and bootlaces, but my feet stayed cold. Willi offered to rub them. We removed boots and socks and planted both my feet against his stomach. No sensation returned.

Tired by the awkward position, and frustrated by the result, we gave it up. I slid my feet back into socks and boots, but couldn't tie them. I offered to warm Willi's feet. Thinking that his freedom from pain was due to a high tolerance of cold, he declined. We were too weary to realize the reason for his comfort.

The night was overpoweringly empty. Stars shed cold unshimmering light. The heat lightning dancing along the plains spoke of a world of warmth and flatness. The black silhouette of Lhotse lurked half-sensed, half-seen, still below. Only the ridge on which we were rose higher, disappearing into the night, a last lonely outpost of the world.

Mostly there was nothing. We hung suspended in a timeless void. The wind died, and there was silence. Even without wind it was cold. I could reach back and touch Lute or Barrel lying head to toe above me. They seemed miles away.

Unsignalled, unembellished, the hours passed. Intense cold penetrated, carrying with it the realization that each of us was completely alone. Nothing Willi could do for me or I for him. No team now, just each of us, imprisoned with his own discomfort, his own thoughts, his own will to survive.

Yet for me, survival was hardly a conscious thought. Nothing to plan, nothing to push for, nothing to do but shiver and wait for the sun to rise. I floated in a dreamlike eternity, devoid of plans, fears, regrets. The heat lightning, Lhotse, my companions, discomfort, all were there—yet not there. Death had no meaning, nor, for that matter, did life. Survival was no concern, no issue. Only a dulled impatience for the sun to rise tied my formless thoughts to the future. About 4:00 the sky began to lighten along the eastern rim, baring the bulk of Kangchenjunga. The sun was slow in following, interminably slow. Not till after 5:00 did it finally come, its light streaming through the South Col, blazing yellow across the Nuptse Wall, then on to the white wave-crest of peaks far below. We watched as if our own life was being born again. Then as the cold yellow light touched us, we rose. There were still miles to go.

᠎᠎᠎᠎᠎᠎᠎᠎᠎᠎᠎᠎᠎᠎᠎᠎᠎᠎᠎᠎᠎᠎᠎᠎᠎᠎᠎᠎ ⸭   ⸭   ⸭

The rest is like a photograph with little depth of field, the focused moments crystal sharp against a blurred background of fatigue. We descended the gully I had been unable to find in the dark. Round the corner, Dave and Girmi were coming toward us. They thought they heard shouts in the night and had started up, but their own calls were followed only by silence. Now, as they came in search of the bodies of Lute and Barry they saw people coming down—not just two, but four. Dave puzzled a moment before he understood.

The tents at Camp 6—and we were home from the mountain. Nima Dorje brought tea. We shed boots. I stared blankly at the marble-white soles of Willi's feet. They were cold and hard as ice. We filled in Emerson's diary for the last time, then started down.

With wind tearing snow from its rocky plain, the South Col was as desolate and uninviting as it had always been described. We sought shelter in the tents at Camp 5 for lunch, then emerged into the gale. Across the Geneva Spur, out of the wind, on to the open sweep of the Lhotse Face we plodded in somber procession. Dave led gently, patiently; the four behind rocked along, feet apart to keep from falling. Only for Willi and me was this side of the mountain new. Like tourists we looked around, forgetting fatigue for the moment.

At Camp 4 we stopped to melt water, then continued with the setting sun, walking through dusk into darkness as Dave guided us among crevasses, down the Cwm. It was a mystery to me how he found the way. I walked along at the back, following the flashlight. Sometimes Willi stopped and I would nearly bump into him. We waited while Dave searched, then moved on. No one complained.

At 10:30 P.M. we arrived at Advance Base. Dick, Barry, and Al were down from the Ridge, waiting. Frozen feet and Barrel's hands were thawed in warm water. Finally to bed, after almost two days. Short of a sleeping bag. Willi and I shared one as best we could.

May 24 we were late starting, tired. Lute, Willi, and Barrel walked on thawed feet. It was too dangerous to carry them down through the Icefall. Willi, ahead of me on the rope, heeled down like an awkward clown. The codeine wasn't enough to prevent cries of pain when he stubbed his toes against the snow. I cried as I walked behind, unharmed.

At Camp 1 Maynard nursed us like a mother hen, serving us water laboriously melted from ice samples drilled from the glacier for analysis. Then down through the Icefall, past Jake's grave—and a feeling of finality. It's all done. The dream's finished.

No rest. The next day, a grim gray one, we departed Base. From low-hanging clouds wet snow fell. Willi, Barrel, and Lute were loaded aboard porters to be carried down over the rocky moraine. It was easier walking.

At Gorak Shep we paused. On a huge boulder a Sherpa craftsman had patiently carved:

IN MEMORY OF JOHN E. BREITENBACH,
AMERICAN MOUNT EVEREST EXPEDITION, 1963.

Clouds concealed the mountain that was Jake's grave.

As we descended, the falling snow gave way to a fine drizzle. There was nothing to see; just one foot, then another. But slowly a change came, something that no matter how many times experienced, is always new, like life. It *was* life. From ice and snow and rock, we descended to a world of living things, of green—grass and trees and bushes. There was no taking it for granted.

Spring had come, and even the gray drizzle imparted a wet sheen to all that grew. At Pheriche flowers bloomed in the meadows.

Lying in bed, Willi and I listened to a sound that wasn't identifiable, so foreign was it to the place—the chopping whirr as a helicopter circled, searching for a place to land. In a flurry of activity Willi and Barrel were loaded aboard. The helicopter rose from the hilltop above the village and dipped into the distance. The chop-chop-chop of the blades faded, until finally the craft itself was lost in the massive backdrop. The departure was too unreal, too much a part of another world, to be really comprehended. Less than five days after they had stood on the summit of Everest, Barrel and Willi were back in Kathmandu. For them the expedition was ended. Now all that remained was weeks in bed, sitting, rocking in pain, waiting for toes to mummify to the time for amputation.

Up over barren passes made forbidding by mist and a chill wind, we traveled. Hard work. Then down through forests of rain-drenched rhododendrons, blossoming pastels of pink and lavender. Toes hurt. Two weeks to Kathmandu. Feet slipped on the muddy path. Everything was wet.

We were finished. Everest was climbed; nothing to push for now. Existence knew only the instant, counting steps, falling asleep each time we stopped to rest beside the trail. Lester, Emerson, and I talked about motivation; for me it was all gone. It was a time of relaxation, a time when senses were tuned to perceive, but nothing was left to give.

Pleasure lay half-hidden beneath discomfort, fatigue, loneliness. Willi was gone. The gap where he had been was filled with a question: Why hadn't I known that his feet were numb? Surely I could have done something, if only . . . I was too weary to know the question couldn't be resolved. Half of me seemed to have gone with him; the other half was isolated from my companions by an experience I couldn't share and by the feeling that something was ending that had come to mean too much. Talk of home, of the first evening in the Yak and Yeti Bar, of the reception that waited, was it really so important? Did it warrant the rush?

We'd climbed Everest. What good was it to Jake? To Willi? To Barrel? To Norman, with Everest all done now? And to the rest of us? What waits? What price less tangible than toes? There must be something more to it than toiling over the top of another, albeit expensive, mountain. Perhaps there was something of the nobility-that-is-man in it somewhere, but it was hard to be sure.

Yes, it satisfied in a way. Not just climbing the mountain, but the entire effort—the creating something, the few of us molding it from the beginning. With a lot of luck we'd succeeded. But what had we proved?

Existence on a mountain is simple. Seldom in life does it come any simpler: survival, plus the striving toward a summit. The goal is solidly, three-dimensionally—there you can see it, touch it, stand upon it—the way to reach it well defined, the energy of all directed toward its achievement. It is this simplicity that strips the veneer off civilization and makes that which is meaningful easier to come by—the pleasure of deep companionship, moments of uninhibited humor, the tasting of hardship, sorrow, beauty, joy. But it is this very simplicity that may prevent finding answers to the questions I had asked as we approached the mountain.

Then I had been unsure that I could survive and function in a world so foreign to my normal existence. Now I felt at home here, no longer overly afraid. Each step toward Kathmandu carried me back toward the known, yet toward many things terribly unknown, toward goals unclear, to be reached by paths undefined.

Beneath fatigue lurked the suspicion that the answers I sought were not to be found on a mountain. What possible difference could climbing Everest make? Certainly the mountain hadn't been changed. Even now wind and falling snow would have obliterated most signs of our having been there. Was I any greater for having stood on the highest place on earth? Within the wasted figure that stumbled weary and fearful back toward home there was no question about the answer to that one.

It had been a wonderful dream, but now all that lingered was the memory. The dream was ended.

Everest must join the realities of my existence, commonplace and otherwise. The goal, unattainable, had been attained. Or had it? The questions, many of them, remained. And the answers? It is strange how when a dream is fulfilled there is little left but doubt.

Never let success hide its emptiness from you, achievement its nothingness, toil its desolation. And so keep alive the incentive to push on farther, that pain in the soul which drives us beyond ourselves.

Whither? That I don't know. That I don't ask to know.

—Dag Hammarskjold

"ALL THE WINDS OF ASIA"

FROM
Everest: The Mountaineering History
BY WALT UNSWORTH

THE SUMMIT OF THE HIGHEST MOUNTAIN ON EARTH TURNED OUT to be a fitting place for Doug Scott and Dougal Haston to usher in a new age of Himalayan climbing. In the years between the Everest traverse by Tom Hornbein and Willi Unsoeld in 1963, and the decade of the 1970s in which Reinhold Messner changed the very nature of Himalayan climbing, Englishman Doug Scott and Scotsman Dougal Haston became the first British climbers to reach the top of Everest. The pair established a new benchmark for technical climbing in the process.

Scott, at 32, already was one of the most free-thinking climbers of his generation, and the more experienced Haston was by then at the pinnacle of the profession. The pair reached the summit of Everest via the Southwest Face, a difficult and technical new route, to arrive at what Haston called a "unique moment in our lives." For Scott, that summit was "everything and more than a summit should be."

But the climbers had reached the top too late in the day to descend, and had actually tarried there to enjoy the sunset, leaving them to face a deadly experiment. Haston and Scott would discover that night whether human beings could survive, intact, a night above 28,700 feet without oxygen. "Dougal and I were so wrapped up in our own personal miseries, we hardly noticed each other," Scott told me in 2001, "but I did find myself talking to my feet."

Inside a hastily constructed snow cave, the men rubbed their extremities, had conversations with imaginary partners, and drifted into a psychological dream state of oxygen deprivation. When dawn finally came, the two climbers were not only still alive, but virtually unscathed, a tribute to the purity of purpose that Scott says comes only from "total commitment." The next day the exhausted men descended to the safety of high camps, and eventually to international acclaim.

The courage and commitment displayed by Haston and Scott is by now part of Everest legend. But they did not climb the route alone. Their achievement came on the heels of gutsy, technical climbing at altitude by team hard-men Nick Estcourt and Tut Braithwaite. Perhaps less appreciated is the contribution of Chris Bonington, who had proven his leadership on large, technical Himalayan challenges such as the successful ascent of the South Face of Annapurna in 1972. A leading player in the British climbing scene since the late 1950s, Bonington was by the time of the 1975 Southwest Face attempt, a consummate master of expedition leadership.

His job was a daunting one. From the seemingly impossible task of raising the money, to picking the perfect team, to applying all of the tricks and hard lessons he had learned in a decade of Himalayan expeditions, Bonington saw the 1975 expedition through to success. He was so wired during the crux of the effort that the expedition doctor worried he was in a "state of hypermania," resulting in Mick Burke's applying the moniker, the "Mad Mahdi," to their leader. Tragically, Burke disappeared high on the mountain at the conclusion of the expedition.

Walt Unsworth, the tireless and meticulous Everest historian, devotes an entire chapter in his comprehensive *Everest: The Mountaineering History* to this expedition, arguably the most important British attempt on the mountain since the first ascent in 1953. The excerpt below picks up Unsworth's reporting of the West Face climb with the controversy over the expedition's "outrageous" expense—more than £100,000, to be paid primarily by the lead sponsor, Barclay's Bank International. In those tough days, economically speaking, of the mid-1970s, a number of critics thought the money could be better spent else-where. This piece is from *Everest: The Mountaineering History,* by Walt Unsworth, on pages 446–458.

T he critics really hadn't thought it through. How can you measure in terms of cash the national euphoria engendered by, say, the successful Everest ascent of 1953, made when the country was still recovering from the war and in even worse financial straits than it was in 1975? After it was all over, Bonington said:

> . . . *if we said these are stringent times—which was one of the criticisms which was made—therefore, it is a waste of money to go off on mountaineering expeditions and therefore, in par- allel really, it is a waste of money to do absolutely anything which isn't tied up with the direct productivity of the country, then what an appalling, boring, dreary country we should have,*

and if we had such a boring, dreary country we should be deeper
in the mire than we already are.

The climbing world itself was not mute. Some critics merely echoed the
sentiment that £100,000 was too much to spend on a single expedition and
that the money would have been better disbursed among a number of lightweight expeditions with less prestigious objectives—failing to understand that
in such circumstances the money would not have been forthcoming at all.
Others, no doubt bored by the repeated failures and the media coverage which
the Face had received, dismissed the route as an ugly one of no consequence,
a subjective assessment which only history can confirm; while some criticized
Bonington because he seemed to favor a tightly knit little group which ex-
cluded some equally good climbers—though in fact only eight out of the final eighteen members were close acquaintances. All the conservatism which
is so rampant in climbing rebelled against the giant publicity machine that
the South-West Face invariably provoked, and it was this more than anything
else which was the cause of the criticism. Bonington had more than the Face
to climb: old Cassius Bonafide would be hacked to death by vitriol-dipped
quills if he didn't get this one right!

Bonington laid his plans carefully, unhampered by financial constraints and
with sufficient time in hand to do a much more thorough job than had been
possible in 1972. Men, food, and materials were fitted into a logistical pyramid
the apex of which was to be two men sitting in a lonely tent—placed in the
right spot at the right time—ready for the final summit dash. It was an exercise
in a vast yet precise upwards funneling of resources—and it was perhaps a sign
of the times that it was done with the aid of a computer. It was probably the
most meticulous preparation of any Everest expedition since Hunt's.

In order to achieve the speedy ascent he thought essential, Bonington reckoned on expanding his team to eighteen front-line members—that is, those
who were to be actually engaged in the climb, either as lead climbers or in
support roles.

The core of these came from the 1972 expedition and the Annapurna expedition: forty-four-year-old Hamish MacInnes (who became deputy leader),
the inaugurator of the madcap Creagh Dhu expedition to Everest twenty-two

years earlier, who had twice been on the South-West Face, Dougal Haston, Doug Scott, Mick Burke, Nick Estcourt, Martin Boyson, and Mike Thompson. Only the last two had not been on the Face before.

Newcomers to the team were Paul Braithwaite, a twenty-eight-year-old interior decorator from Oldham who looked like a character from *Dr. Zhivago*, who had an impressive Alpine record, and who was invariably known as Tut; Allen Fyffe, also twenty-eight, was a Scot, a bald, broad-shouldered man who had also done some outstanding Alpine routes, and was a climbing instructor; Ronnie Richards, twenty-nine, a bespectacled chemist from the Lake District who had climbed the West Ridge of Pic Lenin in the Pamirs the previous year; and Dave Clarke, thirty-seven, who was the owner of an equipment shop in Leeds—sandy haired, solid and no-nonsense. Barclays Bank (which has its own climbing club) nominated Mike Rhodes, a twenty-seven-year-old clerk from Bradford. Youngest of them all was Peter Boardman, twenty-four years old and the National Officer of the British Mountaineering Council; broad shouldered and genial, he had already acquired a considerable reputation for accomplishing big climbs.

The two doctors were Charles Clarke and Jim Duff, both experienced mountaineers, and to complete the team there was Adrian Gordon, a fluent Nepali speaker who lived in Kathmandu, who was to look after Advanced Base Camp, and Mike Cheney, Base Camp manager, a small, sharp-featured man who was deeply involved in the trekking business and was acquiring the mantle of Jimmy Roberts as a Nepali expert.

Behind them there was a considerable support team: the Sherpa corps of thirty-three high-altitude Sherpas led by their sirdar, the twenty-seven-year-old Pertemba, who came from Khumjung, and twenty-six Icefall porters under Phurkipa, whose job it was to keep the route into the Cwm open and see that the supplies got through. There were more Sherpas to do the cooking and general chores.

In addition there was a four-man BBC TV team, a *Sunday Times* reporter, a liaison officer (each with *their* Sherpas) and, working from England at the outset of the expedition, Bob Stoodley and his drivers, whose job was to transport all the equipment to Kathmandu in two sixteen-ton vans.

And right at the base of the organizational pyramid was a small army of secretaries, media men, and general helpers to ensure that everything was coordinated both on and off the mountain.

This was the extent of the manpower that Bonington had to influence and control. "Perhaps I am a frustrated field marshal," he wryly commented.

Naturally enough, the gear and food were the best available and in ample quantities. The tents in particular were given thorough attention in view of the previous disastrous experience, when much of the tentage had been wrecked by gales. MacInnes was given the job of redesigning them, and produced a strengthened box for the lower Face camps and a more compact "assault box" for Camp 6, which Bonington confidently expected to be placed above the Rock Band. Bulletproof mesh to deflect stonefall was provided for the roofs of the lower boxes.

With sufficient men and materials under his command it only remained for Bonington's judgment on timing and the route to be followed to be borne out in practice. If he got those wrong, then no amount of skill and determination, no vast quantities of superlative gear, would be of any avail. A degree of luck was needed as well, for mountaineering is essentially a gamble, and the winner is the one who correctly calculates the odds.

And the odds were not reckoned great, even amongst the team members. Fifty-fifty was the optimistic view—the pessimists were quoting ten to one against.

Influenced by the experience of the Japanese, Bonington planned to be at Base Camp ready to begin the climb by the end of the third week in August. Normally this would have meant transporting tons of material over the long trek from Kathmandu during the height of the monsoon, which was a far from pleasant prospect, but Bonington hit upon the idea of sending the gear out *before* the monsoon and storing it in one of the Sherpas' houses at Khunde, a village near Namche Bazar, and only four or five marches from Base Camp. Two somewhat overloaded trucks left Barclay's city headquarters (sped on their way by a farewell cocktail party) on April 9 and arrived in Kathmandu on May 3. From there the gear was airlifted to Lukla airstrip, a tilled grass field perched on an alpine shoulder over the gorge of the Dudh Kosi, and portered from there to Khunde. It was safely established in its monsoon storage by June 10.

Meanwhile, the route to be followed on the Face had been discussed and analyzed by the climbers. It eschewed the rightwards traverse that led to the Whillans Chimney and concentrated instead on a deep gully to the left of the great central couloir. This was the area that had first attracted the Japanese when they pioneered the Face, but it had since been unaccountably neglected. Bonington and Scott had observed the gully during their previous outing and felt that it held promise.

If the gully led them through the Rock Band, as they hoped, they would find themselves at the left-hand extremity of the curious snowy shelf that is such a prominent feature of the upper Face. Here they planned to establish Camp 6. To reach the summit from there would mean traversing right across the shelf, then climbing a gully to the summit ridge and following the ridge, over the Hillary Step, to the top. It would be a long, long day, with a more than likely chance of an enforced bivouac on the return. But the Japanese had shown such a bivouac to be feasible, and the risk had to be accepted.

Base Camp was established on August 22. Already the weather signs were favorable, for during the walk-in—despite the season—they had been blessed with fine mornings, and rain only in the afternoons. Estcourt and Haston, who had gone ahead of the main parties, were already at work on the Icefall, which proved to be in a rather better condition than on the previous occasion.

In five days they were through the Icefall and two days later Camp 1 was established. The monsoon was not really at an end and there was still much soft snow around, with frightening avalanches roaring off Lhotse and Nuptse. It was conditions such as these that had destroyed a French expedition to the West Ridge the previous autumn, and Bonington was concerned about making a premature entry into the Western Cwm with the risk of being hit by an avalanche. Nevertheless by September 2 Camp 2 (Advanced Base) was established in the Cwm at 21,700 feet.

There had been some discussion as to how to tackle the lower slopes of the Face—the great central couloir. Haston and Scott had discovered what they believed to be a new and more direct line sloping up to the couloir from the left, with rocky outcrops beneath which camps could be sheltered, but in the end Bonington decided it would be preferable to follow the established route, which kept just to the right of the couloir and out of the main avalanche danger.

There was, however, a change in the disposition of the camps. Camp 3 occupied its traditional site at 23,000 feet, but Camp 4, which had been a very exposed camp sited in the heart of the big couloir, was pulled back almost a thousand feet to 23,700 feet and a more sheltered position, and Camp 5, previously sited at 26,000 feet, was lowered to 25,500 feet. Tactically the new sites were an improvement—the long, exhausting carry from Camps 3 to 4 was much reduced, and Camp 5 was in a better position for attacking the left-hand side of the Rock Band.

Things were going remarkably well. The weather was good, supplies were flowing, and tensions amongst the lead climbers, though always near the surface, were not breaking through. Bonington himself spent much of this period at Advanced Base: the frustrated field marshal now in full battle command, disposing of his troops. Later he analyzed his command philosophy:

> *I try to be as democratic as I possibly can and in this was very aware of what the other members of the team felt. Whenever I possibly could I would consult and discuss how we were going to do it.*
>
> *I think in a strong expedition and a large expedition it must come back to one person, the leader, in the final analysis to make a decision. If you don't do that I don't think you are doing the job as the leader, but at the same time you can do this in an easygoing, relaxed kind of way. I think we succeeded in being democratic in the sense that as far as possible people were consulted right the way through the expedition and could also make their voices heard and known, but someone has got to make a decision in the end and I made it.*

Back at Base Camp, Dr. Charles Clarke viewed his leader—and others— with a shrewd eye.

> *Chris is in a state of hypermania at Camp 2 in the Western Cwm, drawing charts of stores, oxygen, men, being uncontrollably effusive down the radio and Mick has christened him the "Mad Mahdi." He is desperate that the master plan unfolds smoothly*

and above all that the route from Base to Camp 2 is safe, for it is here that the Sherpas go alone and much can go wrong.

He really is a great leader in spite of all the criticism leveled at him. Nobody else has the personality to command us and deep down we respect him. I have a very good relationship with him particularly as I, thank God, am not in the raffle—i.e. the great decision of who goes to the top. This sadly alienates him from most of the lead climbers. Even a little is enough and it's just beginning to show itself. No splits, no factions, no nastiness, but it's all there in their hearts.

By the time MacInnes, Boysen, and Boardman occupied Camp 4 on September 11, the expedition was well ahead of the schedule Bonington had set. Six days later the leader, with Richards, established Camp 5 at 25,500 feet and they were joined there next day by Scott and Burke. Progress was almost unbelievably smooth and swift. Bonington, Scott, and Richards ran out fixed rope from Camp 5 to the Rock Band, while Estcourt and Braithwaite moved up in support. The very next day the assault on the Rock Band started.

Moving across the ropes fixed by their companions on the previous day, Estcourt and Braithwaite approached the dark gully that they hoped might prove the key to the ascent. When they reached the end of the ropes Tut Braithwaite won the "toss" to decide who should lead in the unknown territory ahead and soon found himself clambering over awkward sloping rocks to the gully entrance. Estcourt followed, and behind them in support came Bonington and Burke.

The gully was a dark and narrow slit cleaving through the Rock Band. It had a good snow bed which gave a firm grip for their crampons, and Braithwaite and Estcourt alternated leads, taking in their stride a snow-covered boulder that blocked the chasm at one point. The rock was not too good for pitons and there were no natural anchors, but the standard of climbing was not technically difficult—"about Scottish Grade III" was how Estcourt described it. "Scottish Grade III at 27,000 feet isn't something to be taken lightly," commented Bonington.

Estcourt wasn't taking it lightly at all. His oxygen ran out and he climbed on without it, feeling "like a hundred-and-five-year-old war veteran." And, as they neared the head of the gully, Braithwaite's oxygen also ran out:

> *I don't think I shall ever forget the feeling of suffocation as I ripped the mask away from my face. I was on the brink of falling, beginning to panic, felt a warm trickle run down my leg. God, what's happening? Scrabbled up the rock arête until at last I reached some firm snow. I collapsed exhausted.*

Had he fallen off he would have bounced two hundred feet down the gully and almost certainly been killed.

Braithwaite had halted just below a ramp, which sloped off to the right and seemed to lead to the upper icefield above the Rock Band. Estcourt joined him, then pushed on to tackle the ramp. It was easy at first but then it became a precarious struggle: the ramp was narrow, sloped outwards, and was largely composed of rubble cemented together by ice. It was overhung by a steep wall that thrust out at the encumbered climbers.

Estcourt clawed his way forward, desperately striving to keep his balance, while his companion watched anxiously. He managed to knock a shaky piton into a crack, pulled on it cautiously, and, digging desperately into the snow, snatched at another hold. He knew he just had to keep going: no stopping, no turning back, for to try either would be fatal. After a further twenty feet he reached a good crack, banged home a secure piton, and heaved a sigh of relief. "Given the conditions, it was the hardest pitch I've ever led," he said.

And as they had hoped, the ramp led to the upper icefield. Nick Estcourt and Tut Braithwaite had solved the problem of the Rock Band.

Bonington now had to give serious thought to the summit attempt. Initially he had envisaged only one attempt, and though he would not commit himself on who the summit pair would be, it was widely expected to be Haston and Scott. Such had been the progress of the expedition, however, that there was time in hand for a second and even third summit attempt. The problem was that, whereas the first attempt by Haston and Scott was more or less tacitly accepted by the team, there were a lot of anxious contenders for the subsequent placings. Whatever Bonington's choice, somebody was going to be disappointed.

He had promised to give the Sherpas a place in any subsequent summit attempts after the first, but by juggling the logistics a bit he could make these ascents with four-man rather than two-man teams. His final decision was that the second attempt would be made by Burke, Boysen, Boardman, and the Sherpa sirdar, Pertemba, and the third attempt by Estcourt, Braithwaite, Ang Phurba, and himself.

He placed himself ahead of other contenders, justifying it on the grounds of experience and fitness, but in reality it was that old Everest syndrome at work again—"the glittering prize"—which had tempted earlier leaders like Hunt and Dyhrenfurth. Bonington perhaps had more justification, but was that enough? Charles Clarke, the team doctor, thought not. By the time any third attempt took place, Bonington would have been at Camp 5 for almost two weeks—far too long for anybody to stay at 25,500 feet. Other problems were pressing too, lower down the mountain, so reluctantly Bonington gave up his place to Ronnie Richards.

The announcement of the summit parties was met with varying degrees of disappointment by those who might have expected a chance and didn't get one, none more so than Hamish MacInnes, who had had such a long and close association with attempts on the Face and was Bonington's second in command. But MacInnes had had a close shave with a powder snow avalanche that had swept over him, filling his lungs with icy particles, and he was really too ill for a summit attempt. Nevertheless, it is hard to watch a lifetime ambition slipping by, so he left the expedition quietly, to return home.

On September 22, Haston and Scott established Camp 6 on a small snow ridge just beyond the exit from the gully. Next day they ran out 1,500 feet of fixed rope across the upper snowfield toward a snowy gully that led up to the distant ridge. It proved nervy work, with inadequate anchors, and in the early section of the traverse there was an awkward rock step that required five pitons to overcome. There was no accommodating ice into which crampon claws could bite: only soft snow overlying shaley, downward-sloping rock. Long before the exit gully was reached the rope ran out, so they anchored its end and returned to Camp 6.

The climbers were pleased with their hard day's work—particularly as it had not seemed to exhaust them unduly, which gave them added confidence in their own strength and ability. Next morning at 2:30 A.M. they prepared for their summit bid. Haston wore his bulky duvet suit, but Scott, preferring greater freedom of movement, wore only his windproofs. Realizing they might have to make a forced bivouac, they also packed a tent-sack and a stove. Each had two oxygen cylinders, various pitons, personal gear, and between them three 50-meter ropes. There was no room in their sacks for sleeping bags.

At 3:30 A.M., while it was still dark, they set out on their great adventure. By the time dawn tipped the surrounding ridges they had reached the end of the fixed rope and were embarked on virgin territory, leading into the gully below the South Summit. Suddenly Haston stopped, fighting for breath. A quick investigation showed that there was plenty of oxygen left in his cylinder and therefore it must be the set which was malfunctioning. Only by partially dismantling the apparatus did they discover that a lump of ice had formed in the junction of the mouthpiece tube. They prised it out with a knife, reassembled the set, and continued on their way. Had it been a more serious fault their attempt would have been finished, as the repairs took more than an hour to complete.

Scott tackled a steep rock step in the gully and brought up his companion. Ahead there seemed two possible alternative routes—directly up a gully to the Hillary Step, or more or less straight up toward the South Summit. They decided to go straight up, and immediately ran into waist-deep powder snow of the most tiring, frustrating kind. With Haston in the lead they floundered upwards, thrashing the snow and gaining a couple of feet every few minutes. Although the angle was 60 degrees and the snow in classic avalanche condition there was no hope of belays. Scott was hard behind his leader, sometimes pushing him in the small of the back to prevent him sliding down and losing what little he had gained.

They stepped onto the South Summit at 3 P.M. The climb had taken them eleven and a half hours.

Now they were on ground made familiar by books and photographs. The ridge between the South Summit and the top of Everest undulated away toward the Hillary Step and the goal of their ambition, for although they had climbed the Face, the ascent could not be counted as complete unless they reached the summit of the mountain. However, it was already late in the day, and the snow on the ridge promised to be little better than the awful powder snow in the gully. Should they bivouac and tackle the ridge early next morning, when the night temperatures might have hardened the snow? It was a tempting idea, and while they considered it Scott put on a brew and Haston dug a bivouac snow hole.

But it is hard to have a prize within one's grasp and not reach out for it immediately. Supposing the weather changed before morning? There might be disadvantages as well as advantages in waiting. Tentatively, Haston moved off along the ridge and found conditions not perfect, but acceptable, and that was stimulus enough.

The Hillary Step was banked up with steep, soft snow, and as Haston clambered up it Scott had a growing feeling of elation: " . . . it gradually dawned on me that we were going to reach the summit of Big E."

At 6 P.M., side by side, Scott and Haston stepped onto the summit of Everest. The Southwest Face had been climbed.

On the top they found a tripod, five feet high, with a bunch of red ribbons fluttering from it—proof positive that the Chinese had indeed made the ascent they claimed in the spring. Scott stood in front of it and handed his camera to Haston. "Here you are, youth," he said. "Take a snap for my mother."

The two men were in a precarious situation. They were on the roof of the world, with night fast approaching. Analyzing the situation they reckoned they could get back to the South Summit in the gloaming, and, if the moon came out, possibly all the way back to Camp 6. The going would be firmer than it was on the ascent—already the snow was hardening as night approached.

They set off back along the ridge, abseiled down the Hillary Step, and reached the South Summit. The expected moonlight did not materialize, and a tentative exploration of the descent gully convinced them that it would be too risky to try returning to Camp 6. There was nothing for it but to bivouac on the South Summit at a height of 28,750 feet—the highest bivouac ever undertaken.

They enlarged the snow cave that they had begun earlier in the day until by about 9 P.M. it was large enough for them to crawl into and lie down out of the wind. Their oxygen was exhausted and before long the fuel in their little stove was used up too. The cold gnawed into their bones.

Scott, lacking his duvet suit, hacked away at the cave for much of the night in an effort to keep warm, but without the life-giving oxygen nothing eased the appalling coldness.

"There was no escaping the cold," Haston wrote. "Every position was tried. Holding together, feet in each other's armpits, rubbing, moving around the hole constantly, exercising arms. Just no way to catch a vestige of warmth."

They began to hallucinate under the stress. Scott wrote, "Our minds started to wander with the stress and the lack of sleep and oxygen. Dougal quite clearly spoke out to Dave Clarke. He had quite a long and involved conversation with him. I found myself talking to my feet."

"I don't think anything we did or said that night was rational or planned," Haston wrote. "Suffering from lack of oxygen, cold, tiredness but with a terrible will to get through the night all our survival instincts came right up front. These and our wills saw the night to a successful end."

And with the first light they began their descent, moving cautiously at first, aware of the dangers brought on by tiredness and oxygen deficiency. Yet the warmth of movement was itself a pleasure. When at 9 A.M. they stumbled into Camp 6 they were not only safe, but sound. They had not slept or eaten for thirty hours, they had survived the highest bivouac ever made—and without oxygen—and they were not even frostbitten.

That same day, September 25, the second assault team of Boysen, Boardman, Burke, and Pertemba occupied Camp 6. Burke was climbing slowly and giving cause for concern; he had already spent eight nights at Camp 5 and Bonington was worried that this might have caused deterioration. But Burke explained over the radio that he had been delayed by various things—and in any case he was determined to fulfill his role as cameraman by filming the route to the summit.

At 4:30 on the following morning the four men set off individually for the summit, protected by the fixed rope. Boysen went first, then Boardman and Pertemba, with Burke fetching up the rear.

Misfortune struck quickly. Before he had gone far, Boysen's oxygen set stopped working, and to compound his misery he lost a crampon. There was nothing he could do but go back, passing the others in turn; he finally crawled back into the tent and "howled with anguish, frustration, and self-pity."

Through the open door of the tent he could see the others making progress.

Boardman and Pertemba were climbing rapidly. The snow was in much better condition than it had been two days earlier, and when they reached the end of the fixed ropes they continued to climb solo, not feeling the need to be roped together. At 11 A.M. they reached the South Summit, where they were delayed for an hour by the malfunctioning of Pertemba's oxygen set, which, like Haston's, had an ice blockage. Once this was corrected, however, they continued along the ridge, to reach the summit of Everest at 1 P.M.

They mumbled into a miniature tape recorder and Pertemba fixed a Nepalese flag to the Chinese survey pole, but they were denied the superb views that Haston and Scott had witnessed two days previously. In fact, all through the day the clouds had been boiling up, obscuring the surrounding mountains. At first, Everest and Lhotse had remained above the cloud, like islands in a troubled sea, but gradually the vapor had swirled higher until even the summits of these mighty peaks were covered in mist.

Earlier in the day Boardman had been aware of a tiny figure a long way behind them, and had presumed that it was Burke watching their progress before rejoining his partner, Boysen, in the tent. As they descended from the summit, however, they were surprised to come across Burke sitting in the snow.

We were amazed to see him through the mist. Mick was sitting on the snow only a few hundred yards down an easy angled snow slope from the summit. He congratulated us and said he wanted to film us on a bump on the ridge and pretend it was the summit, but I told him about the Chinese maypole. Then he asked us to go back to the summit with him. I agreed reluctantly and he, sensing my reluctance, changed his mind and said he'd go up and film it and then come straight down after us. He borrowed Pertemba's camera to take some stills on the top and we walked back fifty feet and then walked past him whilst he filmed us. I took a couple of pictures of him. He had the Blue Peter flag and an auto-load camera with him. He asked us to wait for him by the big rock on the South Summit where Pertemba and I had dumped our first oxygen cylinders and some

rope and film on the way up. I told him that Pertemba was
wanting to move roped with me—so he should catch us up fairly
quickly. I said 'See you soon' and we moved back down the ridge
to the South Summit. Shortly after we had left him the weather
began to deteriorate.

At the South Summit the two men waited for Burke to return but as time
went by and there was no sign of their companion the anxiety over his fate—
and theirs—began to grow apace:

All the winds of Asia seemed to be trying to blow us from the
ridge. A decision was needed. It was four in the afternoon and
the skies were already darkening around the South Summit of
Everest. I threw my iced and useless snow goggles away into
the whiteness and tried, clumsily mitted, to clear the ice from
my eyelashes. I bowed my head into the spindrift and tried to
peer along the ridge. Mick should have met us at least three
quarters of an hour before, unless something had happened to
him. We had been waiting for nearly one and a half hours. There
was no sign of Doug and Dougal's bivouac site. The sky and
cornices and whirling snow merged together, visibility was re-
duced to ten feet and all tracks were obliterated. Pertemba and
I huddled next to the rock of the South Summit where Mick had
asked us to wait for him. Pertemba said he could not feel his
toes or fingers and mine too were nailed with cold. I thought of
Mick wearing his glasses and blinded by spindrift, negotiating
the fixed rope on the Hillary Step, the fragile one-foot windslab
on the Nepal side and the cornices on the Tibetan side of the
ridge. I thought of our own predicament, with the eight hun-
dred feet of the South Summit Gully—guarded by a sixty-foot
rockstep halfway—to descend, and then half of the two-thou-
sand-foot great traverse above the Rock Band to cross before
reaching the end of the fixed ropes that extended across from
Camp 6. It had taken Doug and Dougal three hours in the dawn

sunshine after their bivouac to reach Camp 6—but we now had
only an hour of light left. At 28,700 feet the boundary between
a controlled and an uncontrolled situation is narrow and we
had crossed that boundary within minutes—a strong wind and
sun shining through clouds had turned into a violent blizzard
of driving snow, the early afternoon had drifted into approach-
ing night and our success was turning into tragedy.

After ten minutes Boardman decided that is was too risky to wait any longer.
With the storm increasing in fury and the darkness closing in, to delay their
departure any further meant almost certain death; a bivouac under such conditions was out of the question. So they cast about for the way down, fumbling and half blinded. For one instant the storm lifted and revealed the South
Summit. There was no sign of Burke. The time was 4:30 p.m.

Boardman and Pertemba then began a descent that was to prove every
whit as dramatic as that of Hornbein's party in 1963. The young climber
plunged down the exit gully as fast as he could, belayed to a "dead man,"
then yanked Pertemba down after him. The Sherpa was unaccustomed to
climbing without the assistance of fixed ropes, and though he had performed
nobly on the way up, the storm and the disappearance of Burke had temporarily unnerved him, making him cautious. But Boardman realized there
was no time for niceties: speed was essential if they were both to survive.
What worried him most was a bagging fear that he had chosen the wrong
gully and they were off route . . . the sight of an abandoned oxygen cylinder, which marked the rock step in the gully, came as a great relief. They
rappelled down the step. Pertemba was going more strongly now and they
fought their way through the dusk and storm across the open face for a
thousand feet toward the fixed ropes.

During our traverse we were covered by two powder snow ava-
lanches from the summit slopes. Fortunately our oxygen cylin-
ders were still functioning and we could breathe. It was a miracle
that we found the end of the fixed ropes in the dark, marked by
two oxygen cylinders sticking out of the snow. On the fixed rope

Pertemba slowed down again and I pulled him mercilessly until he shouted that one of his crampons had fallen off. The rope between us snagged and in flicking it free I tumbled over a fifteen-foot rock step to be held on the fixed rope. At one point a section of the fixed rope had been swept away. At half past seven we stumbled into the 'summit boxes' at Camp 6. Martin was there and I burst into tears.

For thirty hours the three men were trapped at Camp 6 by the raging storm. Pertemba was snowblind, Boardman was worried about possible frostbite in his feet, and the luckless Boysen, who looked after them both, got frostbitten hands. On the second night, when the storm abated, they could hear avalanches roaring down the Face. Next day they began their sad descent.

So the Southwest Face was climbed at last. Not once, but three times, for everyone agrees that Burke must have made the summit and that the accident occurred on the descent, when, blinded by the storm, it would have been so easy for him to lose his way and stumble to his death over the South or East Faces of the mountain.

Bonington had told them all over the radio to stick together and if anything went wrong to turn back. But when a lifetime's ambition is within grasp, some men tend to ignore such orders. Everyone on the expedition, Bonington included, has agreed that if they had been in Burke's position that fateful morning they too would have gone for the top.

"TO THE ULTIMATE POINT"

FROM
Everest: Expedition to the Ultimate
BY REINHOLD MESSNER

IN 1970, AN UNKNOWN 25-YEAR-OLD CLIMBER FROM SOUTH TIROL named Reinhold Messner ventured for the first time to the Himalaya. Already an accomplished climber with an impressive list of solo ascents and the big north walls of the Alps behind him, Messner felt ready for the Rupal Face of Nanga Parbat. Still, the huge face was so intimidating that Hermann Buhl, who made the first ascent of the mountain, had called it "unclimbable."

After weeks of slow progress in bad weather, Messner and his brother Gunther finally climbed to the top of the daunting face, and the summit of Nanga Parbat. But they were unable to descend the difficult technical ground they had come up, and were caught out in a bivouac high on the mountain. Eventually forced to descend via the Diamir Face, on the other side of the peak, the climbers became separated. Gunther was not seen again, and was presumed lost in an avalanche. Messner barely survived the epic, suffering frostbite that cost him his toes, and nearly his life.

Despite the tragic outcome, the climb made an indelible mark: a difficult new route and a traverse of an 8000-meter peak. It was the beginning of the single greatest Himalayan climbing career of the twentieth century. In 1975, Messner changed the very style in which Himalayan peaks were climbed when he made an Alpine-style ascent of an 8000-meter mountain, Hidden Peak in the Karakoram of Pakistan. In the next few years, Messner would so torque the world of big-peak mountaineering as to make it unrecognizable.

Perhaps nothing was more stunning than Messner's 1978 ascent of Everest without oxygen, a feat many believed to be physiologically impossible. From the earliest attempts on the mountain through the Everest expeditions in the 1930s, whether or not to use oxygen had been continuously debated. Mallory and Irvine used it in 1924; Smythe and Shipton in 1933 did not. The question was always the same: Is the advantage of oxygen sufficient to overcome the weight of the apparatus?

Early methods of carrying and delivering oxygen were awkward, heavy, and of dubious efficacy. That changed after World War II, when technological advances in supplemental-oxygen use from both the aviation and medical arenas clearly tipped the balance. The result: Everest was climbed. The first men to the top, Edmund Hillary and Tenzing Norgay, both used bottled gas—

as did all sixty-three climbers who successfully reached the summit between 1953 and 1978. The sixty-fourth and sixty-fifth summiters were Messner and Peter Habeler; they would be the first to the top without supplemental oxygen. "Everest by fair means—that is the human dimension," Messner was to say, "and that is what interests me. In reaching for the oxygen cylinder, a climber degrades Everest. A climber who doesn't rely on his own strength and skill, but on apparatus or drugs, deceives himself."

In preparation for their experiment, Messner and Habeler attached themselves to an Austrian expedition in 1978. Messner and Habeler would use the camps and other infrastructure provided by the expedition, but climb without oxygen. No one knew how the men would fare. Would they die? Would they damage so many brain cells that they might live but pay a terrible price?

Neither Messner nor his partner knew if they could survive the gamble, a fact that lends dramatic import to Messner's unadorned narrative of the ascent. In the excerpt below, the story picks up as Messner and Habeler awake at the South Col on the dawn of their historic climb. The piece is from Messner's *Everest: Expedition to the Ultimate,* pages 174–192.

May 8. Shortly after 3 o'clock I begin to brew up some coffee. The huge lump of snow, as big as a man's head, that's been lying in the tent all night, I now break into pieces and put into the billy. It takes a long time before the water is warm. We drink in turns.

Still lying in our bags, we put on two pairs of socks and our inner boots. I try to warm up my stiffly frozen outer boots between my legs. Dressing oneself at 8000 meters is a protracted, breath-consuming struggle.

Between 5 and 6 o'clock we are finally ready. I am wearing silk underwear, then a fleecy pile undersuit, over that a complete down suit, with double-layer boots and gaiters of strong insulated neoprene; in addition, three pairs of gloves, two hats, storm goggles. In case of emergency, I have another pair of gloves, another hat, and some more goggles in my rucksack.

Other than that I only carry the barest essentials—a length of rope, cameras, altimeter, and a miniature tape recorder.

The hoar frost that crumbles off the inside of the tent, and the fact that my sleeping bag is rigidly frozen and my beard encrusted with ice, these things worry me less than they did. For the six weeks since we have been in Base Camp and above, these have been the facts of life, and we have learned to live with such discomforts.

As Peter and I leave the tent, a squall of sleet hits us in the face. No! It can't be true—the sky is overcast, and there is only the barest strip of blue in the western sky. A sharp wind blows from the west and all the valleys are filled with mist. We are horrified, at first sight it looks as if we are beaten. But then, in the certain knowledge that we won't get another chance, I resolve that come-what-may, I shall still go as far as is humanly possible.

Peter still hesitates and I do my best to encourage him. "We can always turn back if it gets too bad," I say.

When one, like he, has a wife and child to consider, these decisions are very much harder to make. In one's subconscious mind a barrier of apprehension builds up quite naturally. It was the same for me when I was still married. But since I have been on my own again, I feel much easier in my mind when confronted with life or death situations. I just direct all my concentration toward the immediate problem—there is no before or after in my mind. I have nothing to lose except my own being—and I still live.

Despite our light rucksacks, we only make slow progress, then our pace quickens as we cross the crevasse-torn icefield. From the top of the ice with the summit pyramid rearing directly in front of us, we can see for the first time Makalu out to the East, a massive granite peak. A huge fish-shaped cloud shrouds its summit. It is snowing there already and above us too, the wind is plastering everything with snow. The blue stripe on the horizon has disappeared. Endless emptiness of sky.

The snow beneath our feet is hard, and the teeth of our crampons bite into it well. But in this rarefied air, we have to frequently pause and rest. Higher up, where the drifting snow lies knee-deep, we frequently take to the ridge of rock, which, although it offers more difficult climbing, spares us the heavy work of breaking trail.

We converse in sign language. Every time Peter scratches a downward-pointing arrow in the snow, meaning "We should turn back," I reply with another pointing upwards—a discussion without words.

After four hours we reach the fifth high camp, which for us is only a staging post. Through an occasional break in the clouds, we can see the summit of Lhotse, which is level with the height at which we are now, and the sharp, finely detailed ridge of Nuptse. We brew tea. Again I dictate a few impressions into my tape recorder.

"Peter and I are at 8,500 meters in the last camp. Considering the conditions, we have reached here quite quickly but the weather is extremely bad. We don't know if we'll be able to go on or not. The snow is so deep, the work of breaking trail so back-breaking that we can't see very much hope of success. We are now trying to melt some snow to drink. Earlier today, when we saw that the weather was not as good as we had hoped for, we didn't bring our sleeping bags with us. We confined ourselves to the barest essentials so that we could move as quickly as possible. But now we are faced with a dilemma. To sit it out here and bivouac is a risk we should only take in the direst emergency. To go on—for we are still quite early—is an equally chancy business. Looking across at Makalu, sometimes wearing its cloud, sometimes clear, I sit inside the tent drinking my tea, and feel a little better. When we are climbing, talking is out of the question, dictating too, it would be too exhausting. We need every last bit of oxygen. It's practically certain we can't reach the summit. But we could perhaps get a bit farther. We'll try anyway. We are both in good heart and spirits. Even if this frightful weather should finally thwart us—we would still like to go a bit farther."

"Peter, what's the weather doing at the moment?" I ask from inside the tent.
"Still bad."
"Is it snowing?" And without waiting for an answer, "do you still want to try and get a bit farther?"
"We can but try."
"If we can keep up the speed we've been making and the snow is not too deep, we perhaps have a chance of getting as far as the South Summit in three or four hours. To get any farther than that won't be easy."

After half an hour's rest, we continue our cautious way. Our climbing gets even slower. The snow is hard on the Chinese side, the east side, of the ridge.

But soon we have to cross back to the Nepalese side when it gets too steep on the other. Frequently, we are wallowing in knee-deep snow. The steep rock spur to the left of the Hillary Route looks impossible, but we cross over to it nevertheless, and with the help of the points of our crampons, climb gingerly up the ledges. After every few steps, we huddle over our ice axes, mouths agape, struggling for sufficient breath to keep our muscles going. I have the feeling I am about to burst apart. As we get higher, it becomes necessary to lie down to recover our breath.

I am convinced now that we can reach the summit. There is still mountain in front of me so I keep on climbing. Automatically now, without thinking very much about it. We don't put the rope on until we're on the South Summit. A little later it pulls taut, and I turn around to see Peter taking off his rucksack. He wants to climb unfettered. I fumble in my rucksack for my camera and film him as he storms up. In front of us stretches an enormous snow ridge, the most beautiful ridge I have ever seen. Enormous cornices overhang it on the Tibetan side. Toward Nepal, the angle is easier. The main summit still seems to be enormously distant. I tell myself—so far as my condition and concentration allows—that distances are deceptive at altitude. The thin air makes everything seem a long way away.

There is still my ax in my hand as a balancing aid. For hours without ceasing I plunge it into the snow or slide its point along the surface of the hard snow. It has become essential to my support. If I had no ax, I should simply fall down. As I anticipate reaching the summit, I dare not look ahead anymore for I don't want to know how far there is still to go. Some of the time I feel full of purpose and self control, in the face of the storm; but at other moments I am filled with despair and try desperately to clench my teeth despite my wide-open, gasping mouth. The storm chases along the corniced summit ridge. Peter and I, trying our hardest to be cautious in our movements, seem nevertheless to be unusually clumsy, and completely exhausted with the effort. There is insufficient air for talking in the summit zone, and as if we had pledged ourselves to silence, we continue our sign-language with the points of our axs in the snow. Each buffet of wind, hurling sleet into my eyes, leaves me more awkward than ever.

Apathy mingles with defiance. Is this the weather we must contend with all the way? Peter seems to be scribbling in the sky with his ax. I watch carefully and finally laugh as he reaches the end. In the South, Ama Dablam has broken clear of the clouds, it is bathed in sunlight. Perhaps the weather will yet hold.

I climb down into the notch that separates the South Summit from the Main Summit, and with a wary eye for the edge of the cornices, gingerly advance. Immediately below the Hillary Step, the most difficult pitch on the summit wall, I stop. Peter catches up; then I climb the steep step, resting three or four times on the way. Once up, we alternate leads. From the south a stiff wind blows crystals of ice into our faces. Between photographing and filming, I sometimes forget to pull my goggles back over my eyes.

Now, shortly after midday, and at a height of 8800 meters, we can no longer keep on our feet while we rest. We crumple to our knees, clutching our axes, the points of which we have rammed into the hard snow. We are no longer belayed to one another, climbing quite independently, but each aware instinctively of the other's presence and confident that he is making no mistakes. The harmony of our partnership has grown up over the years through a repeated sharing of delicate situations. Now neither of us has any doubts about the other.

Breathing becomes such a strenuous business that we scarcely have strength left to go on. Every ten or fifteen steps we collapse into the snow to rest, then crawl on again. My mind seems almost to have ceased to function. I simply go on climbing automatically. The fact that we are on Everest, the highest mountain in the world, is forgotten—nor does it register that we are climbing without oxygen apparatus.

The only thing that lures me on is that little point ahead, where all the lines come together, the apex, the ultimate. The exertion now must be terrible, and yet I am insensible to it. It is as if the cortex of my brain were numb, as if only deeper inside my head is there something making the decisions for me. I don't want to go on. I crawl, I cough, but I am drawn on toward this farthest point as if it were some magnetic pole. Perhaps because to be there offers the only solution. My mind is disconnected, dead. But my soul is alive and receptive, grown huge and palpable. It wants to reach the very top so that it can swing back into equilibrium.

The last few meters up to the summit no longer seem so hard. On reaching the top, I sit down and let my legs dangle into space. I don't have to climb anymore. I pull my camera from my rucksack and, in my down mittens, fumble a long time with the batteries before I have it working properly. Then I film Peter. Now, after the hours of torment, which indeed I didn't recognize as torment, now, when the monotonous motion of plodding upwards is at an end, and I have nothing more to do than breathe, a great peace floods my whole being. I breathe like someone who has run the race of his life and knows that he may now rest forever. I keep looking all around, because the first time I didn't see anything of the panorama I had expected from Everest, neither indeed did I notice how the wind was continually chasing snow across the summit. In my state of spiritual abstraction, I no longer belong to myself and to my eyesight. I am nothing more than a single, narrow, gasping lung, floating over the mists and the summits.

Only after I have drawn a couple of deep breaths do I again sense my legs, my arms, my head. I am in a state of bright, clear consciousness, even if not fully aware of where I am. In the instant that Peter joins me and flings his arms around me, we both burst into tears. We lie in the snow, shaking with emotion. The camera is cast aside. Our tears express everything we feel after such a concentrated effort of will, they are our release.

We lie next to each other, there on the summit, lost to oblivion. And so we remain for some while, up to our necks in drifted snow, mouths open, recovering. When I do stand up, Peter stares at me as if he wants to impress my face on his memory, as if indeed he doesn't recognize my face at all.

Standing now in diffused light, with the wind at my back, I experience suddenly a feeling of completeness—not a feeling of having achieved something or of being stronger than everyone who was ever here before, not a feeling of having arrived at the ultimate point, not a feeling of supremacy. Just a breath of happiness deep inside my mind and my breast. The summit seemed suddenly to me to be a refuge, and I had not expected to find any refuge up here. Looking at the steep, sharp ridges below us, I have the impression that to have come later would have been too late. Everything we now say to one another, we only say out of embarrassment. I don't think anymore. As I pull the tape recorder, trancelike, from my rucksack, and switch it on wanting to record a few appropriate phrases, tears again well into my eyes. "Now we are on the summit of Everest," I begin, "it is so cold that we cannot take photographs. . . . " I cannot go on, I am immediately shaken with sobs. I can neither talk nor think, feeling only how this momentous experience changes everything. To reach only a few meters below the summit would have required the same amount of effort, the same anxiety and burden of sorrow, but a feeling like this, an eruption of feeling, is only possible on the summit itself.

Everything that is, everything I am, is now colored by the fact that I have reached this special place. The summit—for the time being at least—is the simple intuitive answer to the enigma of life.

There is no sense of triumph, no feeling of potency, only of being, and of thankfulness toward my partner. Everything else is forgotten in a wave of happiness. For a short while all reason is lost and emotion holds sway; my feelings have taken over and will no longer be resisted. Peter and I don't speak; we take a few photographs. All at once Peter feels a tightness in his fingers, just as he had done earlier on the Hillary Step. Cramp? Or might it signify something much worse? He remembers the Sherpa who a few days earlier had to be carried down the mountain half-paralyzed following a stroke brought on by exertion at great altitude. Peter grows very uneasy and wants to get down.

He starts back alone, without the rope. I see him reach the South Summit while I am still talking into my tape recorder. I unpack a film cassette and, instead of throwing away the wrapping paper, I toss the film over the edge. Only as it disappears do I realize what I have done. I take a second cassette from my rucksack and load it into the camera. After so much concentration, I am again overcome with emotion. I take a deep breath, then I drop everything back into the rucksack, one thing at a time—recorder, ciné camera, still camera—I tie the spare batteries onto the Chinese summit emblem and squat down again. I am no less aware than I was, but I am now able to think about the business of going down.

It is only early in the afternoon, but the light gives the impression that it is already evening, and I feel as if I have been sitting on the summit for a long, long time—a few hours even. And yet I am still reluctant to leave; descent, it seems, was not any part of my plan at all. In all the preparations I made for this climb—and they stretch back over several years—I have always only concerned myself with getting up, or at most, with being on the summit. I have never given a thought to going back down again. I have now to summon every last ounce of resolve, and make myself stand up and leave this place.

I say to myself, "Now, you must climb down, but slowly. Take care on the Hillary Step. Remember how exposed it is, so go carefully! In a few hours you will be down where the air is richer, and then it will go a lot easier." I force myself to look ahead, to look down, so that I can climb down. Then with one last touch of the length of rope and the batteries hanging on the tripod, I set off after Peter in the hope that he is waiting for me on the South Summit.

Despite myself, I turn around just a few steps below the top, almost sad to be leaving. I feel I belong sitting there and regret that I must depart without going back just one more time. There are fine scratches in the snow where Peter went down, the marks of his crampons. Unlike the ascent, I now seem able to think as I go. When I pause to rest, I have no difficulty in keeping on my feet, and can stretch and breathe deeply. Sudden realizations come to me— looking at the Nuptse Ridge, swimming in mist, I am struck with a deep sense of loss. It dawns on me that this is a sad day for me. Something irrevocable and final has taken place. My long-cherished dream is gone. The mountain from which I descend is now but a shattered illusion. . . .

I look back along the summit ridge, I see the footprints in the snow, I feel the ax in my right hand. All these things belong to me; all these things are part of me. I reach the South Summit half an hour after Peter, but he is no longer there. He must have been desperate to get down. As I plod slowly on through the deep snow, letting one foot fall in front of the other, I can see the marks of a slide away to my left on the steep 50-degree snow slope. The tracks disappear somewhere in cloud. And I realize with a jerk—for logical thought has now returned—that that east flank falls away for 4000 meters and is riven with crevasses. Once past the South Summit, it remains only to go down. Down, down, one step in front of the other, face to the valley, trampling the snow, planting the crampons, unwavering concentration—but down. That is all that is left. I take one last look back at Everest summit. I have really climbed it after dreaming about it for so long. I experience a little thrill of pride.

There is no trace of Peter, in fact hardly anything to be seen even of our ascent; it would seem to be a totally different mountain from the one we climbed; that has seemingly vanished into the mist. Yet I feel Peter is still close, as if the mountain and Peter and I were one. Unthinkable to have one without the others. As I peer ahead for a sight of him, I realize how our friendship has grown. I am not annoyed that he did not wait. Only concerned for him.

Just below the South Summit, I see the slide marks again, just like those disappearing into the mist on the Chinese side of the ridge; but the possibility of a catastrophe is not yet in my mind. I think only how close death still is to me. I follow the ridge down, keeping to the right of the tracks, almost proud of the apprehension that prevents me from following Peter's example and sliding down on the seat of my pants. I look forward to catching him up and hearing from him the story of his bizarre descent. Again I have the conviction that he is the only person who could have shared this experience with me. I need not feel too concerned on his behalf. Peter does not make mistakes.

Here now I have discovered how alone I am. Loneliness seems to be reaching out and enveloping me from all sides. There is nothing but emptiness far and wide. The great sky above me is formless, with no scurrying clouds. Just above the spot on the ridge where the fifth high camp is situated, the slide-marks suddenly end. Peter must obviously have crossed farther over to the right onto the southeast flank, and continued his glissade down this too, to the South Col. Tramping past the deserted camp alone, I nod to myself, as if to convince myself, "You have really done it."

I frequently stop to wait for the mist to blow over. Then below me I can make out two yellow specks, the tents. Nothing else. Though I cannot see him, I am sure that Peter is in the camp already, or if not, will soon be there.

When I am tired, I simply plump down into the snow. At long last, within me, I feel a tight concentration of joy at our success. And this pleasure spreads and grows and seeps through everything as I sit there in the snow, oblivious of my tiredness. At last a mountain on which I don't "anticipate." Content to do only what I really do do. Even 100 meters below the summit I was still thinking ahead, anticipating that I would soon be up there. Now I no longer plan; now, it is only the here and now that matters. Beyond that, I cannot think nor yet do I wish to. I have no doubts that I can reach the camp, but I don't allow myself to think about it yet—what little there is to think about, that is, like crawling into a warm sleeping bag.

I am so tired that I can't hurry my thoughts along. I cross the last snow slope above the South Col like a sleepwalker. Whenever I sit down to rest, I automatically look at my watch but I don't register what time it is. Now, with the last few steps to the tent, I have the feeling of having done something once that I will never more achieve again. The tents offer a sense of security that is quickly lost in the desolation of the South Col. Only inside the tent does it really feel safe. Peter is there, and Eric too. As I crawl into the tent and see Peter, I feel triumphant: We have done it!

And we shall climb other eight-thousanders without oxygen also! I am now so overcome with happiness that I even forget to pause for breath. My excited conversations over the radio with Base Camp are only occasionally punctuated by deep intakes of breath.

And in between I turn to Peter: "Tell me again what you thought after the Hillary Step, when you were no longer yourself?"

"After the Hillary Step, it was no longer me that was climbing—it felt like someone else on the steep face, climbing for me."

"Peter—If we left between 5 and 6 this morning, we must have been on the summit at something like 1 or 2 o'clock. It must have taken us eight hours to do the climb. You came down in one hour—that is crazy, really crazy! I took an hour and a half, or an hour and three quarters."

"Shall we sleep in the same positions as last night?"

"Yes, yes that's—fine."

"I don't need to cook so much today."

"Tell me—this morning, did you believe we'd do it?"

"I wasn't a hundred percent sure."

"When were you absolutely sure, then, that we would?"

"On the South Summit."

"On the South Summit I began to shoot more and more film. For a long time I didn't know if it was you I had in the picture, or a crevasse, the wind was blowing so hard. There was just this black blur and a wild storm. It looked tremendous. Did you notice?"

"I didn't notice."

To start with, we are both in incredibly high spirits, euphoric. But as the evening progresses my eyes begin to ache, and Peter's ankle, that he knocked earlier, starts to swell badly. My eyes get dimmer by the minute and the pain becomes excruciating. My first fear is that I am going blind. We have been warned that nerve damage is not infrequent at altitude, and irreversible brain damage possible. But then I feel as if I have sand in my eyes and realize that I am merely snowblind.

There follows a fearful night. I have the feeling that in place of my eyes, there are now just two gaping sockets. I keep sitting up and pressing my fists into my eyes, weeping and crying out. The tears help to soothe the pain and Peter comforts me as if I were a small child.

※   ※   ※

The descent the next day, May 9, from the South Col down to Camp 2 is a nightmare. Snowblind, as I am, I stumble behind Peter. I cannot see more than a meter in front of me.

On May 10 we stagger back into Base Camp like a pair of invalids. We are still, according to our friends at least, out of our minds.

Our undertaking, we know, could just as easily have turned out very differently. We don't think about that. In the Death Zone, success and disaster run as closely together as storm and lull, hot and cold.

Of the seven times I have attempted an eight-thousand-meter peak, I have only four times reached the summit. Nowadays I appreciate that—as in all true adventure—the path between the summit and the grave is a very narrow one indeed. That there is no way of telling in advance which way it will finish doesn't mean that life up there is any more significant than elsewhere, but it is certainly more intense.

"SISYPHUS ON EVEREST"

FROM
The Crystal Horizon: Everest—The First Solo Ascent
BY REINHOLD MESSNER

REINHOLD MESSNER'S UNCOMPROMISING RELATIONSHIP TO EVEREST was unlike that of other climber. Not content to just climb the world's highest peak, he felt compelled to climb it "by fair means," without oxygen. Even after that accomplishment, he was unsatisfied. Messner would later say of his 1978 oxygenless ascent that he and Habeler climbed unsupported for only "the last 900 feet." Below that, they had enjoyed the succor of the expedition, and the psychological ease of knowing their friends were nearby. For Messner, the "ultimate" ascent—to climb the mountain without support of any kind—had not yet been done.

Messner returned to Everest in 1980 to remedy that. This time, he journeyed to Tibet, without the support of any Sherpa or any expedition, to make an attempt in what he considered a pure style. Messner's successful solo ascent of Nanga Parbat two years before had given him the confidence to attempt Everest alone, as he put it, "for the fun of it." In the space of a decade, the "taboos of mountaineering," as Messner called them, would fall before him: Everest without oxygen, Everest solo, and the ascent of all fourteen of the 8000-meter peaks without supplemental oxygen. But perhaps no achievement surpasses that of his 1980 ascent, when he would solo Everest without oxygen by a new route. His unsupported climb was a breakthrough by any standard, and would cement his standing as a climber without peer.

When Messner approached the Rongbuk Glacier to begin his solo attempt, the Tibetan approach to the mountain had only just opened to Westerners for the first time since the British attempts in the 1930s. Since then, only the Chinese, a Japanese expedition, and perhaps the Russians, had attempted the peak from the north. The terrain was largely unfamiliar when Messner, his girlfriend Nena Holguin, and a Chinese liaison officer arrived at the northside base camp. Relying on early British accounts to show him the way, Messner would climb Everest absolutely alone in three days, like a weekend climber doing a peak in the Cascades.

But even for Messner, the climb was desperate. At the North Col, he fell in a crevasse, where he might easily have died or disappeared to become another northside mystery in the vein of Mallory and Irvine. Higher up, he followed the ghosts of Edward Norton and Frank Smythe into the lonely, hypoxic reaches of the Great Couloir, where the solitude weighs on him: "How much easier it is to climb as a pair. The knowledge that someone is standing behind you brings comfort. Not only is solo climbing far more strenuous and dangerous, above all the psychological burden is more than doubled."

In his stream-of-consciousness account, Messner invokes the spirit of Maurice Wilson, a religious fanatic who in 1934 had attempted to solo Everest despite a total lack of training as a climber. Wilson, trusting in God to show him the way, was tenacious, but human: his body was later found at the foot of the North Col.

Messner's utterly fascinating account of the climb is excerpted below, from his book *The Crystal Horizon.* The narrative is rambling but oddly focused, honest, and engaging. He spares the reader nothing of his torments, joys, or fears, and the writing resonates with an authenticity uncharacteristic of his other works. We join Messner as he rouses himself from sleep in his camp, with Nena, at the foot of the North Col. It is predawn, August 18, and the lone climber sets out toward the North Col, where he has stashed his "15-kilo"—38-pound—rucksack with essential items, but no radio. From Messner's *The Crystal Horizon: Everest—The First Solo Ascent,* pages 205–249.

When it is time to get up I pick up socks, boots, breeches, and top clothes like a sleepwalker. Each movement is quick and sure as if I had practiced them a hundred times. No wasted movement.

In front of the tent I stretch myself, sniff the night air. Then I continue my ascent of the previous day. I am soon well up. I reach the ice hollow and pick up the rucksack.

The snow suddenly gives way under me and my headlamp goes out. Despairingly I try to cling on in the snow, but in vain. The initial reaction passes. Although it is pitch-dark I believe I can see everything: at first snow crystals, then blue-green ice. It occurs to me that I am not wearing crampons. I know what is happening but nevertheless remain quite calm. I am falling into the depths and experience the fall in slow motion, strike the walls of the widening crevasse once with my chest, once with the rucksack. My sense of time is interrupted, also my perception of the depth of the drop. Have I been falling only split seconds or is it minutes? I am completely weightless, a torrent of warmth surges through my body.

Suddenly I have support under my feet again. At the same time I know that I am caught, perhaps trapped forever in this crevasse. Cold sweat beads my forehead. Now I am frightened. "If only I had a radio with me" is my first thought. I could call Nena. Perhaps she would hear me. But whether she could climb the 500 meters up to me and let a rope down to me in the crevasse is more than questionable. I have consciously committed myself to this solo ascent without a radio, and discussed it many times before starting.

I finger my headlamp and suddenly everything is bright. It's working! I breathe deeply, trying not to move at all. Also, the snow surface on which I am standing is not firm. Like a thin, transparent bridge it hangs fragile between both walls of the crevasse. I put my head back and see some 8 meters above the tree trunk–sized hole through which I have fallen. From the bit of black sky above a few far, far distant stars twinkle down at me. The sweat of fear breaks from all my pores, covers my body with a touch that is as icy as the iridescent blue-green ice walls between which I am imprisoned. Because they converge obliquely above me I have no chance of climbing up them. With my headlamp I try to light up the bottom of the crevasse; but there is no end to be seen. Just a black hole to the left and right of me. The snow bridge that has stopped my fall is only one square meter large.

I have goose pimples and shiver all over. The reactions of my body, however, are in stark contrast to the calm in my mind: there is no fear at the prospect of a new plunge into the bottomless depths, only a presentiment of dissolving, of evaporation. At the same time my mind says, that was lucky! For the first time I experience fear as a bodily reflex without psychological pain in the chest. My only problem is how to get out again. Mount Everest has become irrelevant. I seem to myself like an innocent prisoner. I don't reproach myself, don't swear. This pure, innocent feeling is inexplicable. What determines my life at this moment I do not know. I promise to myself I will descend, I will give up, if I come out of this unhurt. No more solo eight-thousanders!

My sweaty fear freezes in my hair and beard. The anxiety in my bones disappears the moment I set my body in motion, as I try to get my crampons out of the rucksack. But at each movement the feeling of falling again comes over me, a feeling of plunging into the abyss, as if the ground were slowly giving way.

Then I discover a ramp running along the crevasse wall on the valley side, a ledge the width of two feet in the ice that leads obliquely upwards and is full of snow. That is the way out! Carefully I let myself fall forward, arms outstretched, to the adjoining crevasse wall. For a long moment my body makes an arch between the wedged snow block and the slightly overhanging wall above me. Carefully I straddle across with the right foot, make a foothold in the snow that has frozen on the ledge on this crevasse wall on the downhill side. I transfer weight to the step. It holds. The insecure spot I am standing on is thus relieved. Each of these movements I instinctively make as exactly as in a rehearsed ballet. I try to make myself lighter. Breathing deeply my whole body identifies itself with the new position, I am for a moment, a long, life-determining moment, weightless. I have pushed myself off from the snow bridge with the left foot, my arms keep me in balance, my right leg supports my body. The left foot can get a grip. Relieved deep breathing. Very carefully I move—face to the wall—to the right. The right foot gropes for a new hold in the snow, the left boot is placed precisely in the footstep which the right has vacated a few seconds before. The ledge becomes broader, leads obliquely upwards to the outside. I am saved!

In a few minutes I am on the surface—still on the valley side to be sure— but safe. I am a different person, standing there rucksack on my shoulders, ice ax in my hand as if nothing had happened. I hesitate for a moment longer, consider what I did wrong. How did this fall happen? Perhaps my left foot, placed 2 centimeters above the underlying edge of the crevasse, broke through as I tried to find a hold with the right on the opposite wall.

Down below in the crevasse I had decided to turn round, give up, if I got out unharmed. Now that I am standing on top I continue my ascent without thinking, unconsciously, as if I were computer-programmed.

The first glimmer of dawn illuminates Everest's North Col. I look at the time—shortly before seven. How long was I down there? I don't know. The fall into the crevasse is already wiped from my mind. The vow to descend could not have been fundamentally serious. I don't ask myself how I came to deceive myself thus. Determinedly I go back along the lower edge of the crevasse, my mind totally fixed on the summit, as if this perilous incident had only shaken my body, but not that identification which has for weeks constituted my being—my identification with Everest. The fall into the crevasse has put me into a far greater state of alertness than normal. I know this is the only place where I can cross the crevasse which runs right across this 500-meters-high ice wall below the North Col. During my reconnaissance ascent four weeks ago I discovered the snow bridge, just 2 meters wide, which today proved almost my undoing. Then it had borne my weight. It may hold up now as well, if I only put weight on the outside edges.

On my solo climb I have no aluminum ladder and no rope, which larger expeditions would use to overcome hindrances of this sort. Two ski sticks and the titanium ice ax are my sole aids. Trance-like, I turn back to the hole I fell through. I shine my light down. Black as night. This time I must watch like hell so as not to make any mistake. On the other side of the crevasse is a steep snow wall. Soon decided, I bend forward and thrust the ski sticks—handles foremost—into the snow up to the discs. High up on the wall above me they now make two firm anchor points, artificial holds. I must cross the hole with a big straddling step and find a hold up there on the other side of the crevasse with the ice ax and ski sticks. Even though I know that on my descent I must find another route, I am immersed in the ascent as if there were nothing more to follow. With a powerful move I swing myself up, make a few quick steps and feel safe again. All these movements are fast but not hurried.

Slowly it becomes day. Far to the east stands the Kangchenjunga massif. Otherwise there is not much to be seen of this world. Up above a gray-blue sea of mist spreads a firmament that changes with infinite variations from blue to red.

The weather is fine, the air biting cold. What a good thing that I broke off the attempt in July. The snow softened by the monsoon then seemed bottomless, and the avalanche danger was great. It is not without danger now—more than once I have lost the route on the slopes leading to the North Col—but today, August 18, the snow is so firmly frozen that I leave only a light track behind me.

The highest slope is very steep but the previous bad snow has consolidated. What I am climbing on is not iron-hard névé like lower down; shallow crust predominates here. Frequently I break through the splintering surface and sink in up to the ankles. As I step on to the top of the pass, I quite suddenly feel a strong west wind in my face. It takes my breath away, makes my eyes water. I stop briefly. Look, breathe more quickly and intermittently. Then a regular rhythm sets in again. The wind does not penetrate my thick clothes, but occasionally makes me stagger. Instinctively I stoop, thrust firmly on to my ski sticks. I follow the old route exactly, along the north rib, the English route. For the first 500 meters this ridge looks like a steep ski slope. Its rises are slightly undulating and perhaps 30 degrees inclined. Endless masses of névé overhang to the east. An intense dawn seems to enliven the cornices. The shadow colors the snow blue, in the soft light of the rising sun outlines blur. In between on the blunt knife-edge snow crystals flash like diamonds. Now the sun touches the pinnacle of Pumori, the broad flank of Cho Oyu. The nearby North Peak stands like a gigantic wedge between day and night. Also, above the summit of Mount Everest lies a rosy dawn. The mountain appears so clearly against the deep blue sky that I can recognize each separate rock tower on the Northeast Ridge. Up there in 1924 George Mallory and Andrew Irvine were seen for the last time on their bold summit push. . . .

The distance as the crow flies from myself to the "first step" now amounts to perhaps 2 kilometers—a distance at which one would not be able to recognize a person's limbs. Odell, who had stood much higher, said that he was able to see the two climbers for five minutes. He had not spotted them through moving swathes of mist, rather through a sudden clearing of the air, such an air as now lies above me. He saw them on the "first step" and did not mistake rocks for men as has often been put to him. I exclude the possibility of an optical illusion, although I too, as I now stand and stare at the "first step," for moments succumb to the illusion of seeing black points in motion. Mallory did not climb the "second step," he attempted the ascent, but gave up. That I know for certain as I stand and stare.

Where does the ability to look back more than fifty years come from? Or can I no longer distinguish between reality and fantasy because I have read so much? Does this attempt of June 8, 1924, continue to play itself out up here, visible only in a heightened state of consciousness? This is no optical illusion; the sensation of human energy surrounds my body like the wind, like the sunbeams.

As I continue climbing the tiny figures disappear. I place one foot at a time so firmly in the snow that my whole being becomes this step. Leaning on my ski sticks I climb as evenly as possible—fifty paces, rest, fifty paces. When I have rested I cast a glance upward to orientate myself approximately. Thus I never have the feeling of being alone on this slope. As intensely as I now gaze upwards I am observed by Nena from below.

Nena does not know that the most dangerous moment of my expedition lies behind me. She did not see the fall into the crevasse. It was still dark then. Now she follows my route and photographs it. The sun floods the slopes to the North Col. Through the telephoto lens Nena can make out my tracks, which look like a pearl necklace. The hole through which I fell won't strike her, as the chain of pearls runs across the crevasse. I am climbing smoothly now and am at a height of more than 7200 meters. The air quickly warms up. The sun beats full on Cho Oyu to the west and on the North Peak of Mount Everest. Its shadow spans the glistening valleys like a giant black hole. I can allow myself time.

I have already made 700 meters height this morning. Never before in my life have I climbed so easily at over 7000 meters. It is not only the ideal snow conditions that urge me on. It is my mood.

Nevertheless I must not overstrain myself. I always rest before total tiredness goes to my legs like a numbing pain. I must allow myself time, apportion my strength.

Frequently while sitting down I trace the route up the Northeast Ridge. I want to get to just under the shoulder and then across the shallow ridge to the second step. The views that I have during my rest stops impress themselves like pictures on my mind. When I seat myself on the tightly filled rucksack, back to the slope, facing the valley, I photograph, so to speak, with my brain. Only occasionally do I take the camera out of the rucksack, and then I take more snaps than I can really use. Photographing myself—screw camera to the ice ax with the shaft stuck in the snow, set delayed action release, walk a dozen paces, wait for the click, rest, return and dismantle the whole thing— I find, as always, comical and an unnecessary waste of strength. Once, I spot my shadow in the viewfinder of the reflex camera. Involuntarily I have to laugh, as one laughs when one recognizes the clown in one's friend. Now I find the

climbing soothing. It is almost like the rhythm of my very fibers, clearly audible music. Leaning on the two ski sticks I can also rest while standing. On
the move and in uneven snow they help me to balance. With pitiful equipment by today's standards—normally I would not even climb the Matterhorn
with it—on this ridge nearly sixty years ago Mallory and his friends Norton
and Somervell crossed the 8000 meter barrier for the first time in the history
of mountaineering. George Leigh Mallory, that fiery spirit, recognized then
that, even after thorough preparation and a six-week acclimatization, Mount
Everest would have to be stormed in six days from Rongbuk Base Camp.
This early realization seems to me like a vision. Since I reached Base Camp
via Lhasa and Shigatse, more than seven weeks have elapsed. I have been on
the move for four days, I require two more days to reach the summit if all
goes well and the weather holds.

Now I am 7220 meters high. Again I squat down to rest. Haste at this
altitude produces exhaustion, and I have most of my day's work already behind me. However, I want to go on as long as I have the strength for it. Far
below is the valley end of the Rongbuk Glacier. The view to the west is still
clear. To the left under the sky lies Nepal, in front of that a tip of the west
shoulder of Everest. In the distance great ranges of mountains fade away. The
bright light of the morning dissolves mountains and valleys. The rock bastion of Changtse, also known as the North Peak, falling abruptly to the
Rongbuk Glacier, is now a most impressive view. The beautiful pyramid of
Pumori looks supernatural and uncanny. Here and only here is God able to
manifest himself. To the right the Tibetan plateau loses itself in infinity. The
few clouds there, distributed like spiders' webs, are motionless. Up here, too,
no wind. Snow only whirls through the air far below on the North Col; it
seems to me as if this col is a funnel for all the winds in Tibet. Looking down,
the broad North Flank of Mount Everest is slightly sunken and wind protected on the left. Likewise the north-east surface to the right is hollowed out.
The ground plunges steeply down on each side.

The rock slopes on the north side are deeply snowed up, everything looks
gentle and flatter than it really is. Up here everything seems peaceful. Now
I have to rest at shorter intervals but each time my breathing quickly returns to its former rhythm, and I feel myself recover. This change between

going on and stopping, exhaustion and returning energy determines my speed. With each meter of ascent this rhythm becomes shorter phased, more constrained. Higher up above, I know from experience, it will be only will-power that forces the body from complete lethargy for another step. This sort of snail's pace compels me to rest now for some minutes every thirty paces, with longer rests sitting down every two hours. As the air up here contains only a third of the usual quantity of oxygen I climb as the Sherpas do. I climb and rest, rest and climb. I know that I shall feel comparatively well as soon as I sit down but put off this compelling feeling minute by minute. I must be careful to avoid any harsh irritation of the respiratory tracts. The bronchial tubes and throat are my weakest points. I know it. And already I sense some hoarseness. So I am doubly glad that on this windy mountain hardly a breeze is blowing today. A steep rise now costs me more energy than I thought. From below, going over it by eye, I supposed it would require five rest stops. Meanwhile it has become eight or nine and I am still not on top. There, where it becomes flatter, something like deliverance awaits me. I don't want to sit down until I am over the rounded top.

Now and then small snow crystals swirl in the air above me, a glittering and glistening enlivening the space. A whistling and singing comes and goes. Still eighty paces?

While climbing I watch only the foot making the step. Otherwise there is nothing. The air tastes empty, not stale, just empty and rough. My throat hurts. While resting I let myself droop, ski sticks and legs take the weight of my upper body. Lungs heave. For a time I forget everything. Breathing is so strenuous that no power to think remains. Noises from within me drown out all external sounds. Slowly with the throbbing in my throat willpower returns.

Onwards. Another thirty paces. How this ridge fools me! Or is it my eyes? Everything seems so close, and is then so far. After a standing rest stop I am over the top. I turn round, let myself drop on the snow. From up here I gaze again and again at the scenery, at the almost endless distance. In the pastel shades of the ranges lies something mystical. It strengthens the impression of distance, the unattainable, as if I had only dreamed of this Tibet, as if I had never been here. But where I am now, I have been already, that much I know. I stare at the plateau, think I can recognize a village. Tingri perhaps?

In spirit I see before me the whitewashed mud houses with the black window holes. Red scarves wave beside Tibetan prayer flags. I see blunt-featured
faces. The people in Tibet do not laugh as merrily as the people in the mountains of Nepal. All that goes through my mind as if I were standing at the
edge of this village; it is no memory, it is the present. The altimeter shows
7360 meters and it is about 9 A.M. I did the stretch to the North Col in two
hours. By this ploy I have spared myself a bivouac. Now I am climbing slowly,
consciously slowly.

Now and then the snow gives way up to the ankles, and snowdrifts cost
strength. Mostly, however, I can go round the spots of crusted snow. Each
avoidance feels like a personal triumph. I must not waste my energy. This
impulse determines my thoughts and feelings more and more. Tomorrow and
the day after it will be more strenuous. The two adjustable ski sticks really
are a wonderful help here. I can distribute my weight to legs and arms. I
balance myself from up top, not on my legs.

The north flank to the right of me is a gigantic snow slope. Only a few
rock islands lie scattered darkly across this vertical ice desert. Avalanche lines
are distinctly recognizable. For the time being I stay on the blunt North Ridge.
That is not only the safest route, the wind has also blown away a lot of snow.
In spite of all that, there is no trace of my predecessors. Everything is buried
under a thick cloak of snow. Only once, at about 7500 meters, do I see a red
rope in the snow. I go over, touch it. The rope seems fairly new and is anchored to a rock outcrop. That must have been done by the Japanese, I think.
In customary expedition style and teamwork they had set up a chain of high
camps in May. On steep sections they anchored fixed ropes, on which they
could descend to Base Camp when the weather became bad, and on which
they could pull themselves up in order to continue the preparation of the route.
Step by step they pushed forward to the summit with the support of Chinese
high-altitude porters. With exactly these tactics I climbed Mount Everest myself in 1978 by the southern route. On that occasion there were eleven of us
climbers employing two dozen Sherpas as high-altitude porters and taking
turns with building camp. Only for the last 900 meters did Peter Habeler
and I climb on without support—as far as the top.

This time there is no one to help carry; no one to prepare my bivouac; no comrade to help me break trail in deep snow and no Sherpa to carry my equipment. Nobody. How much easier it is to climb as a pair. The knowledge that someone is standing behind you brings comfort. Not only is solo climbing far more strenuous and dangerous, above all the psychological burden is more than doubled. Everything that lies ahead of me, including the descent—while resting this is all often blown up out of all proportion—weighs me down. Like a snail that carries its home on its back I carry my tent in my rucksack. I shall erect it, sleep in it, and take it with me for the next night. I am equipped like a nomad. I can survive for a week. Nevertheless I have scarcely any reserves. After seven days I must be back, nothing can be allowed to go wrong. A second tent would be too heavy, to say nothing of oxygen apparatus which would double my load again. My 18 kilos weighs so heavily at this height that I now stop and stand after every two dozen steps, struggle for breath and forget everything around me.

The stretches between the rest stops become shorter and shorter. Often, very often, I sit down to have a breather. Each time it takes great willpower to stand up again. The knowledge that I have completed my self-inflicted day's stint helps me now. It is as if thinking of that releases energy. "Still a bit more, you can do it," I say to myself softly by way of encouragement. "What you climb today, you won't have to climb tomorrow."

Soloing doesn't feel like isolation now. Only occasionally does a feeling of impotence strike me with the thought of the awful endless exertion that still lies before me. If a friend, a partner, were there we could alternate with breaking trail. Physically I am carrying the exertion alone. Psychologically helpers appear sporadically. There is again someone behind me! Is it my separated ego or some other human energy that compensates for a partner? Thus am I accompanied up to a height of 7800 meters.

The first bivouac spot that I tread down on the snow does not please me. I must camp on a rock and anchor the tent securely. The wind increases. A few meters above me I see the ideal camping place. Once more I hesitate before I make a platform. It is as if it did not smell like a campsite. Several meters lower perhaps. Finally, I feel within myself I have found the correct place. At first strength to unpack the rucksack and put up the tent fails me. I stand there and gaze down at Advanced Base Camp. It must have been warm down there, there is less snow on the mountains.

It is after 3 o'clock, I must cook. Below I recognize a tiny red speck. Nena has placed the sleeping bag on the roof of the tent to protect it from the heat. Or is it a signal for me? I hope that she sees me too. No longing, only the knowledge that she is below, waiting.

Down below the heat is generally worse to bear than the cold, although the thermometer there at night sinks below minus 10°C, and up here perhaps to minus 20°C. The sun and the dry air parch me. I remember that I have with me a tiny bottle of Japanese medicinal herb oil, and put two drops of it on my tongue. For a while that brings relief and opens the airways. Apart from aspirin this herbal remedy is the only medication I carry on the mountain.

The thin air works like a grater on my throat. Each breath leaves a pain in the throat and a feeling of stickiness in the mouth. I take my time setting up the bivouac.

I am tired and glad that I have finally decided to stop. Already the consciousness that no further effort is required works wonders. Was it not myself, but a power from without which drove me on? I feel it to be so. My will returns to normal and I begin to think clearly again. I can perceive again, not merely see. I enjoy a magnificent view to the glacier below me, toward the snow world to the east. Far below is the gloomy form of the North Peak, which looks as if it had turned its head round. Behind it swim soft and wavy ranges of mountains; there, behind the Tibetan plateau, are people. For a long time I search in vain for the ice pyramid of Pumori, more than 7000 meters high, in the sea of summits to the west. It has dwindled to an unimportant hump of snow by the bank of the Rongbuk Glacier. Meanwhile I have unpacked the tent. I fix the rucksack in the snow above the campsite so that it cannot move and roll away. I remain standing between the handles of the ski sticks and peer upward. Still a short rise, then comes the gigantic dip before the ridge. The conviction, a hunch condensed almost to certainty, that I shall reach the summit in a further two days makes me lighthearted. There don't seem to be any serious hindrances in the way. The "second step," the only section which could frighten me, has been secured with ropes and pitons for years now. What a good thing that I know that. Above me I divine a yellow band of rock below the snow; some rock outcrops betray the horizontal stratification of the mountain.

Before starting I had already reckoned that there should be no problem if I made 1200 meters height the first day. I have done at least 1300 meters. During the solo ascent of Nanga Parbat in 1978, which is the psychological support for this solo trip on Everest, I was actually able to climb 1600 meters on the first day, but on that occasion I started from 4800 meters, and there is a vast difference between climbing at 6000 and 7000 meters above sea level. Here, just under 8000 meters, each action becomes a triumph, an ordeal.

My tiny tent, not 2 kilos in weight and constructed so that it can withstand storms up to 100 kilometers per hour, does not need much space. It is just big enough for me to lie with my knees bent. Nevertheless I require a long time to flatten out a site for it. I push the snow backwards and forwards with my boots, stamp it down. I have no shovel. The tent must not be sloping. I have trouble putting it up. Again and again a gust of wind comes and lifts it. Not until I have the tent wall stretched on the light metal tubes do I feel all right. With my ski sticks, ice ax, and the only rock piton I have with me I anchor the bivouac cover. Then I lay a thin foam rubber mat on the floor, and, pushing the full rucksack from behind, crawl inside. For a time I just lie there. I listen to the wind hurling ice crystals against the tent wall. It comes in waves, ebbs to and fro and its rhythm keeps me awake. The wind is blowing from the northwest, that is a good sign. I ought to cook, I must. Again a command that absorbs everything in me and about me. But more tired than before from the many small jobs, from the erection of the bivouac, I cannot brace myself to it. For the last time I go outside the tent, fetch snow in my little aluminum pot and peer down into the valley, as if to dodge the all-important work of cooking. It becomes terribly cold. For a time I sit on the knob of rock which I picked out from below as an "ideal resting place."

Far to the north I see the Tibetan hill country, still farther northwards the gray-brown stone cone of Shekar, and right at the back a chain of white mountains. Clouds fill the valleys to the south. The wind becomes stronger. If Wilson had managed to get up here, I think suddenly, would he have reached the summit? Wilson was tougher than I am, uncompromising and capable of enduring loneliness. The stretch above me seems to be really easy, so Wilson would have been able to climb it, at least as far as the Northeast Ridge. Do I understand this madman so well because I am mad myself? Or do I take comfort in the constancy of this man in my delusion to prove something? I don't know exactly what it is, at least not rationally; I can still look at myself objectively, but I behave like one possessed, who uses himself to express himself.

I know of no mountain, no other region from which there is such an infinite view as from Mount Everest across the Tibetan plateau. With this impression I crawl back into the constriction of the tent. The space about me shrinks to a cubic meter, and I quickly forget where the tent is standing. Feet in sleeping bag I begin to cook on my small gas burner. Taking off the rucksack, leveling the campsite, fixing the tent, all that was a hard piece of work after more than ten hours of climbing. Now follow six hours of chores, and these chores are as strenuous as the climbing was before. I eat cheese in small crumbs and nibble a piece of coarse South Tyrolean brown bread. At intervals I fall asleep. When I wake up again the first pot is full of warm water. The soup tastes insipid. The snow has taken ages to melt.

I am surrounded by so much peace and at the same time so powerfully aroused that I could embrace anyone. Although I have eaten nothing since this morning I am not hungry. Also I must force myself to drink. The feeling of thirst is less than the fluid requirement of my body. I must drink at least four liters; this is a fundamental standard that I have set myself, like the course of the route and weather studies. Again I think of Maurice Wilson who in his fanaticism had ventured a solo ascent of Everest, although he was certainly no mountaineer. He knew little about altitude. Even after terrible snowstorms and several falls Wilson had not given up. I lack nothing, the forthcoming climbing problems are well within my capabilities, and yet I must force myself to believe in success. I know that I can do it. Nevertheless I try to talk myself into not giving up. So long as Wilson was able to remain on his legs he climbed upwards like one possessed, borne aloft by belief and by God. I need so much energy just to fight against fear and inertia. In this I pursue a goal which not only climbers can understand. When shall I finally be able to live without a goal? Why do I myself stand in the way with my ambition, with my fanaticism? "*Fai la cucina*," says someone near me. "Get on with the cooking." I think again of cooking. Half aloud I talk to myself. The strong feeling I have had for several hours past, of being with an invisible companion, has apparently encouraged me to think that someone else is doing the cooking. I ask myself too how we shall find space to sleep in this tiny tent. I divide the piece of dried meat that I take out of the rucksack into two equal portions. Only when I turn round do I realize that I am alone. Now I am speaking Italian although for me the mother tongue is South Tyrol German and for three months I have been speaking English with Nena.

I know I can prepare warm water simply from snow with the heat of the sun. Basically it works on the hothouse principle. I have brought especially for this purpose a plain black plastic bag to fill with snow that is connected by a tube to a transparent plastic bag. But it is too windy, and now in the afternoon the sun is veiled. I therefore cook in the tent on the tiny gas flame. Half outstretched, changing position from time to time, I lie there. The mat is as hard as stone. The wind has become so strong that the tent flutters and is constantly blowing out the flame on my gas burner whenever I open the tent flap a few inches in order to shovel snow with the lid of the cooking pot. It will be a bad night I think. But at the same time the wind is a good sign, so it also comforts me. I need a lot of snow before I have melted a liter of water. Once more I make tomato soup, then two pots of Tibetan salt tea. I learned how to make it from the nomads. A handful of herbs to a liter of water, plus two pinches of salt. I must drink a lot, if I am not to become dehydrated. My blood could thicken up too much if I do not take enough fluid, so I force myself to melt more snow to drink. The cooking lasts several hours. I just lie there, holding the cooking pot and occasionally pushing a piece of dried meat or Parmesan cheese into my mouth. I have no desire to leave the tent. The storm outside gets up even more. Now grains of ice beat like hail against the tent wall. The poles sing. That is good, for the wind will clear snow from the ridge and drive off the monsoon clouds that were advancing during late afternoon. There is no question of going to sleep. Terrible buffets beat at the tent. Or does my over-wakeful sense only deceive me? Tent floor and sleeping bag are lifted up time and again. If the storm becomes stronger it will hurl me together with my lodgings into the depths. I must hold the tent fast. Snow powder forces itself through the cracks. Cooking has now become impossible. I lie down, arms in sleeping bag, and wait. I would like to keep my eyes closed but every time a solid gust of wind comes I open them again involuntarily. Am I still here? This lying here tensely itself takes energy. The tent walls flutter, the storm whistles, howls, presses. Whirling snow beats on the tent like spray on the bow of a ship.

Once when I look out through the tent flap a torrent of ice crystals beats against me. Nevertheless, no panic wells up. My surroundings are completely hidden, extinguished. The black rock outcrops above me appear ghostly. This storm really threatens to catapult me and the tent into the depths. The fine ice dust in the tent, the fingers that stick to metal, all that makes me shiver continually. Nevertheless I manage to remain fairly warm. Whenever the wind allows I put both arms deep into the sleeping bag and hold it down from within. Only my face remains free. Once I fall asleep briefly.

The night is tolerable. The storm has abated. In the sleepless intervals endless thoughts go round and round in my mind. I feel this thinking as something tangible. From the back of my mind springs one fragment of thought after another, to and fro, like points of condensed energy, finding no way out, with a life of their own. As if there were an energy in my field of force which is independent of me. Indeed it belongs to me, but exists without my so much as lifting a finger, without impulse. Even in sleep.

It comes and goes against my will. So it is also with this almost tangible power around me. A spirit breathes regularly in and out, which originates from nothingness and which condenses to nothingness. Only somewhere between these extreme forms do I perceive it, even with my senses.

There is also my plan for tomorrow. Is it possible in X hours to climb Y meters? Over and over again, this question. I answer it irrationally, I answer it emotionally—a game, like the counting of petals—she loves me, she loves me not. Six hundred meters of ascent perhaps? Seven hundred? As far as the "second step"? Then the weather penetrates my half-wakeful consciousness. The wind has not entirely calmed down; nevertheless I feel its decrease as something like peace. The quiet before the storm? The moon shines but still the night is warm. I am no longer freezing. Is the monsoon break over? Is it still ice crystals the wind hurls against the tent or is it snowing already? If it snows suddenly, and a lot, I shall be able to go neither up nor down. Then I shall be trapped. In my inertia I don't know which I prefer, good weather or snow. What should I do in the case of avalanche danger? How long could I survive here? These questions, to which my imagination knows no answer, and also wants to give no answer, pursue me into my dreams. Again chains of thought without conclusion, independent streams of energy in my mind. Certainly the avalanche danger is slight higher up but this grainy new snow is like a morass, it not only holds one back, it also saps one. Once exhausted I am lost forever.

As the morning dawns sluggishly I notice that the wind is dropping again. That lends me wings. I maneuver the gas burner into the sleeping bag to warm it up. An hour later I am drinking lukewarm coffee. With that I chew the hard, coarse brown bread from South Tyrol again. All the small chores in the constriction and cold of the tent add up to a bodily ordeal. I work with numb fingers; uninterruptedly, hoar frost trickles from the canvas. To be able to stretch out fully, or to stand up to adjust my clothes is a luxury that I cannot perform in here. Such a tent would weigh at least three times as much as my special construction. Once more I force myself to cook. The dry lumps of snow produce an unpleasant noise between my fingers. It is an eternity before my fist-sized pot is full of water.

For an hour I lie still with my clothes on in the sleeping bag, drink, and doze off. I don't want to look at the time. When I open my eyes I often don't know whether it is morning or evening.

I feel a driving unrest in my innermost being. It is not fear which suddenly seizes me like a big all-embracing hand. It is all the experiences of my mountaineering life that spread out in me and press for activity. The exertion of thrity years of climbing; avalanches, which I have been through, states of exhaustion that have condensed over the decades to a feeling of deep helplessness. You must go on! Time won is energy saved. I know what can happen to me during the next few days, and I know how great the grind will become below the summit. This knowledge is now only endurable in activity.

I must go, and yet each smallest chore is an effort. Up here life is brutally racked between exhaustion and willpower; self-conquest becomes a compulsion. Why don't I go down? There is no occasion to. I cannot simply give up without reason. I wanted to make the climb, I still want to. Curiosity (where is Mallory?), the game (man versus Mount Everest), ambition (I want to be the first)—all these superficial incentives have vanished, gone. Whatever it is that drives me is planted much deeper than I or the magnifying glass of the psychologists can detect. Day by day, hour by hour, minute by minute, step by step I force myself to do something against which my body rebels. At the same time this condition is only bearable in activity. Only a bad omen or the slightest illness would be a strong enough excuse for me to descend.

As the sun strikes my tent and slowly absorbs the hoar frost from the inner wall I pack up everything again. Bit by bit, in the reverse order to which I must unpack again in the evening. Only two tins of sardines, a gas cartridge, as well as half the soup and tea, do I leave behind in a tiny depot, to make my rucksack lighter. I must make do with the remainder of the provisions. It is almost 9 o'clock.

The weather is fine. Tomorrow I shall be on the summit! The moment I crawl out of the tent my confidence is back once more. As if I am breathing cosmic energy. Or is it only the summit with which I identify? The air above me seems to be thin, of that soft blue that looks transparent. The mountains below me I see only as wavy surfaces, a relief in black and white. Take down the tent, fold it up! I command myself. But now these impulses no longer come from the mind, they come again from the gut.

Each drawing of breath fills my lungs with air, fills my being with self-realization. There can be no doubt. I set out on my way. The first 50 meters I go very slowly, then I find my rhythm again. I make good progress. At an avalanche fracture I hesitate. I climb somewhat to the right of the North Ridge; the ground becomes steeper. There is more snow here than down below.

Suddenly the weather worsens. Like massive wedges, gray-white cloud formations force themselves over the passes from the south into Tibet. Already the valley bottoms are filled with monsoon mist. Instinctively I keep farther to the right. The weather on Everest is often not what it seems. Is it the monsoon or a sudden fall in temperature? Is a storm coming on?

You must have experienced the wind in the region of the summit to know that it can easily sweep people away. Now streaks swim in the sky; this battle with the mountain air makes me nervous. The halts for rest between climbing become longer. Hesitation. Uncertainty. The slopes are not steep, an average 40 degrees perhaps. But above 7900 meters all terrain is strenuous.

Around me the morning air is still clear. Over the Rongbuk Valley, strands of cloud form constantly, shunt as far as the eastern horizon and evaporate.

＊　　　＊　　　＊

As always at great height I need a long time today to get the life-giving energy circulating again. It is as if the harmony had been disturbed. Through movement—right foot placed, weighted, released, dragged, left foot . . . —a field of energy develops in my body. After the initial kick-off the sluices open, guy-ropes slacken. With the reduction of anxiety, currents concentrate throughout my body—immeasurable, intangible forms of energy.

On this morning of August 19 I climb for a long time—much longer than normal—with this power dammed up. It is as if something were blocked, not so much to do with the height but with me, so that I scarcely make headway.

Yesterday it was so easy. Now each step is an ordeal. Why am I so slow? The rucksack weighs more heavily, although it has become lighter. I feel myself lost, vulnerable. However, I cannot make myself believe that there is a God who governs this world, who concerns himself with each single one of us. There is no creator outside of me, outside of the cosmos. I don't know when this faith was lost to me, I only know that since then it is more difficult not to feel myself alone and forsaken in this world. The snow lies deeper here. When my boots sink in an odd noise results: it is as if someone were behind me.

At last I must accept being alone, inevitably alone. In the long stops for breathing something like homesickness comes over me. My need for security overcomes me, and with that I know that all hopes that someone waits for me down below are, like the anxiety before my solo climb, impeding, paralyzing. Only when moving, seeking, and seeing does it become possible for me to accept this loneliness.

When I think, the energy at my disposal is quickly used up. With willpower alone I can get no further now but when I disengage my brain I am open to a power from without. I am like a hollow hand and experience a regeneration. The balled fist or outstretched fingers contribute with exhaustion to helplessness. Only when I am like a hollow hand does an invisible part of my being regenerate, not only in sleep, but also in climbing.

The rhythm of climbing—rest is determined by energy, and this energy determines my rhythm. The stops between climbing are already longer than the fifteen paces I make now each time. This is my measure of time, step by step. Time and space are one.

It is so difficult to cope, to take upon oneself all responsibility, not only for one's actions, but also for being here at all, especially if the whole body is desperate through exertion. In spite of the risk freely entered into I cannot, like Wilson, entrust myself wholly to a God. To what, then? During the ascent I am like a walking corpse. What holds me upright is the world around me: air, sky, earth, the clouds which press in from the west. The experience of proceeding one step at a time. The sense of one's will as something tangible prior to the last two paces before resting. The terrain is easy. Nevertheless it demands my whole attention. That I can stand, that I can proceed, gives me energy to think ahead, to want to get ahead. At least as important as success is joy at one's own skill. It is astonishing how often I have overlooked this part of the pleasure of climbing and have talked solely of loads carried to the summit. High altitude climbing requires a whole range of proficiencies, knowledge, and inventiveness. The higher you go, the more man himself becomes the problem. Ability also to solve problems of this sort is what makes a good climber. I see the usefulness of climbing not in the further development of technique, rather in the development of the instinct and proficiency of man to extend himself. Learning about his limitations is just as important as his claim to be able to do anything.

With my snail-like advance I have lost the ability to estimate distance. Also sense of time. Am I about to break down? As I once said, the development of the self is part of my motive, yet what constitutes development when comparisons cannot be made? If I am frequently said to have a compulsion to succeed, this is characteristic of the people of today, for whom experience of an effort, and not the learning process itself, is what counts. He who only perceives his body as a vehicle for success cannot understand me, cannot follow my thoughts. I carry on—without calculating or anticipating how far I have got. This climbing, resting, breathing has become a condition that completely absorbs me. It is merely movement along a fixed line. The forward-thrusting impulse in climbing is often referred to as aggression; I prefer to call it curiosity or passion. Now all that has gone. My advance has its own dynamic force, fifteen paces, breathe, propped on the ski sticks which are inwardly and up-wardly adjusted. With the knowledge that God is the solution. I confess that in moments of real danger something acts as a defense mechanism; it aids sur-vival, but evaporates as soon as the threat is past. I am not at this moment under threat. It is all so peaceful here around me. I am not in any hurry. I can-not go any faster. I submit to this realization as to a law of Nature.

My altimeter shows 7900 meters. But altimeters have the capacity to be-come inaccurate up high. Generally they show less than the actual height. It is also possible that the air pressure has altered during the night. I no longer take the altimeter seriously.

The weather is still fine, and I want to go on. Retreat no longer comes to mind. About 100 meters above the campsite I decide that climbing up the ridge is becoming too dangerous. Also too strenuous, for there the snow lies partially knee-deep. All the hollows are filled in. And above me a single giant-sized trough. Not only the avalanche danger, but the exertion above deters me. A feeling of hopelessness grips me as I poke the right ski stick into the floury mess. Snow slab danger! The topmost layer is firm but gives way with a crack when I step on it. Underneath the snow is grainy. On my own, under these conditions, I would quickly tire myself out.

Then I see that on the North Face the snow slabs have gone. What luck! There the foundation is hard. Yes, that's the way! Without thinking much I begin to cross the North Face. Instinctively, as if pre-programmed, I want to get to the Norton Couloir and to climb it tomorrow to the summit. The traverse of the North Face extends a long way, and gains little height, but is good going in the firm monsoon snow. I don't need the ice ax; leaning on the ski sticks I cross the slope. The rucksack with the tent, which I have tied on out-side so that it can dry, is still heavy. At almost 8000 meters even standing with this rucksack on my back is an exertion. Without the ski sticks I would stagger, collapse. I rest like a four-legged creature; in this way the weight of the rucksack does not constrict my breathing.

When I continue again, I do it likewise, largely bending forward, having also shortened the ski stick in my left hand, which is on the uphill side. I have completely given up counting my steps; I have not the inclination or strength to take any pictures. Rhythmically—go—rest—I progress like a snail.

And out of this progress energy flows to me; it suffices exactly to maintain this rhythm.

The terrain is inclined and rolling. The stretch as far as the great snow couloir seems short. Without asking myself how many dips must lie between me and my planned bivouac spot I climb unhesitatingly upwards. My confidence grows. I no longer feel the loneliness as isolation, much more as detachment. The bridge of wife and friends, the embodiment in a community—supports that I need—I experience now for what they are: aids to endure the awareness of loneliness.

I am now directly under the "first step." Above me projects a blunt flat-topped buttress shaped like a sickle. It is snowed up, and to the right of it stands an unfriendly steep wall, dark; snow lies only on some of its ledges. The rock outcrops in the monsoon snow increase. With that my perception grows of already having been here before—do I know this route?

What disquiets me is the weather. No wind. The sun burns. Clouds press in from the south. Like wedges they push their gray white masses northwards. Yes, there is no doubt; the monsoon storms are sending out their scouts.

Nevertheless I climb on determinedly. Always upwards to the right. I stop in exact line with the summit; or what I take to be the summit—the final point up there is presumably invisible—makes no overpowering impression on me. I stand close under the Northeast Ridge and the route appears flattened.

The view too is restricted: on one side by the mass of the mountain, on the other by the rising cloud ceiling. The North Peak appears now flat and small; it separates the mist welling up from the valley. Only after longer rest stops am I capable of such observations. Between the North Ridge and the Norton Couloir I am standing on a mountainside which has no equal in the Alps. A slanting trapezium, 2½ kilometers high and almost a kilometer wide.

I progress so slowly! How long my pauses to breathe are each time I don't know. With the ski sticks I succeed in going fifteen paces, then I must rest for several minutes. All strength seems to depend on the lungs. If my lungs are pumped out I must stop. I breathe in through my mouth and expel the air through mouth and nose. And while standing I must use all my willpower to force my lungs to work. Only when they pump regularly does the pain disappear, and I experience something like energy. Now my legs have strength again.

I took the spontaneous decision to follow the North Flank of Mount Everest even though I wanted to be on the lookout for signs of Mallory and Irvine. But I do not resent my change of plan, not only because there is so much snow, but also because I know of their failure. I am on the best route to the summit. The going is at times tiring, at times agony; it all depends on the snow conditions. The downward-sloping slabs luckily lie buried beneath a layer of névé and up to now I have been able to go round all the rock outcrops. I can see the Northeast Ridge above me, but know that at the moment nothing of the pioneers can be found there. Mallory and Irvine climbed along this ridge, exactly on its edge. That is no guess. I am convinced that Odell saw them on the "first step," on that knob which rises out of the line of the ridge. I know now that they failed on the "second step." In the deep trough above me Mallory and Irvine lie buried in the monsoon snow. This hunch absorbs me like an old fairytale and I can think about it without dread.

It is as if I saw now the origin of a legend, as if I have perceived the truth. The observations of the Chinese climber Wang in 1974, who told the Japanese Hasegawa of his discovery five years later before an avalanche killed him below the North Col, appear now just as struck from my memory as the contradictory descriptions of the two steps. "First" and "second step" now lie above me. There Mallory and Irvine live on. The fate of the pair is now free from all speculation and hopes. It is alive in me. I cannot tell whether I see it as on a stage or in my mind's eye. At all events it is happening in my life—as if it belonged to it.

Close up, the "second step" appears to overhang. Only a little snow adheres to it. No, without pitons and ladders like the Chinese installed it is literally impossible to climb over it. Likewise today. A few months back the Japanese climber Kato also used the climbing aids left behind by the Chinese.

Between the two steps, therefore, Mallory and Irvine are presumed dead, without previously having reached the summit. I don't ask myself how they died, I only see them turn back. Mallory and Irvine, decades-long legends, live for me forever up there, and not just in Odell's words.

Disappointed and exhausted they turn round below the "second step." In the failing daylight the difficulties increase. The two force themselves to make the laborious descent. They get slower and slower. Night falls. Only energy from success could have saved them. The vision fades. How the pair died cannot be answered until someone finds Mallory's body or the camera that Somervell had lent him. Perhaps it can never be answered conclusively. That the two of them did not reach the summit is for me, however, beyond doubt.

After a longer rest my breathing is quiet and regular. Is that someone talking nearby? Is somebody there? Again I hear only my heart and my breathing. And yet there they are again. In this silence each sound, each atmosphere-drowning noise sounds like a spoken word. I jump frequently because I believe I hear voices. Perhaps it is Mallory and Irvine? With my knowledge of the circumstances surrounding their disappearance, which has occupied me many years, now each noise brings a vision alive in me. At any rate I believe sometimes that it is their calls that a breath of wind carries to me or takes away. But I do not recognize their voices for I have never tried to imagine them. So, do Mallory and Irvine really live on? Yes, their spirit is still there—I sense it distinctly.

I gaze at the "second step" and already two beings fill my imagination, release phantoms; in the driving mist everything seems so near, ghostly. In spite of my tiredness I stare up again and again at the knife-edge above me. The "second step" rears closer. A relatively easy snow gully leads to a steep groove. Quite distinctly I perceive a barrier at the top. At this moment I do not know that in May 1980 Yasuo Kato and Susumi Makamura took forty minutes over the "second step." I see the real proof that Mallory and Irvine, with their comparatively primitive equipment, failed there in 1924.

Because the swelling mist envelops everything and because I am exhausted by the climbing, everything around me disappears. With my eyes hurrying on ahead a few meters, I look for the way to go. Brightness pierces me when the sun breaks through the clouds: flashing snow crystals move past me like water from a spring.

In spite of the gloomy snowy waste around me which ebbs and flows with the pulsating clouds, I feel no panic. I know the route. And the track behind me is still there. True, it is snowing lightly, but it is warm. I approach the Norton Couloir over enormous, gentle waves—I have two behind me already. I can't see it, I only sense it. Nevertheless I am not for a moment afraid of being too high. Is it the tiredness that makes me indifferent, or is it this feeling of knowing the way that gives me the assurance of a sleep-walker?—I am convinced that all is well.

Every time I cross a rib there are more lumps of rock. In a row above and below me they make a sort of border. Far above and far below they disap-pear into the mist. These are the rock islands that show me the way. Like cairns they all have a definite form and each dark speck has a meaning, each gives support to my eyes and to me.

Meanwhile the mists around me have become so dense that the sun only now and then breaks through. Direction finding becomes more difficult. Some-times the breathless silence after resting fills me for a few moments with ter-ror. Have I already gone too far? When the silence becomes unbearable I have to continue climbing. Always obliquely upwards. The pounding in my body and the gasping for breath after each ten paces lets me forget the emp-tiness about me. For a pain-filled eternity there is nothing at all. I exist only as a mind above a body. While resting I literally let myself fall: with my up-per body leaning on the ski sticks, the rucksack tipped onto the nape of my neck, I go through a period of only breathing out and breathing in. Then I perk up again, and with the first step experience the exertion of the next sec-tion. Onward!

Sometimes I feel as if I am stuck in the snow. Nevertheless, I don't let myself get discouraged. I move continually to the right up the North Face. The whole face is like a single avalanche zone. New snow trickles down from above and it is sleeting. I tell myself that it is only a temporary disturbance; the snow will consolidate itself. "It will hold for two days yet," I say to myself.

The ascending traverse continues endlessly with many but regular pauses. Because of the exertion and concentration I have not noticed that the weather has become so bad that I ought to turn back. All around everything is covered in mist. I squat and rest. Perhaps I should put up the tent. The spot seems too insecure to me. I must bivouac on a ridge. If it snows any more that means avalanche danger. These are not rational thoughts, but come from the instincts that lie deep within me. For at least another hour I force myself on still farther. On a blunt elevation that runs across the face like a giant rib I squat down again. For a while I feel only heaviness, indifference, numbness. Then the clouds tear themselves apart. The valley appears: gray, lightly covered in snow, soon masked again by mists. Not only do the mountains seem flattened, also the slopes beneath me and the snow shield in the big couloir. I see all that with the feeling of no longer belonging to the world below. When I notice it is 3 o'clock in the afternoon, it sinks in: I am still about 200 meters to the east of the Norton Couloir. When I then peer at the altimeter it shows 8220 meters. I am disappointed. It's more than that surely! It's not only that I would be delighted to have got as far as 8400 meters, but that I have exerted myself much more than yesterday. It is misty and snows lightly. I can't go any farther today. And yet that is an evasion: I do not know whether there is a bivouac place higher up.

I am dead tired. Conscious of this I scarcely make it to the next rocks. Earlier than planned I erect my tent. On a rock bollard, safe from avalanches—snow slides would branch off to the left and right of it—I find a 2-by-2-meter big, almost flat surface. While I make the snow firm I remain standing up. I ask myself how I shall find my way back if the weather stays like this. This doubt and the knowledge of all that can happen condense into fear. Only when I work am I inwardly at peace. The quite light snowfall, the stationary clouds, the warmth, all that is sinister to me. Is it the monsoon or only anxiety? A fall in temperature is on the way, it seems to me. If I cannot get back for days my reserves will be soon used up. The avalanche danger on the North Face and below the North Col grows with every hour.

An hour later my tent is standing on the rock outcrop. Once again I anchor it with ice ax and ski sticks. I can camp here protected from the wind. Also, if there is a storm there is scarcely any danger. I place the open rucksack in front of the tent flap, and push the mat in. Lumps of snow for cooking lie ready to hand. All is prepared for the long night. A feeling of relief comes over me.

I take only two pictures then abandon photography again. It takes too much energy to take the camera out of the rucksack, walk away ten paces, rest, press the self-release. Then I must go back. And for what? Documentary proof, reports, all that has become meaningless. It seems to me much more important that I make myself something to drink.

Tonight I keep my clumsy, double-layered plastic boots near all my clothing; they must not be allowed to become cold. I sense my clothes as something alien. The layers between skin and outer covering feel like unpleasant stuffy air: hence the feeling of being in a straitjacket. While I lie in the tent—too tired to sleep, too weak to cook. I try to imagine Advanced Base Camp. Nena will now be making tea. Or is she looking straight up here? Has it cleared up meanwhile? Perhaps the weather is improving. Time passes too fast and too slowly. Only when I manage to switch off completely does it cease to exist.

How does one live at this height? I am no longer living, I am only vegetating. When one must do everything alone each manipulation takes a lot of willpower. With each job I notice the effect of the thin air. Speed of thought is greatly diminished and I can make clear decisions only very slowly. They are influenced by my tiredness and breathing difficulties. My windpipe feels as if it were made of wood, and I am aware of a slight irritation of my bronchial tubes.

Although I have not been able to prepare any really hot drinks, because water boils at a lower temperature on account of the height, I still keep on melting snow. Pot after pot. I drink soup and salt tea. It is still too little. I am not very hungry. I must force myself to eat. Also I don't know what to eat without making myself sick. Should I open this tin of sardines now or something else? The slightest effort requires time, energy, and attention. All movements are slow and cumbersome. I decide on cheese and bread, chicken in curry sauce, a freeze-dried ready-to-serve meal that I mix with lukewarm water. I stick the empty packet under the top of my sleeping bag. I shall need it during the night to pee in. It takes me more than half an hour to choke down the insipid pap. Outside it gets darker. The many small tasks in the bivouac take as much energy as hours of regular climbing. The difference between arriving at a prepared camp, to be cared for by Sherpas or comrades, and evening after evening having to make camp and cook for oneself is tremendous. Perhaps it is the essential distinction between the classic big expedition and the modern small expedition. Going to sleep is by itself a big exertion. Up here I cannot simply get into bed, stick my head under the covers, and fall asleep.

Once more I sit up in my sleeping bag. First I loosen my boots. Tomorrow morning I want to have warm feet and boots not frozen stiff. So I first change my socks, then pull my boots on again. Once more I push feet and boots right back into the sleeping bag. I throw away the damp socks. Then, outstretched, propped up on my arms, I stick the rucksack under the mat as a pillow. I arrange the cooking equipment so that I can get at it next morning from the sleeping bag. Constantly I have to shift my body a little and keep my head up, not in order to sleep well, but only to be able to endure the night.

These movements in the narrow tent make me breathless. I am forced to breathe deeply. In between, I pant again. I have had numb fingers for hours. In spite of the occasional slumber of exhaustion—an inadvertent dozing—I cannot fall asleep properly during the night. I am endless like the night.

In the morning I am just as tired as the evening before, and stiff as well. I ask myself whether I really want to go on. I must! Then I use the little strength I have to move my body. I know well enough from experience that I can still carry on for a time, but I try to push everything aside—to think of nothing, to prolong a deliberate state that allowed me to endure the whole night.

I have only to get going and keep moving in order to have some energy again. The will to make the first decisive move still fails me. When I open the tent flap this morning, it is already day outside. A golden red glow bathes the summit pyramid; to the east, fields of clouds stretch away into the distance. Automatically I remember the monsoon. It is an eternity before I hold the first pot of warm water between my hands. There is ice lying in the tent. I can't eat anything.

While I fish lumps of snow into the tent I peer up into the Norton Couloir. Fairly steep. Smoky gray clouds cling to the mountain sides. The air is glassy, as if it were full of moisture. I feel a bit chilly in spite of the favorable temperature. Ice by the rocks and tent! However, cold is no problem on Mount Everest during the monsoon period. I am sure that it thaws in high summer when it is windless and misty, even on the summit. My three layers of clothing—silk, pile suit, thin down suit—are sufficient when almost undone.

Two years ago in May 1978 I endured up to minus 40°C at night. Now it is minus 15°C maximum, perhaps only minus 10°C. Nevertheless I must not be careless. As long as the sun is not shining I wear gloves, fasten my boots loosely. At this height a few degrees below zero can cause frostbite. Think only of going on. As if retreat, failure, had never crossed my mind. But what if the mist becomes thicker? Ought I to wait a bit? No, that is senseless. In any case I am already very late. I must get outside. At this height there is no recovering. By tomorrow I could be so weak that there would not be enough left for a summit bid. It's now or never. Either/or. I must either go up or go down. There is no other choice.

Twice while melting snow I take my pulse. Way above 100 beats per minute. I feel all in. No more trains of thought. Only commands in the mind. The night was one long ordeal. Painful joints, mucous in my throat. Morning is depressing. On this August 20 I leave everything behind: tent, ski sticks, mat, sleeping bag. The rucksack too stays in the tent. I take only the camera with me. So just as I am I crawl out of the tent, draw my hood over my head and with bare fingers buckle crampons onto my boots. I retrieve only the titanium ax from the snow. Have I got everything? It must be after 8 o'clock already. Without the load on my back things are easier. But I miss the ski sticks as balancing poles. With the short ice ax in my right hand I feel secure, certainly, but for traversing it is a poor substitute.

Only when I climb directly upwards do my gloved left hand and the ice ax fumble about in the snow beneath my head. I proceed on all fours. While resting I distribute my whole weight so that the upper part of my body remains free. I kneel in the snow, lay my arms on the rammed-in ice ax and put my head on this cushion. I can still survey the steep rise above me, orientate myself, weigh up difficulties. Fortunately an uninterrupted snow gully runs up the Norton Couloir. So long as I can see and plod I am confident.

Once, before I reach the bottom of the broad trough, I look out for a longer rest possibility. The tent, a yellow speck, appears as through a weak magnifying glass. Is that only the light mist or are all my senses fooled? I remember the place and then climb up the rise above me to the right. Pace by pace. Step by step. Already after a short while I miss the rucksack like a true friend. It has let me down. For two days it has been my partner in conversation, has encouraged me to go on when I have been completely exhausted. Now I talk to the ice ax. But a friend is little enough in this state of exposure. Nevertheless, the voices in the air are there again. I don't ask myself where they come from. I accept them as real. Lack of oxygen and insufficient supply of blood to the brain are bound up with it, are certainly the cause of these irrational experiences which I got to know two years ago during my solo ascent of Nanga Parbat. Up here in 1933 Frank Smythe shared his biscuits with an imaginary partner.

The rucksack has indeed been my companion. But without it things go easier, much easier even. If I had to carry something now I would not make any progress. I decided to make the ascent because I knew that on this last day I could leave everything behind. In the driving clouds, following my instinct more than my eyes I look for the route step by step. Again the distant memory of this couloir. I live in a sort of half-darkness of mist, clouds, snowdrifts, and recognition of individual sections. I was here once before! A feeling that even lengthy reflection cannot dispel.

An hour above camp I come up against a steep step about 100 meters high. Or is it 200 meters towering up in front of me?

The climbing is made easy by the snow. My whole foot always finds a hold without the crampons hitting the rocks. For hours repeatedly expending oneself, dying, bracing oneself, exerting one's will, letting oneself fall, collecting oneself. The rock islands to left and right of the great gully are yellowish with brighter streaks here and there. Often I see everything double and am uncertain where I should go. I keep more to the right. The slope is now so steep that I rest in the climbing position.

I literally creep along now. Only seldom do I manage to do ten paces without stopping to gasp for air. The view disappoints me. Yesterday morning it was still impressive. Now when I look down on the long glacier with the moraine ridges everything appears flat. The landscape is blunted, deadened by the new snow. Despite the swelling mist I lose all feeling of distance.

Light powder snow on a semi-firm base here. The rock slabs underneath, lying one on another like roof tiles, are approximately as steep as a church roof, and are almost completely snow-covered. I leave the gully where it becomes wider and forms a pear-shaped bay. I take bearings on a blunt ridge up to the right. The going must be easier there.

It is getting steeper. When I move I no longer pound like a locomotive, I feel my way ahead hesitatingly. Jerkily I gain height. This climbing is not difficult but downright unpleasant. Often I can find no hold in the snow and must make out the steps by touch. I cannot afford to slip here. For the first time during this solo ascent I feel in danger of falling, like increased gravity. This climbing carefully with great concentration increases my exhaustion. Besides, the mist interferes more and more. All I see is a piece of snow in front of me, now and then a prospect of blue sky above the ridge. Everything goes very slowly. In spite of the enormous strain that each step upwards requires, I am still convinced that I shall get to the top, which I experience now in a sort of anticipation, like a deliverance.

The knowledge of being halfway there in itself soothes me, gives me strength, drives me on. Often I am near the end of my tether. After a dozen paces everything in me screams to stop, sit, breathe. But after a short rest I can go on. Worrying about the bad weather has cost me additional energy. And the ever-recurring question of the descent. But simultaneously in the thickening mist I experience an inspiring hope, something like curiosity outside of time and space. Not the demoralizing despair which a visible and unendingly distant summit often triggers. It is now all about the struggle against my own limitations. This becomes obvious with each step; with each breath it resolves itself. The decision to climb up or down no longer bothers me. It is the irregular rhythm, the weakness in the knees. I go on like a robot. Against all bodily remonstrances I force myself upwards. It must be! I don't think much, I converse with myself, cheer myself up. Where is my rucksack? My second friend the ice ax is still here. We call a halt.

The way up the Norton Couloir is logical and not so difficult as I expected. I shall find my way back. When I reach the blunt rib above I should be able to see the summit. If the cloud breaks. Up there it seems to be flatter.

The fancy to have climbed here once already constantly helps me to find the right route. The steep step shot through with brightly colored rock lies beneath me. I still keep to my right—not so long ago an avalanche went down here. The snow bears. Under the blunt ridge it becomes deeper, my speed accordingly slower. On hands and knees I climb up, completely apathetic. My boots armed with crampons are like anchors in the snow. They hold me.

As I stand on the rib I hear the wind amongst the stones. Far below this rock rib continues as a buttress. For a short while the mist is so thick that I can no longer orientate myself visually. I continue somewhat farther along the rib, where the least of the snow lies. For an hour. Until a dark vertical rock wall bars the way above me. Something in me draws me to the left, I pass the obstacle, and continue still keeping to the right. How long? My only adversary is the slope, time no longer exists. I consist of tiredness and exertion.

I guess myself to be near the top but the knife-edge goes on for ever. During the next three hours I am aware of myself no more. I am one with space and time. Nevertheless I keep moving. Every time the blue sky shows through the thick clouds I believe I see the summit, am there. But still there are snow and stones above me. The few rocks which rise out of the snow are greeny-gray, shot through here and there with brighter streaks. Ghostlike they stir in the wispy clouds. For a long time I traverse upwards, keeping to the right. A steep rock barrier bars the way to the ridge. Only if I can pass the wall to the right shall I get any higher.

Arriving on the crest of the Northeast Ridge I sense the cornices, stand still. Then I lie down on the snow. Now I am there. The ridge is flat. Where is the summit? Groaning I stand up again, stamp the snow down. With ice ax, arms, and upper body burrowing in the snow, I creep on, keeping to the right. Ever upwards.

When I rest I feel utterly lifeless except that my throat burns when I draw breath. Suddenly it becomes brighter. I turn round and can see down into the valley. Right to the bottom where the glacier flows. Breathtaking! Automatically I take a few photographs. Then everything is all gray again. Completely windless.

Once more I must pull myself together. I can scarcely go on. No despair, no happiness, no anxiety. I have not lost the mastery of my feelings, there are actually no more feelings. I consist only of will. After each few meters this too fizzles out in an unending tiredness. Then I think nothing, feel nothing. I let myself fall, just lie there. For an indefinite time I remain completely irresolute. Then I make a few steps again.

At most it can only be another 10 meters up to the top! To the left below me project enormous cornices. For a few moments I spy through a hole in the clouds the North Peak far below me. Then the sky opens out above me too. Oncoming shreds of cloud float past nearby in the light wind. I see the gray of the clouds, the black of the sky and the shining white of the snow surface as one. They belong together like the stripes of a flag. I must be there!

Above me nothing but sky. I sense it, although in the mist I see as little of it as the world beneath me. To the right the ridge still goes on up. But perhaps that only seems so, perhaps I deceive myself. No sign of my predecessors.

It is odd that I cannot see the Chinese aluminum survey tripod that has stood on the summit since 1975. Suddenly I am standing in front of it. I take hold of it, grasp it like a friend. It is as if I embrace my opposing force, something that absolves and electrifies at the same time. At this moment I breathe deeply.

In the mist, in the driving of the clouds I cannot see at first whether I am really standing on the highest point. It seems almost as if the mountain continues on up to the right. This tripod, which rises now scarcely knee high out of the snow, triggers off no sort of euphoria in me. It is just there. Because of the great amount of snow on the summit it is much smaller than when I saw it in 1978; pasted over with snow and unreal.

In 1975 the Chinese anchored it on the highest point, ostensibly to carry out exact measurements. Since then they state the height of their Chomolungma as 8848.12 meters. I don't think of all that up here. This artificial summit erection doesn't seem at all odd. I have arrived, that's all that matters! It's gone 3 o'clock.

Like a zombie, obeying an inner command, I take some photographs. A piece of blue sky flies past in the background. Away to the south snow cornices pile up, which seem to me to be higher than my position. I squat down, feeling hard as stone. I want only to rest a while, forget everything. At first there is no relief. I am leached, completely empty. In this emptiness nevertheless something like energy accumulates. I am charging myself up.

For many hours I have only used up energy. I have climbed myself to a standstill, now I am experiencing regeneration, a return flow of energy.

A bleached shred of material wrapped round the top of the tripod by the wind is scarcely frozen. Absentmindedly I run my fingers over it. I undo it from the metal. Ice and snow remain sticking to it. I should take some more pictures but I cannot brace myself to it. Also I must get back down. Half an hour too late means the end of me. At the moment I am not at all disappointed that once again I have no view. I am standing on the highest point on earth for the second time and again can see nothing. That is because it is now completely windless. The light snowflakes dance, and all around me the clouds swell as if the earth were pulsating underneath. I still don't know how I have made it but I know that I can't do anymore. In my tiredness I am not only as heavy as a corpse, I am incapable of taking anything in. I cannot distinguish above and below.

Again a shred of blue sky goes by with individual ice crystals shining in the sun. The mountains appear far below and quite flat, between the black-white of the valleys. This time I am too late with the camera. Then clouds, mist again; now their primary color is violet.

Is night coming on already? No, it is 4 p.m. I must be away. No feeling of sublimity. I am too tired for that. And although I don't at this moment feel particularly special or happy, I have a hunch that in retrospect it will be comforting, a sort of conclusion. Perhaps a recognition that I too shall have to roll that mythical stone all my life without ever reaching the summit: perhaps I myself am this summit. I am Sisyphus.

After three-quarters of an hour I have the strength to stand up, to stand up for the descent. It has become a bit brighter. I can still see my track. That is comforting. How much easier is the descent of this great mountain! It takes only a fraction of the effort and willpower compared with coming up.

My whole energy is now concentrated in my senses. I find the smell of the snow, the color of the rocks more intense than in previous days, jump at the occasional sheet lightning out of the clouds far to the west. I want only to get down. Climbing down—once facing inwards—as if I were in flight, I don't ask myself why I undertook all the strain of getting to the summit. I would rather be down already. This long way is a burden.

What disturbs me most is my coughing. It makes my life hell. Even gentle coughing tears at my stomach. Besides, I have not eaten for many hours. I must get to Base Camp as quickly as possible. Just before the onset of darkness I find my way back to my tent and rucksack.

This night I scarcely sleep at all. Also I cannot bring myself to cook properly. I drink a little snow water. Again I eat nothing. The warm flame of the gas burner that buzzes near my face is perhaps only to comfort me. I don't switch it off although I don't manage to sit up in my sleeping bag and fetch in snow. Each activity costs now so much energy! Energy that I have derived from climbing, also the stimulus of reaching the summit. Now it fails me. I lie in the tent as if dead. Only the success keeps me alive. I obey the law of inertia. Between waking and sleeping, surrounded by the living dead, the hours slip away. Without any thoughts. I am not safe yet. Suddenly terror seizes me.

My thinking weaves uninterruptedly further, always at the limit of consciousness. In the early hours I rouse myself with the feeling of having come to a decision, but cannot concentrate. Have I gone mad? Has this emptiness sent me mad? Am I altitude sick? When morning comes I am once again in flight. Without drinking anything I abandon camp. Tent, sleeping bag, everything except the rucksack stays behind. Only the ski sticks do I tear out of the snow. Traversing east I climb diagonally downwards. To the east I look down into the snow basin of the Rongbuk Glacier as I reach the blunt ridge a little above the North Col. No tent stands there. Or is it just snowed up? The new snow is powdery and dry. It flies about when I step on it. It is bitterly cold today.

Not only during the ascent but also during the descent my willpower is dulled. The longer I climb the less important the goal seems to me, the more indifferent I become to myself. My attention has diminished, my memory is weakened. My mental fatigue is now greater than the bodily. It is so pleasant to sit doing nothing—and therefore so dangerous. Death through exhaustion is—like death through freezing—a pleasant one. As I traverse the undulating ridge above the North Col I feel as if I am returning from a shadow world.

I make myself carry on through my tiredness, using the knowledge that I have been on the summit. I offer no more resistance, let myself fall at each step. Only I may not remain sitting. Day after day I have endured the loneliness of the undulating snow surface of the North Face; hour after hour against the wind, the sharp ice grains that swirl with it; for an eternity through the mist which deluded me into thinking each block of rock was a friend. Each breath up there was an ordeal and still I took it as a gift.

Now a feeling attacks me of "having survived," of "having been saved." Little by little I step into something that could be called "place of fulfillment," a "saving haven." Like the pilgrims at the sight of the place of pilgrimage, I forget all the ordeals of the journey.

"THE ENGLISH DEAD"

FROM
Ghosts of Everest
BY JOCHEN HEMMLEB, LARRY A. JOHNSON,
AND ERIC R. SIMONSON

IN NOVEMBER 1998, ERIC SIMONSON APPROACHED ME AT MountainZone.com with an intriguing idea. Simonson and a small group of historians and climbers wanted to undertake a focused search for George Mallory and Sandy Irvine, who disappeared high on the Tibetan side of Everest in 1924. Simonson wanted to know if MountainZon.com was interested. For me, the answer was an easy one.

Two years after the 1996 guided-climbing tragedy on Everest's South Col route, and the media frenzy that followed in its wake, I was eager to expose MountainZone.com's Everest-hungry readership to another side of the mountain, and another kind of story. Even though Simonson's chances of success seemed virtually nil, there was hope: while many climbers had passed over the ground where the famous rope team had vanished seventy-five years before, I knew of only one expedition that had made a serious effort to look for them. With luck, a sense of purpose, and good planning, Simonson and his climbers might succeed.

I handed Simonson a $50,000 check to launch his Mallory & Irvine Research Expedition, to which he later added PBS, the BBC, The Mountaineers, and other sponsors. Simonson departed in March 1999 for Tibet with German Everest historian Jochen Hemmleb, physician Lee Meyers, a team of, current and former Rainier guides—Dave Hahn, Andy Politz, Tap Richards, Jake Norton—photographer Thom Pollard and one wild card, the bold and freethinking climber Conrad Anker.

Their search, as the team moved higher on the northern flanks of Everest, made for a riveting "cybercast." The mystery of Mallory and Irvine was told to millions in the course of their efforts. Assuming the expedition would continue looking until time ran out, then come home, I was taken by surprise when on Saturday night, May 1, Simonson called by satellite-telephone to warn of the team's stunning discovery. When MountainZone.com went live with the news on May 2—with Simonson's own voice announcing via satellite-phone that his team had found the body of George Mallory—more than one million people tried to log on to the site at the same time. The following seven days were a blur of television and newspaper interviews.

There can be no question that the discovery of George Mallory's body by Conrad Anker and his colleagues is one of the seminal moments in

Everest history. The discovery was a lucky fluke, but it was made possible by Simonson's skillful planning, the team's exceptionally early-season arrival, and their purposeful effort focused not on the summit but on sleuthing. Perhaps the most important factor was the lowest spring snowfall in the Himalaya in recent memory.

The story is well told in *Ghosts of Everest,* the book written after the expedition by Simonson, Hemmleb, and Larry Johnson, one of the original partners. The narrative below begins with Hemmleb's ruminations on where best to begin looking for the famous missing climbers, and flows into a step-by-step description of the physical search at 27,000 feet and above by Hahn, Richards, Politz, Norton, and Anker. The climbers, on ground so steep they must take care not to fall, are shocked to find one of the men they set out to find. The excerpt can be found in *Ghosts of Everest,* on pages 111–129.

As Hemmleb had reexamined the history of North Face expeditions, it had become clear to him that the only hard bit of data about Mallory and Irvine themselves (as distinct from artifacts like the ice ax) was that the Chinese climber Wang Hongbao had found a body he had adamantly described as "English, English!" during what he said was a short stroll from the 1975 Chinese expedition's Camp VI.

Wang had been a member of a search party looking for Wu Zongyueh, who had disappeared between Camps VI and VII on May 4, 1975. Wang was at Camp VI with another climber, Zhang Junyan, the day after Wu disappeared and had decided, while waiting for another climber to arrive, to go for a short walk. Returning twenty minutes later, he told Zhang (and, later, others) that he had come across the body of a foreign mountaineer. It wasn't until 1979, while participating in a Chinese-Japanese expedition, that Wang told the story of his discovery of an "English dead" to an outsider, the Japanese climber Hasegawa Yoshinori. Says Hasegawa of the exchange, "He said to me, '8100 meter Engleese' and he made a gesture to sleep. . . . Then Wang opened his mouth, pointed his finger to his cheek, [and] pecked it slightly with his finger. . . ." The cheek, Wang was suggesting, had been pecked at by birds. That was all Hasegawa learned; an avalanche swept Wang to his death the next day. Years later, however, Everest expert Tom Holzel tracked down Zhang Junyan, and he corroborated Wang's story.

Whatever the validity of the other clues amassed over the years, it was clear to Hemmleb that this one was preeminent. The challenge was straightforward: locate the site of the 1975 Chinese Camp VI and search an area with a radius that could be covered in a twenty-minute round trip (or more, to be safe). Pinpointing the camp, however, was no easy task.

The Chinese had released little documentation of the 1975 climb. At the time Wang found the body, their Camp VI had been located at 26,900 feet (8200 m), though it was later moved, but there was no indication of whether it had been placed on Everest's North Ridge or the North Face. "I found one picture of the Chinese Camp VI that showed some background features," Hemmleb says, "and I wondered whether from this picture we could delineate the exact location for that camp and therefore narrow down the search area." When he compared the Chinese picture with pictures taken at other expeditions' Camp VIs, he soon realized that each was on a different site and the pictures had different backgrounds. "So the next question," he recalls, "was whether there was a way to delineate the exact locations of these different camps from the background that was visible. Was there a universal technique to delineate the location from which *any* photograph had been taken of Everest's North Face? And there was."

There is one distinctive reference point in every photograph taken from the upper North Ridge looking toward the summit: a triangular snowfield that, in fact, marks the high point reached by Geoffrey Bruce and George Finch during the 1922 British expedition. The photographer's position on any photograph of this area of the mountain can be determined by taking a back-bearing after vertically aligning features on the skyline with this distinctive reference point. "In the Chinese photo," Hemmleb explains, "the snow triangle is in vertical alignment with the summit ridge immediately beyond the so-called 'Third Step.' If you connect these same points horizontally on an aerial orthophotograph of the ridge, you can figure out a line on which the camp sits. To get the precise spot, you need a second back-bearing, which you get by vertically aligning two other features on the Chinese photo, a ledge on the First Step and a tongue of snow at the foot of the Yellow Band." In this way, Hemmleb was able to predict that the 1975 Chinese Camp VI would be found on an ill-defined rib of rock that bisects the snow terrace—a site too far off today's beaten path to the summit for anyone to have noticed it. "Forget the ice ax," says Hemmleb. "Find the camp and you'll find Irvine."

⋆   ⋆   ⋆

At 3:00 A.M. on May 1, 1999, six climbers from the Mallory & Irvine Research Expedition stirred themselves in their wind-battered tents at Camp V and began preparations to do just that. They had left Base Camp below the Rongbuk Glacier a week earlier and had gotten pinned down by high winds at Advance Base Camp for several days.

On April 29, the wind relented and the search team—Simonson, Hahn, Politz, Anker, Richards, Norton, and Pollard—climbed to the North Col. The next day they ascended to Camp V, though Simonson, who had not had the opportunity to acclimatize at higher altitudes, felt unwell and decided to descend rather than jeopardize the search. Simonson explains: "I went on this expedition planning to participate in the search climb, but I had to spend so much time handling administrative duties—juggling things with the film crews, the Chinese officials, the yak drivers, and the trekking expedition that followed us in—that I didn't get high enough soon enough to acclimatize. I could feel it as soon as we left Camp IV."

On the 30th, the remaining six climbers reached Camp V. Now, at 5:00 A.M., they were ready to go, guided by Hemmleb's search directions. "Once we'd gotten all our gear on and attached our oxygen masks," Dave Hahn recalls, "I realized we'd become as separate from one another as deep-sea divers. Without a word, we began working up the ridge."

Hahn describes the climb to Camp VI: "As we left Camp V, there was a steady 25-mile-per-hour wind blowing—not enough to move you around, but enough to make taking care of yourself in the cold morning air a bit more stressful. Actual air temperature is almost irrelevant at this altitude; it feels much colder than it is because the body can't heat itself very efficiently when there's so little oxygen. It's like any fire: you need more than fuel and a spark; you need oxygen too."

Once they got moving and got out of the wind, though, Jake Norton recalls, "It seemed surprisingly warm; it was going to be a beautiful day." Groping along in the dimness of the shadow cast by the North Ridge, the team began the traverse toward the North Face. "The footing was uncomfortable with so little snow," Hahn says. "It was a mix of loose rock, rock frozen in place, and bedrock here and there, all of which was steeply pitched and none of which felt too good when you're walking on the points of your crampons. Eventually, you follow a traversing ledge that takes you around a corner and out onto the North Face proper. It's pretty exposed; if you look down off the edge of the ledge, you see all the way down to the main Rongbuk far below." It was at about this point that Thom Pollard, complaining of problems with his oxygen set, decided to turn around.

Then, Jake Norton made a discovery. "This was my first trip on this route, and the exposure was pretty extreme; it doesn't encourage you to look down," Norton recalls, "but at one point I did, and saw something out of place: a piece of wood in a landscape that was nothing but rock and snow. I climbed down and discovered it was a very old wood-handled piton hammer." Norton picked up the hammer and put it in his pack. Later, it would prove to be an important clue to the history of the old camp Andy Politz had found on the East Rongbuk Glacier.

While four of the climbers continued across the traverse, Politz decided to take a direct line up the North Ridge itself because that was understood to be the route that Mallory and Irvine had taken. Politz had another purpose as well. "I wanted to get to the area where Odell had seen Mallory and Irvine early that afternoon in 1924. There's been so much controversy over the last seventy-five years about what he did or did not see that I wanted to see the mountain from his perspective. No one had ever done that before and, given how vital his observations were to the question of how high [Mallory and Irvine] got, I figured it was time somebody checked out that view."

When he reached the area where Odell had stood, the result was dramatic: "The First, Second, and Third Steps were each clearly separated; you had no trouble distinguishing them. You are really close to them at that point. From the area where Odell stood, there was only one place that anyone could see as being 'a very short distance from the base of the final pyramid,' and that was the Third Step. The First Step is out of the question; the Second is also too far away to fit Odell's description. I took slide photos, digital stills, and video and, afterward, it was really obvious you couldn't confuse one with another, even in bad weather."

After about five hours of climbing, the remaining four climbers reached the area today used as Camp VI. "We hadn't yet established a Camp VI for our expedition," says Norton, "but we were carrying a tent and a few supplies, which we left at what seemed a good site, and then waited for Andy to rejoin us. We could see his red parka coming across from the North Ridge, though he had to climb almost as high as the Yellow Band to find a safe route across."

"We were all pretty excited," Hahn remembers, "and we were optimistic. The ground conditions were excellent, we had Jochen's guidance, and the weather was good. It had taken us a month and a half to get to this point, and now it was time to go to work at last. It was also a bit of a thrill to know we would be going away from known terrain into some new and sporty parts of the mountain."

At 10:30 A.M., after a half-hour rest, the five climbers headed west across the sharply tilted North Face toward the "ill-defined rib" identified in Hemmleb's search instructions. Within only fifteen minutes, Jake Norton hit pay dirt again. He radioed Base Camp that he'd found a distinctively painted, bright blue 1975 Chinese oxygen cylinder, proof that they were near the vicinity of the old Chinese camp, which they estimated to be higher up the sloping rib.

Hemmleb had laid out four possible search routes; they began with the first, fanning out vertically and horizontally along the North Face and walking west. "The plan was simply to keep each other in sight and keep the radios on," Politz says. "From there on we knew the terrain would tell us the plan." Hemmleb agrees: "Once they reached that spot, my job was over; they had to decide what was right from the landscape they found there."

"The idea that this was a 'snow terrace' quickly became a joke," Hahn remembers. "This wasn't like a bunch of guys fanning out across a field. Beyond the rib, the North Face was a consistent 30-degree-plus slope of loose scree and discontinuous ledges and walls, all of it wildly exposed to a long fall to the glacier below. And the area we were trying to cover was immense, maybe the size of twelve crazily tilted football fields."

Politz adds, "Maybe at sea level it wasn't that big an area, but at 8000 meters, when your heart is working at jogging pace but your feet are working at a crawling pace and you're taking three breaths per step, it's a huge area." Climbing higher than he'd ever been before, Jake Norton was also taking great care: "Walking around looking for bodies is kind of an eerie job, especially when you're on slopes where a slight misstep could turn you into another victim."

As they fanned out, each of the climbers was guided by his own private sense of what might have happened to Andrew Irvine. "I was looking for someplace hidden that he might have either fetched up against or sheltered in," says Hahn. Politz confesses, "I wanted Mallory and Irvine to have climbed down, run out of light and strength, sat down, and died of exposure. So I was looking up the mountain to see what route I might have chosen to come down." Politz also quickly realized that looking uphill was impractical; the slope was too steep and stair-stepped to be able to see much; it was better to be looking downslope. He climbed high, partway into the Yellow Band, to get a better downhill view. "I was also trying to pick a line where the Chinese climber, Wang, might reasonably have 'gone for a stroll' for ten or twenty minutes. I thought I'd read that he was a geologist and I figured the Yellow Band was the most geologically interesting part of the surrounding terrain, so that's where I went."

Anker took the opposite extreme and ranged far down the slope, quite near the point where the "terrace" ended in the long drop to the central Rongbuk Glacier. "I couldn't figure out what Conrad's logic was," Politz said later. "It seemed to me that anything that had fallen that far would have just kept on going."

Norton was roughly midway between them: "I had looked at the face of the Yellow Band and just picked an area down on the terrace where I thought a falling body that had picked up a good bit of speed might come to rest. It had always been assumed Irvine had fallen from the point where the ice ax had been found in 1933, so I traced a line down from there and started looking, like I had with the piton hammer, for anything that didn't belong there."

Only a half hour into the search, Richards, Anker, and Norton stumbled into a virtual graveyard of mangled, frozen bodies. "We found ourselves in a kind of collection zone for fallen climbers," Richards recalls. "We'd radio Jochen down in Base Camp and describe what we'd found, and he would immediately know who it was and when they'd died. It was pretty amazing how Jochen had all this information filed away. He could just about tell you what kind of socks that person would have been wearing on that day. I wasn't eager to get close to these bodies; besides, once I saw colorful Gore-Tex or plastic boots I knew it was neither Mallory nor Irvine. Death is like a fog that looms in the air over the North Face of Everest; it hit me really hard. Seeing those first few bodies was eerie, grim, and humbling."

In all, they found the bodies of a half dozen climbers, all relatively contemporary. The bodies troubled Dave Hahn: "I had chosen to believe that most of the fatalities on Everest had come about as exhausted climbers simply sat down to die. I was convinced that falls were rare. It was clear I had miscalculated."

They shook Jake Norton too. "Just seeing these twisted, broken bodies was a pretty stark reminder of our own mortality. I knew that in just a few days, we'd be up on that Northeast Ridge walking along the same route these climbers had fallen from. It was obvious from the contorted condition of their bodies that these climbers had suffered long and terrible falls."

Aware that other expeditions would be listening in to their radio transmissions and concerned about protecting anything they found from the curious, the search team had agreed on a series of code words if they found something from the 1924 expedition. "A boulder would mean either Mallory or Irvine," explains Richards, "and a gorak on a boulder meant a camera. But the truth is that, in the heat of the search, most of us forgot all about that."

Like Hahn, Andy Politz had stopped paying attention to his radio and had stuffed it into a chest pocket in his down suit. "The airways were full of cell phone calls, voice-mail messages, answering machine recordings, and other babble," he recalls, "so I just turned the radio way down and kept searching. I vaguely heard Conrad saying something about Snickers and paid no attention. Then I heard 'Mandatory group meeting!' and started looking around. Farther down the face, I could see the other guys already converging on Conrad."

Down at Base Camp, his eye glued to a telescope, Jochen Hemmleb could see them too. "When I saw Andy climbing down hundreds of feet from his high point," Hemmleb remembers, "I knew he wasn't climbing down just for tea and Snickers. No one at that altitude would climb down so far for that; it was too much effort. Something was up."

Something was indeed up.

> > >

Conrad Anker had been going on intuition, and his intuition had told him to look low. He had climbed down to the lower edge of the terrace, the point where it dropped away some 6600 feet (2000 m) to the main Rongbuk Glacier, and had started zigzagging back up the slope when he saw "a patch of white that was whiter than the rock around it and whiter than the snow." Climbing toward it, he realized the patch of white was another body. But this one was different: " . . . this wasn't a body from recent times; it was something that had been there for quite awhile."

Norton was the first to reach Anker. "I'm afraid I wasn't very eloquent," he recalls. "I just sat down on a rock next to Conrad, looked at this perfect alabaster body, and said to myself, 'Holy shit!' I had harbored no hope that we'd find anything this first day. We just expected to do a reconnaissance of the area. It was just amazing."

As Dave Hahn approached the site and saw the body, he recalls: "There was absolutely no question in my mind that we were looking at a man who had been clinging to the mountain for seventy-five years. The clothing was blasted from most of his body, and his skin was bleached white. I felt like I was viewing a Greek or Roman marble statue."

There was no exultation when the climbers all reached the site, no "high fives" signaling that, only an hour and a half into a search of a vast section of the North Face of Mount Everest, they had found their man. Instead, the five modern climbers stood or kneeled around the ancient body, speechless.

The body itself did the speaking. For here was a body unlike the others crumpled in crannies elsewhere on the terrace. This body was lying fully extended, facedown and pointing uphill, frozen in a position of self-arrest, as if the fall had happened only moments earlier. The head and upper torso were frozen into the rubble that had gathered around them over the decades, but the arms, powerfully muscular still, extended above the head to strong hands that gripped the mountainside, flexed fingertips dug deep into the frozen gravel. The legs were extended downhill. One was broken and the other had been gently crossed over it for protection. Here too, the musculature was still pronounced and powerful. The entire body had about it the strength and grace of a dancer. This body, this man, had once been a splendid specimen of humankind.

"We weren't just looking at a body," Hahn explains, "we were looking at an era, one we'd only known through books. The natural-fiber clothes, the fur-lined leather helmet, the kind of rope that was around him were all so eloquent. As we stood there, this mute but strangely peaceful body was telling us answers to questions that everyone had wondered about for three-quarters of a century: the fact that a rope had been involved; the fact that the hands and forearms were much darker than the rest of the body; the nature and extent of the broken leg and what wasn't broken, and what that said about this person's last moments; the fact that there was no oxygen apparatus."

The hobnail boot, of course, was the giveaway. No Westerner was permitted on the Tibet side of Everest from 1949 until 1979; Tibet, the "Forbidden Kingdom," was forbidden to outsiders. No one had died at this altitude on Everest between 1924 and 1938, and hobnailed boots had given way to crampons and more advanced boot construction by World War II. The body had to be Andrew Comyn Irvine. Jake Norton went so far as to begin scratching out a memorial stone with the words, "Andrew Irvine: 1902–1924."

⊱   ⊱   ⊱

"This isn't him," Andy Politz said to the rest of the climbers when he arrived at the spot where the others waited.

The rest of the team looked at Politz as if he were daft.

"Oh, I think so," Anker said.

"I don't know what made me say it," Politz now says. "Here was this very old body, perfectly preserved, with very old clothing and the hobnailed boots. I knew it had to be Irvine; Irvine was who we were looking for, and that's who it had to be."

But it wasn't.

Tap Richards, who had training in archeology, and Jake Norton began gently separating the ragged layers of clothing that were left around the protected edges of the body: several layers of cotton and silk underwear, a flannel shirt, woolen pullover and trousers, a canvaslike outer garment. Near the nape of the neck, Norton turned over a piece of shirt collar and revealed a fragment of laundry label: *G. Mallory.*

The climbers looked at each other dumbly for a moment, and finally someone said out loud what everyone else was thinking: "Why would Irvine be wearing Mallory's shirt?" Then they found another name tag: *G. Leigh Ma[llory]*. Then a third.

"Maybe it was the altitude and the fact that we'd all put aside our oxygen gear, but it took a while for reality to sink in," says Hahn. "Then it finally hit us: we had not found Andrew Irvine. We had not rediscovered Wang Hongbao's 'English dead.' We were in the presence of George Mallory himself . . . the man whose boldness and drive we'd grown up in awe of."

"Now I realized why I had said it wasn't Irvine," Politz explained later. "It was the position of the body. Somewhere back in my subconscious, my intuition remembered that Wang had found a body that had been in a position where his mouth was agape and his cheek was exposed to the goraks. But this body was facedown. The head was almost entirely covered, and it had not been moved. What's more, it was too far from the 1975 Chinese Camp VI to have ever been found on a short walk. I just sat down. My knees literally got weak. My jaw dropped. Next to me, Dave was saying, 'Oh my God, it's George. Oh my God.'"

It had been an article of faith that if anyone had fallen, it would have been the inexperienced Andrew Irvine. "Throughout the seventy-five years since they disappeared," explains Jake Norton, "it had been understood that George Mallory was infallible, he didn't fall, he couldn't fall. It was a shock to discover that he was fallible, he did fall. We couldn't quite get used to the idea."

Meanwhile, however, time was passing. The climbers had a responsibility to document as professionally as possible what they had found, search for artifacts, provide Mallory a proper burial, and perform a Church of England committal service provided by the Anglican Bishop of Bristol, England. After that, they still had a two- to three-hour descent to Camp V to negotiate safely. "It would have been nice to have been able to leave the work for another day," says Hahn, "but on Everest, there are no guaranteed second chances; the monsoon could start tomorrow."

There was another issue as well: "We knew we were going to have to disturb him to do our job," Hahn explains, "and we only wanted to disturb him once. Then we wanted to leave him in peace. We knew if we did not do a thorough search for the camera and other artifacts, people would keep coming back and disturbing him again."

The first thing the climbers had done when they discovered the body—before they touched it, before they discovered who it was—was to document photographically both the site and the body. Then they discussed what to do next. "It came down to trying to decide what Mallory himself would have wanted," explains Politz. "In the end, Dave put it best: 'If we can find some evidence of what he accomplished, especially whether he and Irvine had made it to the summit, I think he'd want the world to know.'" As they stood around this man, this icon of Everest itself, the others agreed, and it was time to go to work.

Their main objective, of course, was to find the famous camera, the collapsible Kodak Vest Pocket camera that Howard Somervell had lent Mallory for the summit attempt—the mechanism that would answer, it was hoped, the question of whether Mount Everest had been summited in 1924, more than a quarter century before Edmund Hillary and Tenzing Norgay did it by another route in 1953. In the cold, dry air of the mountain, Kodak officials had said, there was every reason to believe the film, if intact, would still be able to be developed.

The camera was not beside George Mallory's body and it seemed reasonable to assume that, if he had it, it would be in a pocket or around his neck—neither of which were immediately accessible, as Mallory was effectively locked in the icy embrace of the North Face.

The task before them was formidable. "It was immediately apparent," Hahn says, "that this was going to be neither simple, easy, or quick." Politz elaborates, "If you took a one-pound ice ax and started chopping concrete with it, you'd get the same effect as what it was like to try to chip away at the frozen gravel and rock that encased roughly half of George Mallory on that slope," Politz explains. "It was just brutally hard work."

It was also dangerous. The ground was uneven and very steeply sloped and, says Hahn, "a single misstep could easily send you down the slope and over the edge. When you got up off your knees, you wanted to be very sure where your feet were going to be. To keep things interesting, every once in a while a rock would go whizzing past our heads."

Progress was slow and, since the climbers had taken off their oxygen sets in order to work, exhausting. The advantage of this pace was that it gave them plenty of time to study Mallory carefully. The tibia and fibula of his right leg were broken above the top of his boot, and his right elbow was either broken or dislocated. There were a number of still-visible cuts, abrasions, and bruises along his right side as well, and the climbing rope in which he was tangled had compressed his rib cage and tugged at his skin. The rope had been passed twice around his waist and the frayed trailing ends were wrapped around his leg and upper body. Though the body was remarkably intact, Everest's goraks had pecked at it and damaged one leg, his buttocks, and the abdominal cavity.

As they worked on the ice, the climbers could not get used to how little Mallory had been wearing during his attempt to reach the highest point on earth. "We're standing there in down suits so thick that I couldn't even see the climbing harness around my waist," Hahn explains. "In our packs we had food, water, electronic gear, and extra mittens, and here was this man before us who was wearing what maybe added up to the equivalent of two layers of fleece. Hell, I walk out on the street in Seattle with more clothing than he had on at 28,000 feet on Everest! Clearly they were tough climbers, but there wasn't any room for anything to go wrong for these guys, no margin at all."

After an hour of chipping at the ice and rock with their axes, the climbers, working in shifts in the thin air, first were able to free one jacket pocket, in which they found an altimeter, good to 30,000 feet; its crystal was broken and the hands were missing. Soon afterward, they removed enough of the frozen gravel around Mallory's torso to be able to free his right shoulder. Jake Norton, doing the delicate excavating with a penknife, reached underneath and discovered that Mallory had a pouch hanging from his neck. Norton looked up at the other climbers: "There's something hard and metallic in here." Carefully, he cut open the bottom of the pouch with his knife: "I just knew it was the camera."

In fact, it was a tin of "Brands & Company Savoury Meat Lozenges" (a kind of bouillon cube). Next, a pair of nail scissors in a leather case emerged. Then, most astonishing of all, a letter in an envelope, perfectly preserved, the ink script crisp and clear, not the slightest bit faded or smudged, as if it had just been written.

Other items emerged from a pouch on Mallory's right side and from various pockets: a beautiful handkerchief with a burgundy, blue, and green foulard pattern, monogrammed *G.L.M.*, carefully wrapped around another group of letters; a second monogrammed handkerchief in a red, blue, and yellow pattern; a white handkerchief wrapped around a tube of petroleum jelly; a single fingerless glove; a pocket knife with an antler handle; an undamaged box of matches, still useable; an assortment of boot laces and straps; adjustable webbing straps attached to a metal spring clip (to hold an oxygen mask to the flying helmet); a note from fellow expedition member Geoffrey Bruce; scraps of paper with gear checklists penciled in; and, deep in one pocket, a pair of sun goggles, intact. One by one, the artifacts, including samples of each layer of clothing, were placed in resealable plastic bags and put in Andy Politz's pack.

The climbers barely spoke to each other. "There was this intense feeling of reverence," Politz remembers. "At one point, I thought about how proud I was of my partners. We were walking a very fine line, trying to do a responsible job archeologically while still treating the body itself with the dignity it deserved. This was one of our great heroes, after all, and in an odd sense we felt we were working with Mallory the person, not Mallory the body. It was humbling."

"At one point, I just stood back," says Tap Richards, "and thought: here we are at 27,000 feet on the north side of Everest and no one else in the world knows anything about this but the five of us. Now we would be able to help George Mallory do something I knew he would have wanted: write a new chapter in the story of his life.

Before the expedition had begun, BBC's Peter Firstbrook reported that he had spoken to the families of both Mallory and Irvine and received their support for the search and for photographing what was found. In addition, he said, the families had asked that the climbers take a DNA sample of whomever they found. Accordingly, the last thing the search team did was take a small skin sample from Mallory's forearm for the DNA analysis.

Then they began the arduous process of burying a legend, of drawing a protective cloak of stone over George Leigh Mallory.

"And that," Politz recalls, "turned out to be quite a project. The idea was to gather rocks and cover the body with them, but rocks turned out to be hard to come by. Any loose rocks had obviously tended to avalanche down the slope and over the edge, and everything else was frozen solid. So we were ranging all over the slope to find, pry up, and haul rocks. Finally we got enough to be sure that Mallory wouldn't be bothered by the birds ever again."

The burial took nearly forty-five minutes. Then Andy Politz read the committal ceremony, and afterward the climbers gathered their gear. "It seems an odd thing to say," said Norton later, "but I don't think any of us wanted to leave him. We were very comfortable being with 'George.' We wanted to spend more time with him; he was so impressive to be with, even in death."

Finally, they shrugged on their backpacks and, at about 3:00 P.M., began working their way east across the terrace toward the North Ridge. "And as we were walking away," Politz recalls, "I was thinking to myself, 'Right; if George isn't happy with that ceremony, guess who's the first one who's going to get it?'" The climbers were both physically and emotionally spent, a dangerous combination on a mountain where most accidents happen on the descent. "I was picking a route across this slope," Politz continues, "and every step of the way I was conscious that I have two kids and a wife back at home, and every step matters here. Plus I've got Mallory's stuff in my pack!"

By 5:30 P.M., all five climbers had reached the relative safety of Camp V. "The last twenty minutes to the camp were rugged," Norton remembers. "I was beat anyway, and we were battling 50-mile-per-hour winds that tried to knock us over with every step. I finally crawled into the tent that Conrad, Tap, and I were sharing, and we just sat there for awhile, exhausted, talking about what had happened. Then Tap and I tried to go to sleep, but it was almost impossible; our minds were whirring."

In the other tent, Dave Hahn and Andy Politz radioed Base Camp to say that they had arrived and were fine. Then, choosing words carefully so that they would have meaning only for the expedition members, Hahn said, "Jochen, you will be a happy man now."

The next morning, May 2, they descended from Camp V, continued past Camp IV on the North Col, and walked into ABC at about 3:00 P.M. "Eric came out to greet us and we all just smiled and said, 'You're not going to believe this,'" Norton remembers. They walked straight to the expedition's big "Weatherport" tent, zipped the tent flaps closed, and began pulling artifacts out to show Simonson.

"He didn't know whether we'd found a body, a camera, or what," says Norton, "so the first thing we gave him was the envelope and letter addressed to 'Mr. George Leigh Mallory,' and he just looked up and smiled a very big smile."

"MALLORY & IRVINE— THE PUZZLES"

FROM
Detectives on Everest
BY JOCHEN HEMMLEB AND ERIC R. SIMONSON

THE DISCOVERY OF GEORGE MALLORY'S BODY BY CONRAD ANKER in 1999, 75 years after Mallory and Sandy Irvine had vanished high on Everest in 1924, represented the first concrete information that could be applied to the mystery of the pair's disappearance since the discovery of the climbers' ice ax in 1933. But Eric Simonson, who had organized the 1999 Mallory & Irvine Research Expedition, and some members of his team—German historian Jochen Hemmleb, climbers Dave Hahn, Andy Politz, Tap Richards, and Jake Norton—all believed there might be even more clues frozen into the Tibetan flank of Everest.

Simonson resolved to return to Everest to make a further search. The team members hoped to find a camera that Mallory and Irvine might have carried, or even the body of Irvine himself. A camera might contain film— which Kodak said possibly could be developed despite three-quarters of a century in the open—and that film might reveal if the climbers had reached the summit before they perished. The body of Irvine was an even more tantalizing focal point for the search, for it had reportedly been seen as recently as 1975. In that year, a Chinese climber named Wang Hongbao had reported seeing a body, described as "English dead," near the site of the Chinese Camp VI just below 27,000 feet. Hemmleb had determined that the report was credible.

Despite the fact that team members had thoroughly searched the area in 1999 looking for signs of Mallory and Irvine, Simonson believed there was "unfinished business" on the mountain, and sufficient chance for more discoveries to justify a second expedition. In the spring of 2001, many of the original team members and two new ones—Brent Okita and John Race— returned to the flanks of Everest above the North Col to once again look for clues that might shed light on what had happened so long ago.

Conditions in 2001, however, were not as favorable as they had been in 1999. The slopes that had been relatively dry and free of snow the year of the first search were now covered in the usual blanket of deep snow. Any dramatic find was to elude the team, although they made a number of smaller discoveries which significantly advanced the knowledge not just of Mallory and Irvine's fate, but also of the British attempts during the 1930s, and even the controversial Chinese claim of a summit in the 1960s.

The years since the 1999 search had also given Hemmleb and Simonson a perspective from which to speculate about what might have happened to Mallory and Irvine on that June day in 1924. The fruits of their research and deductive reasoning is offered in Hemmleb and Simonson's latest book, *Detectives on Everest*, which draws on all of their findings high on the Tibetan side of Everest from their two Everest expeditions. The following excerpt deals with the puzzle pieces that make up the disappearance of Mallory and Irvine. In it, the conjecture picks up with the authors mirroring the thoughts of Noel Odell, the 1924 team member who was the last man to see Mallory and Irvine alive, who wonders of "the mystery of my friends." The section is on pages 117–125, *Detectives on Everest*.

Over the days and weeks after June 8, 1924, the snow and wind erased Mallory and Irvine's final steps on the Northeast Ridge—and with them a simple answer to Noel Odell's "mystery of my friends." Had they reached the summit? How did they die?

In the decades after, the mountain revealed pieces of the various puzzles surrounding Mallory and Irvine's last climb. But the picture emerging from the pieces remains incomplete, because the pieces fit in only some parts—in others, they do not fit.

Puzzle #1: When did Mallory and Irvine leave Camp VI? In his last note to Captain John Noel, Mallory stated the intent to "start early to-morrow." But what could "early" have meant? Although a predawn start had certainly been in their minds, none of the climbers from the early expeditions had managed to leave Camp VI earlier than 5:40 A.M. With one exception (in 1938), none of these climbers used oxygen, which made them feel even more strongly the debilitating effects of cold and altitude.

The Pieces: When Odell arrived at Camp VI, he saw oxygen cylinders as well as parts of the oxygen apparatus and of the pack frames strewn around the site. Odell also found magnesium flares inside the tent, and the 1933 expedition discovered a candle lantern and electric flashlight at the site.

From these clues, researchers reconstructed a straightforward scenario. Mallory and Irvine were delayed by a necessary repair of the oxygen sets—for so long that they departed when it was already daylight and left behind all their light sources.

Alternatively, Mallory and Irvine could have used oxygen for sleeping, as Finch had done in 1922. For this, they likely would have unscrewed the bottles and regulators from the bulky pack frames to save space in the tiny tent. As far as the lighting equipment is concerned, it is by no means certain that the items found at Camp VI were all they had. They could have used some light sources that morning and stashed them later en route.

As of 2001, the picture emerging from the puzzle hints at a start *no sooner* than sunrise, which was around 5:00 A.M. on June 8, 1924. But because the morning was clear and not unduly cold, and with the aid of oxygen, a start *no later* than sunrise seems equally possible.

Puzzle #2: What camera or cameras did Mallory and Irvine carry? When looking for ways to solve the mystery of Mallory and Irvine's summit climb, attention has focused mainly on any camera they had carried and the pictures it might possibly still contain. Many accounts speak of only one camera—in fact, there might have been more.

The Pieces: Descendants of Howard Somervell believed that he lent Mallory his camera—a Vest Pocket Kodak (VPK)—for the summit bid. Mallory had forgotten his own in one of the lower camps, where it was found later and returned to his son. Irvine, the more prolific photographer of the two, possessed his own still camera. His diary entry of June 4, 1924, revealed he had also borrowed a small movie camera from John Noel before the climb.

The logbook at the 1924 expedition's Camp IV on the North Col recorded that "Noel's ciné camera" was taken down to Camp III on June 10. It is unclear whether this referred to the camera borrowed by Irvine or one possibly left behind by Noel himself: He had visited the North Col with four porters three days earlier.

No camera was found with Mallory's body when it was discovered in 1999. If he had brought Somervell's camera along, perhaps it was lost in the fatal fall or he had handed it over to Irvine at some stage during the climb. Theoretically, all of this could leave a maximum of three cameras with Irvine (his own, Somervell's Kodak, and Noel's movie camera)—waiting to be recovered.

Puzzle #3: How much oxygen did Mallory and Irvine use? Besides any cameras, there is another item Mallory and Irvine carried that could equally provide clues about the progress they made and the altitude they reached on summit day—their oxygen sets. Each oxygen bottle had a known duration, determined by its capacity and the flow rate at which the apparatus was set. Therefore an oxygen bottle found along a climber's route can yield the time the climber had taken between the point where he started using the bottle and the place where he discarded it when it was empty. This is assuming the climber had used oxygen continuously and at a constant flow rate.

The Pieces: From the last documented conversation between Mallory and Edward Norton, Mallory had originally planned for a full-scale attempt with oxygen. By using most of his porter capacity to carry oxygen and using only little of the supply himself up to Camp VI, he tried to save as many oxygen bottles as possible for the summit day.

A list of provisions for the summit attempt, found with Mallory's body in 1999, noted six spare cylinders in the porters' load. In addition, the last picture of Mallory and Irvine setting out from the North Col shows Irvine carrying two bottles himself, and Mallory at least one.

According to Mallory's last note to Odell, he had used only three-quarters of a full bottle during the two days of climbing to Camp VI—little oxygen indeed. If Irvine had used the same quantity, this would have left the pair with one or two full bottles plus the six cylinders from the porters' load—seven or eight full cylinders, enough for an attempt with the full supply of three cylinders per climber. To this point, everything tallies with Mallory's original plan.

But their low oxygen consumption and good going to Camp VI could certainly have given rise to a different idea: Perhaps they could attempt the summit with less oxygen: "probably . . . two cylinders," as Mallory wrote.

The decision Mallory and Irvine faced that evening was an important one. Would the advantage of more oxygen from a third cylinder outweigh the "bloody load" of the oxygen sets, which was a notable 20 pounds (9 kg) already with two cylinders?

At this point we know how much oxygen Mallory and Irvine *probably* took (two cylinders each) and how much they *could have* taken (three cylinders each).

One of Mallory and Irvine's oxygen bottles was found close to the first step in 1991, from where our search team recovered it eight years later. It was most likely the first bottle one of them had used. Given the bottle's known capacity and the possible flow rates, it indicated that the climber had taken between four and five and a half hours to reach this point from Camp VI. Incidentally, having used one bottle over this distance suggests he (and presumably his partner) had made good progress, which in turn suggests the oxygen sets had been functioning.

The remaining bottles they had carried, as well as the apparatus and pack frames, are still missing. If these are found farther along the route, they could help in reconstructing Mallory and Irvine's progress above this point and eventually determine the pair's chances to have reached the summit.

Puzzle #4: Which route did Mallory and Irvine choose? Mallory left this question unresolved when he instructed cinematographer John Noel "to start looking out for us *either* crossing the rock band under the pyramid *or* going up skyline at 8 [o'clock]" (italics added). On the face of it, "going up skyline" means just that, climbing along the crest of the Northeast Ridge above Camp VI, which is nowadays reached some 400 yards (360 meters) before the First Step. By also mentioning "crossing the rock band under the pyramid," Mallory seemed to indicate that he had not totally ruled out Norton's route as an alternative to the ridge—so he could not say whether the next morning he and Irvine would be moving across the Yellow Band or emerging atop the ridge crest. Expecting an early start and using oxygen, it was not unreasonable for Mallory to assume he could attain either goal from Camp VI by 8:00 A.M.

The Pieces: The oxygen bottle recovered from the Northeast Ridge in 1999 showed that the pair had indeed chosen the crest of the ridge as their line of ascent—at least to the point where they discarded the oxygen bottle, close to the First Step.

To this day, no higher traces of Mallory and Irvine have been found. The oxygen bottle thus marks the *least* altitude the pair (or one of them) had reached, 27,800 feet (8,475 meters). Based on solid evidence alone, we have as yet no knowledge of their route above this point. They could have continued over the First Step and along the ridge or traversed below the step and toward the Great (Norton) Couloir.

Puzzle #5: Where were Mallory and Irvine last seen? At 12:50 P.M. on June 8, 1924, Noel Odell saw Mallory and Irvine for the last time as they were moving along the upper Northeast Ridge. But did he really see them? And if so, where exactly did he see them?

The Pieces: Throughout his life, Odell was adamant that he had seen two moving figures, taking the strongest objection against any suggestions that he had hallucinated or been deceived by an optical illusion. On this, Dave Hahn once commented, "What Odell described—the climb of a significant rock step—must have lasted at least ten or fifteen minutes. By then he would have realized if he'd been tricked somehow."

Unfortunately, Odell was less sure about *where* he saw the two figures. Odell's initial impression, recorded in his diary less than four days after the event, was that Mallory and Irvine were "nearing the base of the final pyramid." In an account for the British *Alpine Journal* in November 1924, he became more precise and placed them at 28,230 feet (8,605 meters), then the accepted figure for the top of the Second Step. In the same account, he termed the location "the last step but one from the base of the final pyramid." It indicated his awareness of another steplike feature above, later known as the Third Step. The First Step entered the debate with Odell's doubts about his initial impression, which he first expressed in Norton's expedition book, *The Fight for Everest*, published in 1925.

The least we can conclude then is that he saw *someone*—Mallory and Irvine—climbing *something* on the upper Northeast Ridge. His reference to a "great rock step" or "prominent rock step" strongly suggests that he saw them on either the First, Second, or Third Step.

There are strong doubts among the climbing community that Mallory and Irvine could have climbed the Second Step (see Puzzle #6), the most prominent and most difficult of the three. The logical place for Odell's sighting would therefore have been the First Step. But if the pair had been going well that morning, as the location of their discarded oxygen bottle suggests, why had they been on the First Step as late as 12:50 P.M.? In this case, a delay of at least two hours would have to be accounted for and explained.

Furthermore, Odell described the climbers moving over a snow crest or slope, then surmounting a short rocky section before emerging on top of the rock step. There is a pronounced snow patch below the First Step, but any route from this point forward either bypasses the true top of the First Step or avoids the step altogether.

So was it the Second Step, after all, where Odell had last seen the pair?

If Mallory and Irvine had been going well, the Second Step would have fit the time frame better than the First. Could they somehow have climbed the crux? Even if they had—perhaps aided by unknown factors such as a higher snow cover or rock features that have been altered by erosion since then—Odell described no belay or the climbers assisting each other, as one would expect on a pitch of such difficulty. Also, the snow patch beneath the crux is comparatively small and, due to its northern exposure, in the shadows for most of the day—not an obvious place to spot two ascending climbers.

What about the Third Step?

It should be pondered heavily why Odell, if he was somehow mistaken, happened to provide a description that matches this particular feature of the Northeast Ridge with almost step-by-step accuracy. At the foot of the Third Step is a snow crest or slope, which is followed by a rocky section sufficiently easy to be climbed within a couple of minutes—and if the Third Step is tackled along the crest, as most parties do nowadays, climbers do pass over the true top of the step.

Andy Politz, who purposely watched the ridge from the vicinity of Odell's viewpoint in 1999, is convinced that Odell meant the Third Step. Politz also noted that from Odell's viewpoint, the three steps are clearly separated, ruling out any confusion—especially if Odell had seen the "whole summit ridge unveiled," as he had maintained throughout his accounts.

Factors that weigh against the Third Step include the time element. To have climbed that far along the ridge by 12:50 P.M., Mallory and Irvine would have to have made a very early start (before sunrise), even if we assume the best possible circumstances for their ascent, such as continuing good weather up high and no routefinding difficulties. Climbing for so long would most likely have put them beyond the duration of two oxygen cylinders per climber. A sighting at the Third Step, if true, therefore has to carry the additional implication that Mallory and Irvine had used a third cylinder each.

Puzzle #6: Could Mallory and Irvine have climbed the Second Step? The Second Step forms the most difficult part of the upper Northeast Ridge. The feature, some 100 feet (30 meters) high, is comprised of steep, brittle rock, the crux being a 16-foot (5-meters) perpendicular slab in the upper part, which is split vertically by three wide cracks. The Chinese expedition of 1975 equipped this pitch with an aluminum ladder.

The Pieces: In 1999, Conrad Anker nearly free-climbed the crux of the Second Step—that is, without using the Chinese ladder, just as Mallory and Irvine would have to have done. He found the corner crack on the left to be the only feasible way, because the rock was too brittle elsewhere. Initially Anker rated the pitch 5.8, but later revised the grading to 5.10—a technical difficulty beyond the standards of Mallory's days. Anker considered it improbable that Mallory and Irvine could have surmounted the obstacle in 1924.

In 1960, however, the first Chinese expedition scaled the Second Step without a ladder by using a shoulder stand on the crux. They showed that climbers less experienced than Mallory *could* overcome the pitch, albeit requiring a total of three hours and many attempts. The Chinese also had the aid of pitons, which the 1924 expedition did not have.

In 1991, Andy Politz checked some of the climbing moves in the corner crack (although he did not free-climb it) and felt it was in the 5.7 to 5.8 range. After repeating some of Mallory's routes in Wales, he was convinced that Mallory had been fully capable of climbing something as difficult as the Second Step crux—especially given the added demands of his routes at the time, such as inadequate protection and loose rock.

All other climbers who surmounted the Second Step had used the Chinese ladder. Their opinions on Mallory and Irvine's chances to have climbed it have to be taken as educated guesses. A majority believes the pair could not have climbed it in 1924; some still think it possible.

It is curious to note that of the few who tried to grade the pitch after look-ing at it, all gave an estimation between Politz's and Anker's. The Catalans in 1985 and Briton Jon Tinker in 1993 thought the crux was around 5.7; Ameri-can Bob Sloezen, who had climbed the Second Step three times, estimated it was around 5.10. Those who gave a lower rating generally thought it pos-sible for Mallory and Irvine to have climbed the step in 1924; those who gave a higher rating all considered it unlikely.

At present, the answer to the question of whether Mallory and Irvine could have climbed the Second Step is a matter of weighing the differing opinions as well as the factors influencing them. A conclusive answer could be found only through the discovery *above* the Second Step of relics from Mallory and Irvine's final climb.

Puzzle #7: How did Mallory and Irvine die? Before the discovery of Mallory's body in 1999, two basic scenarios were considered likely. Either Mallory and Irvine had fallen to their deaths from the point where Irvine's ice ax had been found in 1933, or they had frozen to death in an open bivouac after failing to return to their high camp before dark. Another theory had Mallory and Irvine separating above the Second Step, with Irvine dying in a fall from the ice-ax site and Mallory either falling or freezing to death high on the moun-tain on the descent from the summit.

The Pieces: When Mallory's body was found, it showed unmistakable signs of a fall—a severe head injury over the left eye, a broken right leg, and several cuts and bruises along the body's right side. Mallory was tangled up in a length of broken climbing rope, indicating that he and Irvine had been together at the time of the accident.

Mallory's body lay below, but not necessarily in line with, the ice-ax loca-tion. A fall line from this point (as indicated on the diagrams from 1933), drawn perpendicular to the altitude contours on the aerial photos, runs 40–50 yards to the southwest (right) of Mallory's position, and the configuration of the ter-rain above makes a fall from the gullies leading through the Yellow Band more likely. Because Mallory's injuries were lesser than those of other victims who have fallen from the Northeast Ridge, many believed that his fall must have occurred from lower down, somewhere in or even below the Yellow Band.

Bloodstains on the left front of Mallory's jacket look blotted, and streaks on the left cuff appear as if he had wiped over a bleeding injury with the back of his hand. DNA sequencing of samples from the stains confirmed that the blood is Mallory's. This has led to speculation about whether he might have suffered another accident before the fatal one, or if this is an actual indication that he had briefly survived the fall.

Without finding Irvine's body and knowing its exact location, we cannot say whether he was killed in the fall with Mallory or if he survived the accident only to die later of cold, exhaustion, or injury.

Puzzle #8: Could Mallory and Irvine have reached the summit? Most experts simply believe that their route was too long and too difficult for them to have succeeded—but a true estimation of Mallory and Irvine's chances depends largely on where they were last seen by Odell.

The Pieces: Had Mallory and Irvine been climbing the First Step when last seen, at 12:50 P.M., it would have been too late to reach the summit and return to the site of the fatal accident during the remainder of the day, even if they had found a way around the Second Step.

If Mallory and Irvine were instead seen surmounting the Second Step at 12:50 P.M., they would have done so at a crucial time. Based on the experience of later expeditions, they should have taken about four hours to reach the upper part of the Second Step from below the First Step, where they had discarded their first oxygen bottle. By the time they climbed the Second Step, Mallory and Irvine would thus have been about to finish their second and perhaps last cylinder of oxygen. Without oxygen, it is unlikely they could have covered the remaining distance to the summit *and* back to the accident site before dark, and it seems impossible that they could have survived a night out in the open with only their clothing as protection.

However, if Mallory and Irvine had switched to a third cylinder near the Second Step or been at the Third Step when last seen (which would have been possible only with a third cylinder anyway), they *could have* reached the top—which is still a far cry from saying that they did.

The possibility that Mallory and Irvine reached the summit of Mount Everest before they died remains rooted in both factual basis and idealistic wish. No matter how inconceivable one thinks it might be, the incomplete and conflicting evidence has to allow for the chance that they made it. But the idea is also carried on by the captivating image it holds—two men standing on top of the world, the perfect culmination of a climb that embodied the essence of human endeavor and spirit. Sir Edmund Hillary, who, with Tenzing Norgay, will always remain the first to successfully climb Mount Everest and return, recognized the power and significance of that image. In an interview for the film *The Mystery of Mallory and Irvine* (Arcturus Motion Picture Company/BBC, 1987), Hillary said:

> *Mallory was the one who not only stimulated his companions, but he stimulated the whole world into an interest in the ascent of Mount Everest. . . . It would have been a very fitting reward for all his efforts if on that final day he had set foot on the summit of the mountain.*

Perhaps one day the mountain will reveal additional pieces of the puzzles to complete the picture of Mallory and Irvine's final day. Until then, nobody will know for certain what happened on June 8, 1924.

"EMOTIONAL RESCUE"

BY DAVE HAHN

AT THE CONCLUSION OF THE 2001 EVEREST EXPEDITION TO SEARCH for further clues to the fate of George Mallory and Sandy Irvine on the northern flanks of Everest, the focus turned to mountaineering. Four of the team members were poised high on the mountain after long weeks of searching for artifacts. Tap Richards, Andy Politz, and Dave Hahn, joined by Jason Tanguay, who had been a guide for the climbing and trekking program affiliated with the expedition, were at Camp VI, in position to make a summit attempt in the continuing stable weather. While Politz intended to continue searching for Irvine and the camera that he and Mallory were believed to have had with them in 1924, Hahn, Richards, and Tanguay planned, with Sherpa Phu Dorje and Phu Nuru, to make a summit bid. Hahn already had summitted Everest three times, but Richards and Tanguay still sought their first successful trip to the top. With them were Sherpa climbers Phu Nuru and Fu Dorji. After weeks of sleuthing high on Everest, the climbers were acclimated and strong.

Their well-laid plans would go awry. May 23, 2001, had seen heavy traffic on the upper slopes of the Northeast Ridge from both guided parties and private expeditions. On that day alone, a total of eighty-nine people reached the summit of Everest by all routes, not just a record but a truly staggering number—and irrefutable evidence of the benign conditions on the peak that day. But at least two parties of climbers, including a Siberian expedition and a guide and client for a commercial operation, had run into trouble high on the mountain. They were forced to spend the night of May 23 above 28,000 feet. A bivouac that high on Everest is an often fatal enterprise.

What transpired on the following day is unlike anything else in Everest history. Hahn, Politz, Richards, and Tanguay became heroes, giving up an opportunity for the summit while coming to the aid of five stricken climbers who otherwise almost certainly would have died. Their assistance, made at tremendous risk to themselves, earned them the American Alpine Club Sowle's Award for "unselfish devotion to imperiled climbers." The award also was presented to Lobsang and Phurba, Sherpa climbers working with the stricken guide.

The events of that day are described in *Detectives on Everest*. Authors Eric Simonson and Jochen Hemmleb were at Base Camp, where expedition leader Simonson directed and orchestrated the movement of people and equipment that facilitated the rescue. A first-hand report of that incredible day high on the Northeast Ridge follows below. The piece comes from Dave Hahn, expedition member and the lead climber on that eventful day, and one of the most articulate mountaineering writers of modern times.

I first met Dave Hahn in 1998, when he agreed to send dispatches to MountainZone.com from the Northeast Ridge as he lead a guided climb of Everest for Eric Simonson's guide service, IMG. Being a jaded editor, I had low expectations from this unknown climber and presumed MountainZone.com would receive dutiful but perfunctory reports of the climbing action. Instead, over the satellite email set-up came beautifully written dispatches, funny observations, and perceptive commentary on the human condition at 8000 meters. The next year, Hahn continued to inspire people around the world with his reports to MountainZone.com from the 1999 Mallory & Irvine Research Expedition, after which he became a regular columnist for the site.

Hahn's is an important new voice in high-altitude climbing, direct from the realities of the death zone: authentic, honest, totally without affect or posturing. Hahn's writings were called "eloquent" by *The New York Times* and "important" by the *Manchester Guardian*. The story below appeared on MountainZone.com as one of Dave Hahn's regular columns.

've said it a thousand times: emotions have no place above 8000 meters. And I've mostly lived true to my words. Rarely have I indulged in fear or elation or thoughts of love, envy, greed, hatred, or that other stuff up on high mountains. In such places, I've always contended that us clumsy, average folks need to keep our minds firmly focused on where our feet are hitting the rock and snow. So what was that fogging up my sunglasses at the Third Step of Everest's North Ridge last May?

Tears at 8700 meters? Clearly a violation of Rule #1. Perhaps there was some good excuse for them when Eric Simonson, down at Base Camp, had radioed up a moment before asking finally if there wasn't some way we could still carry on to the summit, and I'd replied throatily that there wasn't a chance that we'd go on. Let's just hope the tears weren't simply for a missed summit.

People already think I'm an idiot for having been on Everest's top three times; nobody would believe I had a compelling reason to be there a fourth. And though I looked around through my tears at my partners and remembered that Tap Richards and Jason Tanguay and Phu Dorje had not yet been to the top of the "Big E" despite being strong and ready at 7 A.M. on a nice day to easily go the last hour. Well, I wasn't crying for them. They were young, they'd be there some day if they continued to want it bad enough.

Sure, I was conscious that after months of hard work on the 2001 Mallory & Irvine Research Expedition we were going to finally come up empty. No camera from 1924, no more knowledge of where Andrew "Sandy" Irvine had finished up, no answer to the great mystery of how high up George and Sandy had gotten, and lastly, no summit after our team had fixed nearly every inch of the fixed rope for the route. But none of that made me weepy.

It was Andy Lapkass and Jaime Vinals sitting there on the rocks with a few empty oxygen bottles and some shreds of a space blanket. Two nice guys who'd spent the night out after making the top the previous day. Just sitting up where jets fly and people die and where I've now cried.

Phu Dorje summed things up nicely when he'd given up his oxygen bottles for the cause and was starting down, shaking his head in disbelief. "Bad luck!" he kept saying to me, "Bad luck!" while pointing back at the summit pyramid, painfully up close and personal.

Despite the succinctness and truthful nature of his assessment, I still needed to check something with Tap and Jason. We'd just tried, after an hour or so of poking and prodding and feeding and administering drugs and O's to combat cerebral edema, to get Jaime and Andy on their feet. The results were deeply discouraging and were most likely the cause of my fogged glasses. But I needed to know how Tap and Jason saw things since such decisive moments could potentially come back to haunt us all.

"You guys realize that there is absolutely no way we can do what Eric is suggesting, don't you?" Their answers came back through tight throats that made me aware that they had some tears of their own.

No. Not a chance of doing what we'd already been able to do before sunrise a few hours earlier when we'd come across three Russians at the Mushroom Rock. There, despite the fact that we'd found them lying about, feebly kicking their feet, out of oxygen, inappropriately dressed and speaking in an unfamiliar tongue about their predicament at 28,300 feet, we'd been able to revive them somewhat and send them down on their own. It hadn't been easy.

Phu Nuru had surrendered his own oxygen and any hopes of the summit then. We'd given out Decadron pills as if they were candy at a Halloween doorstep. We'd parted with a fair amount of our precious food and water. We'd wrestled to get the Russians up and dressed against the cold. But sure enough, as Eric had suggested might be possible then, they'd come around and were once again taking care of themselves while we were going higher. That was important since, in our communications regarding the Russians, we'd become fully aware that both Andy and Jaime had spent the night out even higher. We didn't know if they were alive or dead when we left the Russians.

It probably sounds terrible to say that we were prepared for them to be dead, in which case our response would have been to go on to the summit. Get your head around it if you can, because we would have. And if they weren't so bad off, we'd have helped them to their feet, patted them on their backs as they proceeded down, and we'd have still pressed on for the top. After all, they had their expedition goals, we had ours. The two were separate.

But when Tap and Jason and I were getting all misty eyed, it had become apparent that we were into something far worse. The summit no longer existed. In fact, even the chance of getting these two climbers down alive no longer existed. We had each been horrified to watch them trying to stand and walk. Without those abilities, it was simply "game over" for these two.

In our heads swam visions of the vertical Second Step, the ridiculous traverse back to the Mushroom Rock, the even more ridiculous traverse back to the First Step, the vertical descent of that feature, the treacherous hop down the rocks and gullies of the Yellow Band. And what would it get you if you could somehow carry somebody over all of that? Well, then you'd have a critically ill person at 27,000 feet instead of 28,500 feet. Big deal.

Watching Jaime and Andy collapse back to the rock, Tap and Jason and I knew what nobody watching through a telescope from below could know, not only were these men going to die, but they were going to do it with us as companions. And I think that was what made us emotional. To make matters worse, to really choke us up, they were far from dead at the moment, in fact they were very much alive.

Andy Lapkass was, despite a night fighting to keep his client warm and frostbite free, despite the impaired vision and slurred words caused by the swelling of his brain in his skull, still the kind of guy you look up to for his generosity and strength and experience. Jaime was so alive that it scared us; utterly cheerful and seemingly unconcerned about his predicament.

But both were pitifully unable to walk. Without choices, we simply gave them a little more of everything and kept trying to get them to rally. After a time, Tap and Jason had Andy moving. But it took both of them to support him and keep his feet going in the right directions. That left me and Jaime and my emotions.

I decided then that I'd been wrong about emotions in the "death zone." Everybody probably should have a set. The fact that Jaime was devoid of them struck me as just plain wrong and I set about changing that.

"Jaime, you have a family, don't you?" He cheerfully replied, "Oh yes, my wife is pregnant." My big brainstorm had backfired. I was choking up again and Jaime was merely happy to have his attention diverted to warm, fuzzy thoughts from the cold hell of the Third Step.

"You want to see them again, don't you?" "Oh yes!" So I started trying to shock him with "Then you better start walking. You HAVE to survive this." But I just got back a cheerful, "Oh, yes."

Even so, we began making slow progress back toward the Second Step. Jaime was only able to go a few steps at a time and then I'd feel him tapping me on the pack to stop and sit down. We walked about two feet apart since I had his oxygen bottle in my pack and just the rubber hose connecting us. The terrain between the Second and Third Steps of Everest's North Ridge is by far the easiest ground of that particular climb. Even so, when we'd get walking along, I half expected to just hear a little "pop" of that rubber hose separating as Jaime tumbled off the Kangshung Face a few feet to our right.

In fact, at one point I considered momentarily that Jaime might step off that face on purpose to save me from an unworkable future. But what emotion immediately chased that thought? That was guilt, for sure. I wanted Jaime to live, but I still just didn't have a clue as to how he would live with just my help and 20 feet of progress between protracted sit-down rests. I started telling him that he needed to get it together before the Second Step or he'd die. This information was still getting tangled up in Jaime's struggle to deal with a poorly fitting oxygen mask and glasses that wouldn't stay clear and in place. He was still too happy to be alive to truly think of death.

We'd fallen so far behind Tap and Jason and Andy that I'd lost track of them completely. My world was down to Jaime and my bad thoughts. The Second Step was filling my head with feelings of inadequacy. That's what you get up that way when you legalize emotions.

I've known people who would have been perfectly able, in the same circumstance, to have left Jaime at the top of the Step, rappelled down and found a half-rotten length of rope, cut it out from the climbing route, climbed back up the Step with it, anchored it, lowered Jaime down and gone about their rescue business. But I knew I didn't have all that in me then and there.

My friends and acquaintances down below must have known it too because they started suggesting over the radio that I was going to have to consider leaving Jaime and saving my own bacon. Finally, running out of options and nearing the top of the Step, I heard Eric winding up for a direct order via the radio. I pulled it from the muffling effect of my down suit and held it out a few inches from Jaime's face. Eric didn't sugarcoat it, "Dave, if Jaime can't do any better than he's doing now, you'll have to leave him up there." I watched Jaime's eyes get pretty wide then as emotion flooded back into him. Anger. That is what he later told me he felt. It was actually the first part of that morning that he was able to fully recall afterward. Not a moment too soon, since we'd arrived at the Step. And then it was all Jaime.

He found some deep and as yet untapped source of strength and determination, clipped in, and rappelled the Second Step without oxygen. Not bad for a dead man, I thought as I accompanied him. Upon reaching the lower rappel of the Step, I preceded Jaime and was thus just below him when he neared the bottom of it all and got hung up in ropes just 6 or 8 feet above me. I was mighty tired then and reaching up to scratch my head kind of uselessly when Phurba Sherpa jumped in like Superman.

Phurba, a member of Jaime's team who had summited the day before and then gone all the way down to Camp V at 25,700 feet had now returned with a vengeance. He jumped up past me, placed his own goggles and oxygen mask and oxygen on Jaime and disentangled him from the ropes in about two minutes flat.

"Now why didn't I do that?" I wondered. "Oh yeah, because I'm getting wasted." But I rallied some, out of shame (a timely emotion) and with Phurba and a steadily stronger Jaime, we got our man back across the first ridiculous traverses to the Mushroom Rock. And there was Andy Politz from our own expedition, who'd come up to swing it all in our favor.

Andy, my tentmate at high camp, had decided not to go for the summit that day. Instead, he wanted one last day of searching for Sandy Irvine, despite the new snow still hanging around our search area. Andy had some hunch he wanted to pursue. But on hearing of all our trials and tribulations with errant campers that morning, Andy had grabbed all the oxygen he could and had bolted up to fight the good fight. And when I saw him, I believed we had won the battle.

Joy, a most welcome emotion, started flooding into me there at the Shroom, even as strength was evaporating. I'd given away my food and water and had now been about 12 hours without the stuff, a bad idea for a guy like me. The rescue proceded then with me kind of tagging along. Andy Lapkass and Jaime were gathering speed as yet another of their Sherpa team, Lobsang, got up to help. That left Tap and Jason and Andy Politz and myself following and decompressing. But when we started into the Yellow Band, Andy and Tap and Jason encountered a pair of the Russians we'd tried so hard to help that morning.

One of them collapsed then and sitting just up the slope I myself sat down in defeat. Watching the guys struggle with injectible drugs, with their radio call to our doc, Lee Meyers, and with searches for some signs of life. I can't quite say what my emotions boiled down to. There I was, with all my rescue training, a ski patroller and all that, just watching.

I told myself that it was because I would not be able to climb down the 40-degree slope directly above this operation and onto the crowded slope without kicking rock and ice onto the victim. I told myself that the poor man was dead and that we could do no more. I told myself that it just didn't matter what any of us ever did anyway. But Politz was not encumbered by such useless, nameless emotions, as he worked furiously there at 28,000 feet finally determining beyond all doubt that the Russian, Alexei, had died.

I came down to join my partners then, and together we did our best to deal with what seemed to be the end of a bad day. Back at high camp finally,

Politz, Tap, and Jason decided that they were not sticking around for more epics and a night of thin air. Since Jaime, Andy Lapkass, and the surviving Russians were all in the care of their various teammates, my partners hightailed it down the mountain to make their own lives better.

I lay back in one of our remaining tents, exhausted. Our Sherpa team had taken away much of high camp that day, and it was with only dull concern that I noted that they had pulled all of the odd food that I survive on [Hahn is gluten intolerant and has a special diet]. I had to go down as well. But I just lay there uselessly, drained of emotion, brains, and strength. It crossed my dull mind that this whole saga would be used to further the "Everest Bashing" popular in some circles; the people who drone on to say that us accident-prone riffraff should not be allowed onto such hallowed ground. Save it all for the Ivy League climbing clubs.

There would certainly be much depressing ado made of those who didn't, couldn't, or wouldn't help out today, I thought glumly. And there was death and what a dead climber looks and feels like crowding my brain with darkness.

So I was wallowing in bad feelings and exhaustion when the procession of climbers from the team we'd helped started down past my tent. Andy Lapkass, the accomplished and friendly man I look up to and admire was obviously in great pain from his frostbite and continuing ordeal when he stopped and leaned in to say thanks and that he was sorry we had to miss out on an Everest summit to help him.

Coming to my senses again, I sat up and told him what I'd just realized with his words, that the day would be far more important to all of us than any summit could ever have been. As he moved away, I saw through the tent door the final pyramid of Everest glowing magically in the late afternoon sun. Still a beautiful and worthy mountain. Leaning out, I saw what I'd been missing all day in my frenzy, Tibet and Nepal and a million mountains and cloud tops. I found a little strength of my own then and got my tired body out of high camp and down lower.

I walked on after darkness, rappelling this and traversing that under shimmering stars until I plodded into Advanced Base Camp at 21,000 feet. It was dark and quiet as one would expect at 11:30 P.M., but to my amazement and everlasting gratitude, Kami Sherpa climbed out of bed and started fixing me a plate of fried rice. He went back to bed after setting it in front of me, and I did my best to get it down my neck. Even so, I woke up several times in the next hour, with my face progressively closer to the rice. Passing out with your face in a plate of food after a big day is not an emotion, but it should be. A good one.

PERMISSIONS

Excerpt from *The Wildest Dream,* by Peter and Leni Gillman, © 2000.

Excerpt from *Frank Smythe: The Six Alpine Himalayan Climbing Books* by Frank Smythe, © 2000. Used by permission of Tony Smythe.

"Approach to Mount Everest," excerpted from *Nepal Himalaya,* collected in *H.W. Tilman: The Seven Mountain-Travel Books,* © 1983 by Joan A. Mullins and Pamela H. Davis. Used by permission of Diadem, Great Britain.

"The Icefall," "The Project," and selections from "The March," excerpted from *Eric Shipton: The Six Mountain Travel Books,* by Eric Shipton, © 1985. Used by permission of Nick Shipton.

"The Summit" and "Postscript to this Edition" written by Sir Edmund Hillary, excerpted from *The Ascent of Everest* by Sir John Hunt, first published by Mount Everest Foundation in 1953. © 1993 and 1998. Reproduced by permission of Hodder and Stoughton Limited.

Excerpt from *A Life on the Edge: Memoirs of Everest and Beyond* by Jim Whittaker, © 1999.

Excerpt from *Everest: The West Ridge* by Thomas Hornbein, © 1980. First published in 1965 by the Sierra Club.

Excerpt from *Everest: The Mountaineering History* by Walt Unsworth, © 2000. Used by permission of Walt Unsworth.

Excerpt from *Everest: Expedition to the Ultimate* by Reinhold Messner, © 1999. Used by permission of BLV Verlagsgesellschaft mbH, Munich, Germany.

Excerpts from *The Crystal Horizon* by Reinhold Messner, © 1989. Used by permission of The Crowood Press, England.

Excerpt from *Ghosts of Everest: The Search for Mallory and Irvine,* by Eric Simonson, Jochen Hemmleb, and Larry Johnson, © 1999.

ABOUT THE EDITOR

Journalist Peter Potterfield has covered wilderness adventure and mountaineering for newspapers, magazines, books, and online publishing. He has served as editor and publisher of MountainZone.com from 1996 to present, where he pioneered live reporting of Everest expeditions and other real-time mountaineering events from remote locations. Potterfield has made a specialty of covering mountaineering and wilderness adventure for the popular press, and he has written on these subjects for *Outside, Reader's Digest, Summit, Backpacker, Conde Nast Traveler,* and other national publications. He is the author of four books on mountaineering, including the critically acclaimed *In the Zone* (The Mountaineers Books, 1996) and *The High Himalaya* (The Mountaineers Books, 2001).

ABOUT THE FOREWORD WRITER

Tom Hornbein was born in 1930 in St. Louis, Missouri. He received a B.S. in geology at the University of Colorado, where he minored in mountaineering. Mountain rescue and teaching first aid prompted a change in direction, and he returned to St. Louis to attend Washington University School of Medicine. In 1963, following a brief stint in the U.S. Navy and his journey to Mount Everest, he joined the faculty of the University of Washington School of Medicine, where he is now an emeritus professor of anesthesiology and physiology.

Hornbein's mountaineering includes trips to Alaska and the Himalayas, but it was his and Willi Unsoeld's May 1963 ascent of Mount Everest via the West Ridge that has captured the imagination of subsequent generations of climbers. Unsoeld and Hornbein descended via the South Col route, completing the first traverse of a major Himalayan peak. As Hornbein enters his eighth decade, he remains active in exploring, climbing, and caring for mountain environments and their people.

THE MOUNTAINEERS, founded in 1906, is a nonprofit outdoor activity and conservation club, whose mission is "to explore, study, preserve, and enjoy the natural beauty of the outdoors. . . . " Based in Seattle, Washington, the club is now the third-largest such organization in the United States, with 15,000 members and five branches throughout Washington state.

The Mountaineers sponsors both classes and year-round outdoor activities in the Pacific Northwest, which include hiking, mountain climbing, ski-touring, snowshoeing, bicycling, camping, kayaking and canoeing, nature study, sailing, and adventure travel. The club's conservation division supports environmental causes through educational activities, sponsoring legislation, and presenting informational programs. All club activities are led by skilled, experienced volunteers, who are dedicated to promoting safe and responsible enjoyment and preservation of the outdoors.

If you would like to participate in these organized outdoor activities or the club's programs, consider a membership in The Mountaineers. For information and an application, write or call The Mountaineers, Club Headquarters, 300 Third Avenue West, Seattle, WA 98119; 206-284-6310.

The Mountaineers Books, an active, nonprofit publishing program of the club, produces guidebooks, instructional texts, historical works, natural history guides, and works on environmental conservation. All books produced by The Mountaineers Books fulfill the club's mission.

Send or call for our catalog of more than 500 outdoor titles:

The Mountaineers Books
1001 SW Klickitat Way, Suite 201
Seattle, WA 98134
800-553-4453
mbooks@mountaineersbooks.org
www.mountaineersbooks.org

The Mountaineers Books is proud to be a corporate sponsor of Leave No Trace, whose mission is to promote and inspire responsible outdoor recreation through education, research, and partnerships. The Leave No Trace program is focused specifically on human-powered (nonmotorized) recreation.

Leave No Trace strives to educate visitors about the nature of their recreational impacts, as well as offer techniques to prevent and minimize such impacts. Leave No Trace is best understood as an educational and ethical program, not as a set of rules and regulations.

For more information, visit *www.LNT.org,* or call 800-332-4100.

OTHER TITLES YOU MIGHT ENJOY FROM THE MOUNTAINEERS BOOKS

These books are available at fine bookstores and outdoor stores, by phone at 800-553-4453, or on the World Wide Web at *www.mountaineersbooks.org*.

The Mountaineers Anthology Series, Volume I: Glorious Failures edited by The Mountaineers Books Staff. $16.95 paperbound. 0-89886-825-4.

The Mountaineers Anthology Series, Volume II: Courage and Misfortune edited by The Mountaineers Books Staff. $16.95 paperbound. 0-89886-826-2.

The Mountaineers Anthology Series, Volume III: Over the Top: Humorous Mountaineering Tales edited by Peter Potterfield. $16.95 paperbound. 0-89886-889-0.

Ghosts of Everest: The Search for Mallory and Irvine by Jochen Hemmleb, Larry A. Johnson, and Eric R. Simonson. $24.95 paperbound. 0-89886-850-5.

Detectives on Everest: The 2001 Mallory and Irvine Research Expedition by Jochen Hemmleb and Eric R. Simonson. $19.95 paperbound. 0-89886-871-8.

The Mystery of Mallory & Irvine: Fully Revised Edition by Tom Holzel and Audrey Salkeld. $18.95 paperbound. 0-89886-726-6.

A Life on the Edge: Memoirs of Everest and Beyond by Jim Whittaker. $16.95 paperbound. 0-89886-754-1.

Everest: Eighty Years of Triumph and Tragedy, 2nd Edition by Peter and Leni Gillman. $35.00 hardbound. 0-89886-780-0.

Everest: The Mountaineering History, 3rd Edition by Walt Unsworth. $45.00 hardbound. 0-89886-670-7.

Fearless on Everest: The Quest for Sandy Irvine by Julie Summers. $18.95 paperbound. 0-89886-796-7.

The Wildest Dream: The Biography of George Mallory by Peter and Leni Gillman. $18.95 paperbound. 0-89886-751-7.

Everest: The West Ridge by Tom Hornbein. $19.95 paperbound. 0-89886-616-2.

In the Zone: Epic Survival Stories from the Mountaineering World by Peter Potterfield. $22.95 hardbound, 0-89886-482-8. $16.95 paperbound, 0-89886-568-9.